CW01639112

Investing £100,000 to £10,000,000 for Security and Profit

IAN LOCKE has, for over a decade, worked as a writer, researcher and consultant on a variety of media, financial and historical subjects for a range of corporations and media concerns in the UK and USA. A specialist in alternative investments and intellectual properties, he has written regularly for a number of leading journals and financial papers, including the *Financial Times*. Besides contributions to television documentary research, he is the author of or contributor to a number of educational reference books which have been published in both Europe and North America. He lives in Richmond, Surrey.

ANDREW LOCKE is an accountant, investor and collector and has, over the last fifteen years, developed his own accounting practice specializing in clients with businesses in entertainment and media activities. This has meant working in a variety of international situations and dealing with all aspects of finance and investment. His *modus operandi* demands daily contact with bankers, brokers and lawyers who together create a secure and profitable environment in which high net worth individuals can operate. He is an advocate of a clearer understanding of money matters and supports any means that assist in a better and more straightforward approach to personal finances. He is married and lives in Richmond, Surrey.

Investing £100,000 to £10,000,000 for Security and Profit

IAN AND ANDREW LOCKE

ROBERT HALE · LONDON

First published in Great Britain 1997

ISBN 0 7090 5795 4

Robert Hale Limited
Clerkenwell House
Clerkenwell Green
London EC1R 0HT

2 4 6 8 10 9 7 5 3 1

Photoset in North Wales by
Derek Doyle & Associates, Mold, Flintshire.
Printed in Great Britain by
St Edmundsbury Press Ltd, Bury St Edmunds, Suffolk.
Bound by WBC Book Manufacturers Limited,
Bridgend, Mid-Glamorgan.

Contents

Acknowledgements

The Authors would like to express their gratitude to all those who have helped bring this project to fruition. In particular, they would like to thank Lesley Hadcroft, Ceri Myall Locke, Daryl Myall, Charles Ryan (Ryan, Gray, Hamilton) and Suzanne Taylor for their encouragement, practical help and comments.

Disclaimer

Although this book is intended to be a helpful and useful guide to the background and use of funds for investment, it is by no means prescriptive. Any reader who makes use of any of the suggestions made in the book does so at his own risk and without liability on the part of the authors, publishers or their agents. The overriding approach should be one of care and caution, and independent professional advice should be taken wherever practical and possible. There are no short cuts in investment.

Investment has an entirely fluid momentum, particularly in a world of twenty-four-hour instant communication. The appendices included in the book are therefore indicative; although the authors have made efforts to verify figures given, the appendices should be used as a guide only and have no application for future investment. Throughout the book the authors indicate reliable sources of current information, and readers are encouraged to both identify and investigate such sources with the aim of making an informed decision – again, exercising the care and caution proper to a prudent investor.

Inevitably the content of the book will not please all readers. Perforce, we have had to make a choice of what to include and what to exclude, and naturally the text will reflect our own preferences and prejudices. We could not avoid some technical language but have attempted to simplify the non-simple; if investment were easy, there would be no need for a book on it.

Finally, the book is written from a UK perspective. Although the investment principles are international, and much of the content is entirely without national bias, it is difficult to divorce the entire approach of the book from the nationality and country of residence both of its authors and of its most likely readership.

1 The Character of Investment

Economic Background

Investment can only be carried out in the environment that exists at the time an investment is made – there are legal, political and economic constraints to how investments can be pursued. Each country creates its own set of restraints and incentives for investment based on ideology and broad economic objectives, although there is a current tendency for economic blocs, such as the EC or ASEAN, to merge these objectives into a common ideology. It is therefore helpful to highlight the general background to investments.

Theoretical Framework for Investment

Two schools of thought continue to provide the theoretical framework for the modern economy and thereby influence the conditions for investment. These two schools, termed Keynesian and Monetarist, are principally based, on the one hand, on the work of the English economist John Maynard Keynes, who died in 1944, and, on the other, on the work of Milton Friedman, the American economist of the University of Chicago. Many economists and economic historians have provided supplements or re-interpretations of these basic theories.

The primary principle of Keynes is that the level of national income – and hence effective levels of output and employment – is determined by an interaction of changes in both real and monetary variables; that there is a direct link between decisions taken by individual households and businesses and that the combination of these two elements affect the economy as a whole. Reductions in output and employment occur in expectation of a fall in economic activity. This is self-fulfilling, and itself creates reduced activity. Keynes saw Government as the only actor capable of achieving improvement in the economic climate or expectations, and Government activity directed towards creating such an improvement was labelled 'interventionist'. In Britain, governments were particularly disinclined to accept the need for increased spending that such intervention demanded. Keynes argued that debt was perfectly sensible, so long as there was an intention to repay (i.e. to balance the books over the long haul), but politicians could see no political advantage in taking on debt, especially when stimulating the economy by intervention along Keynesian lines carried a political risk. This risk lay in public perceptions of a government's ability to manage an economy, given that maintaining the high levels of demand that sustained full employment had implications for other policy objectives – not least inflation and the balance-of-payments position.

Although such misgivings existed, successive Labour governments, from 1945, adopted the Keynesian strategy to a greater or lesser extent, with widespread intervention in the economic life of Britain. The case for nationalization was largely derived from the mechanisms identified by Keynes, sustained by Socialist principles. Such intervention paid an initial political dividend, but increasing problems with the control of government borrowing became a cause of national concern.

Milton Friedman's monetarist theories, initiated in the 1950s, proposed an entirely different view of economic welfare. Money supply became the all-important element. Monetarism linked the money supply to the volume of real output at current prices, and real output was perceived as the result of decisions taken predominantly by households and firms in the private (as opposed to the public) sector. This approach imposed fiscal conservatism, i.e. spending was related to taxation and was ultimately rooted in a doctrine of individual responsibility for personal financial well-being. The theory opposed tariffs, social welfare, corporate taxes and wage and price controls. The means to control inflation was not government intervention, but control of the money supply. The concept of personal fiscal responsibility in a liberal government environment was seen as a wealth creator, and the wealth it created would infuse the entire economy at all levels. From this derived the much-criticized concept of 'trickle down', whereby wealth at the top would cascade down through all social classes thanks to its effect on consumption and increased employment opportunities.

On coming to power in 1979 the first Thatcher government chose to make a version of Friedman's monetarism the key plank of UK economic policy. In practical terms this vision assumed that the prime enemy of a capitalist economy – inflation – could be curbed if supply could be created before demand. This assumption sought to break both the 'stop-go' cycle apparently endemic in British post-war economic life and defeat the 'stagflation' of the 1970s. As economist Brian McCormick summed up the aims of the Thatcher approach: 'individual households and firms must be made to stand on their own feet, to succeed or fail. Trade union power to prevent development must be destroyed'. It was considered that among one likely consequence of developing such a non-interventionist economy would be to make wealth no longer socially unacceptable. The assumed trickle-down, or spread, of this wealth in Britain was so implicit that it led to the remarkable declaration that 'to be poor is unnecessary, so poverty must be pushed back into decent obscurity'.

How Does Britain Compare?

Concerns over the British Empire's financial standing in world markets were first expressed in 1900. Britain had headed international production and GDP tables for a generation, but substantial comparative reports were published of its weakening manufacturing position *vis-à-vis* the new industrial empires of the United States and Germany. By 1993 the standing of Britain in major economies was rated 19th out of 22 in the World Competitiveness report, judged by its domestic economy at the micro-economic level. In one sector – quality of financial services – Britain achieved a higher rating of 8th. According to OECD National Accounts statistics, the UK's GDP per head fell from 12th in 1971 (when Switzerland headed the table) to 18th in 1991, at $15,720. However, the correlation of national GDP per head with the health or otherwise of a national economy came under question in the 1990s, most particularly in the USA. One of the arguments against GDP as a primary measure of national economic 'health' was that it was based on the number of transactions within the economy, and so under-rated social and welfare assistance. In effect, the less nucleic a population became (if the divorce or separation rate rose, or individuals set up their own home at a younger age), the greater the number of economic transactions taking place. The number of transactions would also be increased by the machinery of government. It could be argued, in this instance, that the imposition of the Community Charge ('poll tax') on individuals in the UK, was a factor in increasing the

UK's GDP from 1991; at a simplistic level, the devaluation of the pound in September 1992 was also a distortion of the 'real' GDP, since it had the effect, *inter alia*, of uprating competitiveness, especially in export markets. For the individual, a better yardstick of national status was the rate of disposable income. This has fallen consistently in the UK since 1991. The effect of the recession and increase in public-sector borrowing was reflected in a 6% increase in the central-government take as a percentage of GDP in the four years 1988 to 1992, when it rose to a substantial 44%, as against the EU average of 41%. While income tax fell by 2.5% in 1990, indirect taxes increased; taxes on spending rose by nearly 8%, and duties (imposed by Customs and Excise) increased by 11% in 1991 alone. In effect, the UK government has apparently sought to mask tax increases by concentrating on indirect rather than direct taxation, by blurring the distinctions between income and social-security taxes, and by having to fund increased social commitments arising from policies of its own making. The UK is not alone in facing the prospect of having to demand increased contributions from those receiving income in order to pay for both central government and those who have no declared taxable income.

Investment Background

The process of investment is a sequence of decisions concerning the placement of money in categories of assets that, taken together, form a balanced portfolio, so as to provide security of income and capital. The type of investment is partly a matter of personal preference and partly market-driven. A personal weighting of investment can relate to assets such as houses or cars and other possessions which are the result of personal choice within the means available, whereas market-driven investments such as stocks and shares are determined not only by personal choice but by the circumstances of Government regulation and stock market emphasis at the time of purchase.

It is important that the individual investor clearly identifies his or her objectives before starting to compose a portfolio of assets. There are three main factors in investment – income, capital gains and risk – and the level of income is determined by the investor's attitude to the other two elements. In other words, the higher the income, the higher the implied potential for gain, and the higher the risk. The highest returns of income invariably relate to the highest risk. Although there are exceptions, the offer of above-average returns from any investment will reflect above-average risk. In general terms it is unwise to put completely at risk more than 10% of available funds.

Assets acquired in investment are usually considered as of average risk, that is to say, the aim is to maintain their value after taking account of inflation and to show a gain on cost over a period of time. An asset that does not increase in value over time is considered to be depreciating; the most common form of depreciating asset owned by individuals is their car. Since 1945 the most common form of an appreciating asset has been freehold property – although this has not been the case in the UK since 1991. The trick of investment is to balance appreciating and depreciating assets so that only the minimum sum is ever invested in the latter. Successful investments should keep their value against inflation and at the same time produce a gain equivalent to an appropriate index (the FT100 index is often used as a measurement of the performance of UK shares). The choice of measure should be relevant to the type of asset concerned, but this should not prejudice the overall objectives of the portfolio.

2 Common Forms of Investment

Residential Property

The most common form of personal investment is residential property. Approximately 60% of the adult UK population are now owner-occupiers. Of this number, a small proportion now have negative equity (i.e. the value of the property on the open market is less than the mortgage loan against which it is secured). Enthusiasm for investment in property in Britain was encouraged over a long period of time by successive governments, with mortgage interest payments subsidized by tax incentives designed to promote home ownership; in 1994/95 the cost to the taxpayer of tax subsidies on mortgages was £3.6 billion. There is no tax break generally available to other households that is so directly linked to ownership. Politically the encouragement of home ownership has tended to make voters more likely to vote Conservative, and it was therefore strongly encouraged as a 'right' from 1979 onwards.

In the rush to own their own property home owners tended to forget that in lending more than a traditional proportion of a property's value lenders are normally taking higher-than-average risk. Until the 1980s, when the housing market was liberalized through the relaxation of building-society and bank regulations, it was exceptional for a home loan to be granted for more than 85% of the surveyed value of the property. Moreover, the amount of the loan was calculated by reference to an annual earnings multiple that tended to apply to the earnings of the principal owner only (normally the husband of a married couple), with no other earnings source (wife or partner) normally being admitted in the calculation. The removal of such restrictions in the 1980s led to mortgages of up to 100% of the deemed market value of the property being granted, with calculation of the amount based on multiples of up to three times the principal earner's earnings, plus one year's earnings of the joint owner. These calculations meant that, when the residential property market moved down and interest rates moved up, both capital and income were severely pressurized at the same time – the exact opposite of what a prudent investor would plan for. It is unfortunate that the lenders of the time should have allowed normal common sense to have been so completely forgotten in a desire to gain market share.

The conventional wisdom is that loans on property should never exceed 60% of current market value, and most lenders will state that the average settles down at 30%. It is therefore prudent to lend only the minimum against the property, and the gradual removal of mortgage interest tax relief in recent budgets makes it unnecessary and ill-advised to retain a mortgage so as to gain some form of tax relief. Mortgage loans have traditionally been granted for 25 years based on the assumption of full adult employment. Current circumstances possibly make such a long time-span inappropriate and the reduction in the value of endowment policies (as investment returns have followed stock-market reductions) now makes it possible that after 25 years certain not-with-profit policies will not have performed well enough to repay the mortgage in full. In these circumstances the recent moves toward repayment mortgages or pension mortgages have accelerated and anyone considering buying a property should take careful note of their likely future earnings and their likely retirement date before considering how best to structure their property loan so as to fit their individual circumstances. Here it is important to note that agents for investment companies are in the business of selling policies, and rarely in the business of giving clients advice based on their specific individual circumstances and needs. Despite their training, many agents have little knowledge of an overall investment strategy, and their questions rarely go into sufficient detail to enable them to understand how their particular product would fit into a specific client's overall investment approach.

The highly-publicized phenomenon of negative equity has arisen in UK residential property purchased during the years 1988 to 1992; from 1989 to 1994 the average value of houses in Britain fell by 8%. There are estimated to be some 900,000 properties with negative equity in Britain, the average 'negative value' being somewhat below £4,000. This has to be seen in the context of average mortgages of £40,000 being granted during the peak period of property-buying, and the number of properties with negative equity has dropped from an estimated peak of 2 million in 1993 (some of the reduction being the result of forced sales – often at auction, where values below normal market value are likely). There is an argument that the surrender value of endowment policies has helped to reduce the instances of negative equity, as the proceeds from the sale of these policies has gone towards meeting the mortgage debt. At the peak of endowment policy sales in 1988 80% of mortgages were covered by them, in 1969 this figure had been only 10%, rising to 20% in 1979 and to 60% in 1985, which is also the current level.

Nearly two-thirds of Britons are owner-occupiers; of the remainder some 20% rent from councils and 15% from private landlords. There are about 10 million mortgages, and the level of repossessions is historically unlikely to rise above one-third of one percent in normal years (30,000). In 1991 it was above 75,000, with over 200,000 borrowers six to twelve months in arrears in 1992. This unprecedented level of potential default indicates that the housing market had appealed to, and been targeted at, at least 300,000 families who could ill afford it.

After World War II successive British governments devoted a larger percentage of US-provided Marshall Plan funds to the development of domestic housing than any other western European recipient, even though Britain had had fewer properties damaged or destroyed during the war. This politically driven, American-funded development, assisted by legislation in 1948, 1954 and 1962 that relaxed restrictions on wholesale development in urban areas, caused an unprecedented boom in the property market. This was further stimulated by the abolition of height restrictions for buildings in major cities by 1965 and the ongoing development of new towns. In 1968 the property market was hit by a slump caused by collapses in the secondary banking market, and the number of property companies plummeted, reducing the value of their land banks by 59% within three years. Development schemes, epitomized by the supermarket and the housing estate, subsequently stimulated a revival in land values.

Land Prices from the 1980s

In 1981 the recession ended almost a decade of rising land values, which had increased even beyond the record annual rises in inflation. Substantial 'new' acreage came on to the market, as almost 51% of Britain's manufacturing capacity was wiped out. The trend towards higher housing values had escalated in the decade to 1986, increasing the value of the UK housing stock fivefold (from £162 billion in 1976 to £835 billion in 1986) – and that in the south east of England six-fold. From 1986 the main stimulation for rising land values was the Conservatives' promotion of the 'property-owning democracy', giving rise to Margaret Thatcher's boast that 'there is no finer word in the English language than that of freeholder'. The extraordinary stimulation to the domestic property market in the years 1986 to 1990, the result of deregulation and budgetary stimulation, alongside changes in social custom, caused the average value of residential property to rise from £1,200 to £4,000 per acre. The recession, dating from 1989, then caused a dramatic reversal of the market, bringing residential land values down to £1,300 an acre on average by the end of 1994. The fall in the value of an average acre in the UK from 1981 to 1989 was a massive 56% in England, and the number of housing starts fell by 46% from 1988 to 1991. By the end of 1995 the fall in property values across London was even more marked: 71% down on the 1988/89 peak by one survey.

Examination of the entire picture reveals notable regional variations in land values across the British Isles; in 1995 the differential between the average price per acre in the north of Scotland and the south-east of England was over £1,500. There is, therefore, much potential in the depressed residential property market, arising from negative equity problems and general price falls.

Mortgage Risk

In most circumstances, an investor's single biggest asset will be his home. In an ideal portfolio, where risk is spread over many different types of investment, the maximum invested in residential property might be between 25% and 40% of assets before liabilities, but for most investors the proportion is more likely to be 60% or more. Once any mortgage is taken into account, the proportion of net assets that the property represents can be very high indeed – possibly the entire net worth. In many cases the home is the only asset that individuals have which has any substantial value at all.

For a long period after World War II UK house prices rose faster than inflation, boosted by tax relief on mortgage interest payments. As a result, the impact of a mortgage loan on the ultimate value of a property was not very significant; in effect inflation took care of things, eroding the real capital value of the loan and, as wages increased, reducing the real impact on disposable income of the mortgage interest payments. A loan of £2,000 taken out in 1945 would be the equivalent in real terms of a loan of £40,000 taken out today, so a large commitment at the end of the war would, by 1995, have become relatively very small indeed.

The 1990s, however, have been an unusual period, in which inflationary factors have been reduced considerably, and this has substantially reduced the cushion that inflation used to provide against the effects both of paying mortgage interest and repaying the mortgage loan. A decade earlier investors could have taken out a mortgage-protection plan, which, in return for monthly premiums of no great cost, guaranteed the payments of their mortgage interest (and possibly their mortgage loan) in the event of unemployment or other circumstances causing earnings to fall suddenly or disappear altogether. In the 1980s, when these plans came into existence as part of a normal mortgage package their cost was not very high. With the onset of the 1990s, when house prices across the UK fell by an average of 15% from a historically very high level, the cost of the plans to the insurance industry increased enormously (as accelerating unemployment led to high claims to pay off mortgage arrears); the premiums for these plans was therefore adjusted, and they became relatively expensive.

At the same time the government has committed itself to a series of changes in the law that withdraw the relief provided under social security benefits from high mortgages (over £100,000) and prevent the unemployed from claiming for their mortgage as a right. These changes have created a very significant and unexpected risk that affects the ownership of residential property where the loan taken out can only be repaid on the assumption of a very long period of constant employment. Most mortgages vary only according to the interest rates used by the banks, which are agreed by the Government in consultation with the Governor of the Bank of England. There is therefore a political, as well as an economic, risk involved in the ownership of property where the amount of the loan is uncomfortably high (representing 60% or more of the actual market value of the property). This risk represents the setting of interest rates to achieve political rather than economic goals – for instance, when the £ doggedly tracked the DM in the ERM, UK interest rates were held artificially high to achieve this political objective. The fundamental assumption that lending secured on bricks and mortar was always safe has now been shown to be unreliable in recession for the first time since the early 1970s, and for only the second time since 1945.

In addition to the risk of being unable to pay mortgage interest when due, there is also the possibility of not being able to pay the mortgage capital, if it is secured on an endowment policy for which the underlying equity investment (without profits) has performed unusually poorly, or if the premiums have not been maintained throughout the period of the mortgage. For a long time stock market values were moving upwards, partly in response to inflation and partly reflecting real growth in the value of the assets underlying stock-market investments. However, in periods of recession this growth can go into reverse – for instance the UK stock market fell 10% in 1994. During such periods payments into an endowment policy to cover the mortgage capital can become less valuable, as the underlying investment markets decline. (There are additional risks attached to mortgages taken out in foreign currencies or based on markets other than the UK stock market.) So, despite increased choice in the type of investments that endowment policies can reflect, their value has, if anything, become less certain. In the end, the value of an endowment policy on maturity is linked to the performance of the fund managers of the life company with whom the endowment policy is placed. League tables, published on a regular basis, show the performance of the various funds, and there can be significant differences in the level of performance.

When you take out an endowment policy, there is no absolute guarantee that its value on maturity (normally after twenty-five years) will repay the mortgage loan. In past times, though, when the combination of inflation and stock-market gains was more assured, endowment policies would mature providing enough to repay the mortgage and a substantial surplus as well. In those circumstances such policies represented a welcome and valuable form of tax-free long-term saving. However, the circumstances seem now to have changed. One of the key elements is the date when your mortgage matures – if this coincides with a poor year on the stock market, you could be disappointed at the performance of your endowment policy.

The additional risk that endowment policies carry is that, if you fail to maintain premiums throughout the term, the policy can be cancelled. On cancellation or surrender it is unlikely to be worth the sum of the premiums paid – particularly if this happens in early years. It is estimated that endowment policies only become worth more than the premiums paid after fifteen years of a twenty-five-year policy, and the true gains in the policy are most likely to arise in only the last five years. One of the reasons for this is that front-end commissions on premiums paid reduces the actual amount being invested – so that the assumption that the value of these policies reflects amount paid is untrue. Rarely do sellers of endowment policies make it clear to investors that this is what is actually happening – although, after the shocks of recent times, there are moves to force selling agents to disclose much more information.

Mortgage interest is often seen as an advantageous substitute for rent that would have to be paid if you didn't own your own property. But borrowing to buy a property is now highly unlikely to show a genuine profit, once the costs of borrowing are taken into account. What does mortgage interest actually amount to, and how do total mortgage costs relate to a property's value? If you took out a £100,000 endowment mortgage at a rate of, say 8% (against a bank rate of 7%), then – assuming that this stays fixed throughout the twenty-five-year term of the mortgage – you would end up paying £200,000 in interest against that loan and still have the capital to repay. If you took out an endowment policy to cover the £100,000 loaned, that would cost approximately £125 per month to fund, which over twenty-five years would add up to a further £37,500. Assuming that the endowment policy grew three times over that period this would generate £112,500, or sufficient to repay the capital with a small surplus to offset part of the mortgage interest cost. If we assume that the £100,000 mortgage represents 80% of the house's price at the outset (£125,000), this simple example shows that in reality the total cost of the house is getting on for twice its original purchase price. This hardly makes a house a good investment, since any increase in its value over twenty-five years is often only masking the true cost of the purchase in the first instance.

Obviously one could argue that there are other financial and non-financial benefits involved in owning your own house but the impact of paying mortgage interest on the use of earnings in Britain is massive. As there are currently 10 million UK mortgages at an average of £40,000, £400 billion is tied up in this way. In countries with a higher proportion of rented property than in the UK, such as Japan and Germany, it may well be that this is a contributory factor to the growth of their economies: substantially less of consumer earnings is directed into an owner-occupation syndrome that reduces expenditure on other areas. Given recent disillusion with property prices, we may be seeing the end of the British enthusiasm for owning one's own property – an Englishman's castle may have started to become a wasting asset.

Throughout developed western economies demographic changes are producing a rapidly ageing population. In the UK, where an average age for purchasing a property with a mortgage might be twenty-five, this will mean that, as mortgages are repaid by house-owners reaching fifty, the amount of cash available for investment (providing the owners are still working) will increase substantially as a result. At the same time, these house-owners are likely to have adult children (themselves now looking for property to buy), and the size of their homes may be in excess of what they now need.

Where populations are also decreasing as birth rates fall, the percentage of owner-occupiers is likely to increase without further government incentives. The impact of all these changes is likely to be a continuing division of large houses into smaller units and a greater emphasis on property for retirement. In the light of the disenchantment caused by the change in property values in the 1990s, it may well be that the distinction between those living in rented accommodation, those in mortgaged accommodation and those whose mortgages have been paid off will be emphasized. Those who rent may have a high proportion of their net income available for other purchases, while those who mortgage will have a lower proportion. The older owner-occupier, who has paid off his mortgage, will have greater spending power than any other category, and it is likely that, in the gap between the age of fifty and retirement, money formerly used for mortgage payments will be redirected towards pensions or health policies.

It is difficult to speculate whether the residential market in the UK will recover from its present doldrums in the short term, since every bank-rate rise is a further disincentive to purchase. Sellers continue to expect prices above market value and are reluctant to accept a sale for less than the purchase price. No doubt the situation is exacerbated by the increased rate of divorce and division among families.

For many years personal lending in the UK has been geared towards residential property, and this trend may now decline. There is little incentive now to invest in UK residential property, except where high-quality, and usually expensive, properties with unique features in exceptional locations attract investors who wish to buy without lending (this has been the case recently in prime residential sites in London, with a high proportion of purchasers coming from abroad). There has also been recent growth in repossessed properties selling at below market value and then being reused for rental by property speculators. Perhaps the UK is seeing a slow return to a property market with a smaller proportion of owner-occupiers and more people living in rented accommodation – reflecting the gradual removal of political and financial distortions brought about through the policies of the 1980s. The 'you can't lose' argument for UK residential property has been abruptly countered, and policies on property lending are now returning to the more prudent norms that restricted violent fluctuations in prices during most of the period from 1945 to 1985.

The emphasis that the British put on their homes sometimes puzzles our Continental counterparts. Since Britain has not been invaded since 1066, property has largely been spared the ravages of war outside large conurbations. Although there are architectural styles mocked for their suburban normality, and we seem to naturally distrust modern architecture, each home presents an individuality that testifies to the belief that an Englishman's home is his castle. The stability, location and security of British property attracts buyers from other countries: in 1994 60% of buyers of prime London residential property were foreign (falling to 50% in 1995). Osborne House, near the Boltons in London SW5, a Grade II Georgian house with one-third of an acre of garden, sold for £5.25 million. When the pound was devalued in 1992 foreigners – mostly from Hong Kong, Singapore and Malaysia – rushed to buy in London, and prices per square foot for prime London flats (apartments) rose to £650 in Central London, £500 in Kensington and £400 in W1. Flats at the appropriately named Peninsula Heights (one home of Lord Archer) were priced at £1.6 million to £3.25 million. It is now estimated that only one-third of Mayfair is now British-owned, Far Eastern and Middle Eastern owners accounting for one third and 10% respectively. One-third of lettings go to Americans, and a twenty-year lease in Eaton Square, London SW1 can cost over £1 million, not including ground rent and service charges, which can add up to £10,000 a year.

In contrast to the foreign interest in the prime city properties, in 1994 over 90% of country homes were sold to wealthy, mature, equity-rich Britons, three-quarters of them over 40, who paid an average of £500,000 (though over one-third of buyers for properties over £1 million were foreign). Prime property tends to rise in value (by an average of 7% in 1994), against other housing trends, and the market is fuelled by the normal reasons for sale – death, divorce and debt. Country properties are normally sold with between 10 and 20 acres. One of the major London estate agents defines a perfect estate in terms of 1,000 acres, three or four cottages and a large, attractive, central house with easy access to

London but a long way from road noise. Such an estate would cost some £2.5 million. When the entire village of Salperton on the Salperton Pick estate was sold in 1994 it was offered at £8–10 million, a price that would buy about forty average British homes.

Cash Savings

After residential property the most common form of personal investment is savings – in banks, building societies and government National Savings products. All these investments are by definition 'liquid': in other words, they are cash products. Liquidity is an important element in an investment strategy, and the expression 'cash is king' applies as much today as it ever did. The importance of cash is that it avoids borrowing (together with its associated costs) and ensures the minimum time lapse between making an investment decision and carrying it out so that opportunities to exploit unusual but advantageous circumstances can be taken without delay.

Since the liberalization of bank and building-society regulations and definitions in the late 1980s and early 1990s, UK banks and building societies have become increasingly competitive in offering investors high rates of return, in order to increase their market share and attract a database of investors to whom they can offer other products (whether they want them or not). Often these high rates of return on interest-bearing accounts are offered subject to a time factor – in other words, the investor has to keep his money in that account for a minimum period of time in order to earn the promised rate and, if he withdraws the money early, is penalized by either the deduction of a fixed sum or the payment of a lower interest rate. It is therefore important, if you are to invest in high-rate products, to be certain that you will not need these funds during the fixed period for which you must invest to earn the highest return. It is part of the design of these products that some investors will be forced to withdraw before the rate can be earned – this benefits the bank or building society. This is similar to early surrender of endowment policies, where the return in the early years can be particularly poor, because the commission charged by the agent who sold the policy can reduce its surrender value to virtually nothing for the first 3–5 years.

Many funds now offer index-linked rates of return to ensure that investors are protected from the ravages of inflation. Since UK inflation in recent years has fallen to between 3% and 5%, this is far less relevant than it would have been in the late 1970s, when annual inflation could exceed 20%. When investing in so-called high-rate accounts, it is therefore far more objective to look at the rate you are earning and then deduct inflation – only then will you realise what your 'real' rate of return is. In this context one should also be aware that banks and building societies all operate on margins to earn their profits, so that what they pay to investors has perforce to be less than what they charge to borrowers. For instance, bank base rates are currently 6.75% (the lowest charge for any inter-bank borrower). Savings rates are 6.5% maximum for a fixed one-year term, giving a profit (margin) to the bank before costs of nearly 4% (0.25% over 6.5%) Secured borrowers will normally be charged 3% above base rate: 9.75%. In recent years the margins have been increased to try and recover profitability, and this is particularly true of the high-street banks, whose profits were dented by the huge debts incurred by the businesses and property-buying clients to whom they lent so willingly in the 1980s. It will always be a fact that banks and building societies can exert pressure on a small investor much more readily than on a major corporation.

Keeping funds in interest-bearing accounts should be viewed with caution. It implies that there is no better place to put your money – often the fact of the matter is that such 'investors' are too wary of other forms of investment, or too lacking in knowledge of them. With the massive choice of investment available today, it is highly unusual to find any serious investor with more than 5% to 10% of funds in liquid form at any time. (Indeed, there is an argument that investments themselves are partly liquid, both because there is a valid market, where you can always buy and sell, and because of the underlying liquidity of the companies in which the funds are invested – such as GEC, whose cash pile was the source of much criticism by brokers.) There is no capital gain available from interest-bearing accounts, and the rate of return after inflation is often very poor – and even highly-valued customers of banks and building societies will not necessarily get the highest rate unless they ask for it. Moreover, unless funds are kept on what is described as a Treasury or Bid account (where it is directly held by the Bank of England), or in an offshore account (in the Channel Islands, for example) interest is subject to deduction of basic-rate tax at source, so the government receives a share of tax on your money on a quarterly basis. For most investors this simply goes as a credit against an eventual tax bill, but non-taxpayers have to apply for a repayment of the tax deducted at the appropriate time – usually when they submit their annual tax return.

National Savings

National Savings is a term used for a variety of Government schemes to encourage regular savings by individuals.

The National Savings Bank offers traditional banking facilities. Interest on sums in ordinary accounts is payable at a predetermined rate which is varied periodically. For a current account the maximum balance is £10,000, rising to £100,000 for an investment account, which pays a higher, variable rate of interest. The current rates paid are available at any Post Office and printed regularly in the financial press.

Premium Bonds are a non-performing form of Government security. Any purchase gives entry to the monthly, tax-free, cash prize draw, funded from the interest earned by each bond; the 350,000 prizes range from £50 to £1 million. The scheme began in November 1956, and draw numbers are made by computer, originally called ERNI. The bonds (which can be redeemable at face value) are in units of £1, the current minimum purchase being £100; above this, purchases must be made in multiples of £10, up to a maximum holding of £100,000 per person. Parents, guardians and grandparents may make purchases for children under 16. Prizewinners in the draw have an option to reinvest, by returning their prize warrants.

Bonds only become eligible for entry to the prize draw from the second calendar month after purchase. On the death of a bondholder, the bonds remain eligible for entry to the prize draw only up to and including the twelfth month after the month in which the bondholder died; they are then redeemable.

The advantages of the Premium Bond over other forms of prize-generating payments, not least the National Lottery, are the greater probability of winning something and the certainty of recouping the initial investment. In December 1995, for the second month running, a new bond holder won the £1 million monthly premium bond prize with a stake of only £1,000, while in October 1994 a £50,000 winner had a holding of a mere £18! On average, a holding of £1,250 worth of bonds will provide one prize per year. While the odds on winning the million-pound prize remain extreme (1 in 566 million, as against the odds on winning the National Lottery jackpot of 1 in 16 million), regardless of the number of tickets purchased, each £1 bond has a 1 in 15,000 chance of winning one of the prizes available.

National Savings Income Bonds (NSIB), introduced in 1982, produce regular monthly interest payments while maintaining the capital. They are sold in multiples of £1,000 (with an initial minimum purchase of £2,000) up to a maximum holding of £250,000; the interest rate is higher for holdings of £25,000 or more. The interest, which is calculated daily and paid (or credited) monthly, is taxable, though tax is not deducted at source. NSIB last for ten years but are repayable earlier on three months notice (if you give less notice, the bonds will still be repaid, but you will lose three months' interest). Should a holder (or the remaining holder in a joint account) die, there is no penalty or loss of interest on repayment.

FIRST (Fixed Interest Rate Savings Tax-Paid) Options Bonds, were introduced in July 1992 and offer guaranteed twelve-month fixed-interest-rate returns without the necessity of long-term commitment (they can, however, be held indefinitely). The minimum purchase is £1,000 and the maximum holding £250,000. There is no penalty for withdrawal provided this is made on an anniversary of purchase; nor is there any notice period for withdrawal. Interest on the holding (net of basic-rate tax) is added to the holding on each anniversary of its purchase, and holders are then advised of the fixed interest rate that will apply for the next twelve months. As with any other investments that can mature at a fixed period in the future, it is advisable to be aware of current interest and inflation rates, to avoid a negative return on capital on reinvestment.

A fixed-rate bond, the Capital Bond, was introduced in January 1989. This offers capital growth over five years by adding the fixed-rate interest to the value of the bond on each anniversary of its purchase (although it is taxable, the interest is added without deduction of tax). Purchases start at £100 and increase thereafter in £100 multiples up to a maximum holding of £250,000. Each issue is given a series letter relating to the year of issue. The capital, plus all accumulated interest is repaid at the end of five years. No interest is added to bonds redeemed in the first year.

Gilts (or gilt-edged securities) are essentially IOUs issued by the Bank of England. The majority pay a fixed annual rate of interest over a life that extends until a stated maturity date. On that date the government will repay the nominal capital – though some gilt issues are index-linked, and capital payments are adjusted to reflect Retail Price Index (RPI) fluctuations. The range of change in the RPI has been substantial in the 1990s; in January 1993 it fell below 2.6% for the first time, to 1.7%, having reached a high of 10.9% in autumn 1990.

The cheapest gilts are available through the National Savings Stock register. Dealings are by post, and gilts are available at Post Offices; interest is paid through the National Savings Register without tax deduction at source. The cost of buying through the National Savings register is 0.6% up to £5,000, subject to a minimum of £5. Above this sum, commission is £30 and 0.35% on an amount above £5,000. For larger sums quotes are available from stockbrokers.

Share-Based Products

After property and cash, the most frequent form of investment is in share-based products. These cover a large area including direct equity investment, personal equity plans, personal pensions, investment trusts and unit trusts. Generally speaking, an investor with a substantial sum available will take advantage of tax breaks as far as possible and will spread risk in equities by having a balance of funds in all of these areas.

Equities (Stocks and Shares)

Direct equity investment is usually done via a bank in conjunction with a stockbroker, possibly their own (for instance, Barclays Bank own brokers BZW). Larger investors can deal with a broker direct. Stockbrokers are the only firms licensed to buy and sell equities on behalf of their clients, and as intermediaries in this way they charge broker's commission on each transaction they undertake. This is on a sliding scale and in accordance with stock-market regulations; a fixed minimum charge (currently £20 per transaction) is applied to smaller transactions and 1% of the value of the transaction is charged for larger ones. It is therefore not worthwhile to trade directly in equities unless the transaction cost forms only a small part of the overall equity investment, otherwise you are paying the broker a high proportion of value. When the government privatized industries in the 1980s and 1990s by selling their shares on the stock market, one of the incentives to small investors was that no brokerage was payable on the new issues, and there were usually arrangements for an advantageous fixed charge on sales made within a certain time of the date of issue

(£10 instead of the normal £20). Transaction charges are often ignored or underestimated in making equity purchases or sales, and any prudent investor should always bear such costs in mind when evaluating and changing their portfolio.

Many brokers will not accept an equity portfolio of less than £250,000, since that is the 'break-even' point at which there are sufficient funds available, and sufficient transactions resulting, to make it worthwhile for them. The average equity portfolio would consist of between twenty and twenty-five shareholdings, and therefore the size of a single investment might average £10,000. Given that the average 'Sid', who invested in the British Gas privatization in 1989, might have had funds of only £500 available, this indicates the gulf between the man in the street and the 'serious' investor – and the transaction costs incurred in selling 'Sid's' few shares represent a high proportion of his portfolio value. There are therefore marked differences in the proportional cost of share transactions, depending on the size of the transaction. Investors should also be aware that there is a difference in the price of the same share at any given time, depending on whether you are buying or selling it (bid to offer). The selling price will be lower than the buying price, and this 'spread' is also part of the cost of any transaction.

Historically stock market investment has proved better value than other forms of investment, and many individuals have funds invested in the stock market through a third party (such as a pension fund). However, the proportion of direct individual investors has fallen considerably in the last thirty years – from the 54% of quoted shares owned by individuals in 1963 to 18% in 1993. Typically a UK stock market investor is male and 50. (Even taking unit trusts, a less direct form of investment, only 4% of UK households have investments in unit trust funds, compared to 27% in the US.) These statistics indicate that the appeal of direct investment is becoming narrower, not broader as might be expected, given that standards of living have generally improved over the last three decades. Some commentators point to this shrinkage in private investors as an institutional failing of the City. They say that huge blocks of shares, owned by the larger pension funds, dominate the market and have an adverse effect on shareholder democracy and corporate governance. This in turn enables a mutual admiration society of highly-rewarded top executives in public companies, whose performance-related pay is calculated in such a convoluted manner that it rarely depends on performance during the year in question.

Equities (shares) are either quoted or unquoted. Quoted shares are those whose prices are published on a daily basis on an authorized stock exchange; stock exchanges now exist in all developed and developing countries. Where a stock market has been in existence for a long time – the British stock market started to exist officially in the 1860s – it is described as a 'mature market', as opposed to stock markets in developing countries, which are described as 'emerging'. When considering an equity portfolio, there is less risk in a mature market than in an emerging market; conversely, the latter offers more opportunities for gains.

The experience of 1992/3 showed that where considerable sums of money (many billions of dollars) are all of a sudden placed in an emerging market the laws of supply and demand mean the value of the shares shoots up, since there is only a limited number of shares available in the emerging market. This gain can be ephemeral, since it is only the 'weight of money' that is driving the market higher, not the underlying investment value or 'fundamentals'. What happened in the early 1990s was that US investors, in particular, faced with lower interest rates at home and a dull Dow Jones index, sought to increase the value of their holdings by pushing into hitherto underdeveloped markets. This is extremely risky, since many of these markets quote only a few shares, are relatively unregulated and are prone to classic insider dealing (those close to the market can have the ability to manipulate it). For instance, when the Bombay market crashed in 1993, one man was to blame. The most recent example of sudden collapse was in Mexico in 1994, when the stock market declined by 45% in a period of weeks.

Despite the foregoing, brokers spent a lot of time and money influencing investors to go into the emerging markets during 1992/3, with the result that unwise investors became overexposed in these comparatively risky markets, and spectacular gains turned to spectacular losses. As with the South Sea Bubble in the 1720s, investors did not appreciate that it is the value of the underlying assets of a business that they should be putting their money on, and not the aspirations of broking houses or the speculators who first placed their money in that market. A cautious approach is therefore necessary when a new product or a new market is being promoted – brokers who promote these products often have little direct experience of the market they are seeking to encourage you into. The proliferation of 'niche' investments has been particularly marked after the UK market became relatively moribund in the early 1990s (it has since perked up, though).

The expression 'emerging market' came to be applied in the 1980s to countries where there was perceived be the potential for economic growth that was not yet fulfilled. At first, the areas identified as emerging were in the Far East and Latin America. The Turkish stock market rocketed by 1,000% between 1988 and 1989. The Venezuelan market rose sixfold in 1990, and that of Argentina fourfold in 1991. As Eastern Europe turned its back on Communism the Polish market went up eight times in 1993. Like a butterfly, a market can only emerge once – its sudden take off gives huge gains, but only over a short period, before the normal economic pattern reasserts itself. Emerging countries are short of foreign ('hard') currency and are inefficient; as a result the sudden inflow of much-needed investment has an exaggerated impact on values – the investment money can be misallocated, or the market can be too inefficient or restrictive. Such inflows are the cash equivalents of colonial conquests, and, like conquests, they can go wrong or be only the forerunners of other changes. When you look at potential emerging markets for the future – Bangladesh, Egypt, Iran, Myanmar (Burma) – you realize that a lot has to change there before an investor can expect to indulge in anything more than a gamble or speculation. In true emerging markets genuine local knowledge is an absolute necessity, as is a good (and trustworthy) local agent, and both are hard to come by in such markets. When foreigners placed nearly $50 billion in emerging markets (including some that had already emerged) in 1993 the markets soared by 60%, only to fall back heavily when the investors realized they had created a bubble. To get solid value in emerging markets you must be buying your investment for a price equivalent to less than 10 years' earnings (a P/E ratio of 10 or less), and you must be buying realizable assets. In addition, some of these markets will have accounting standards that are well below the minimum Western requirements, so the buyer should beware.

It is always safer to place the majority of one's direct holdings in equities in the domestic market. Firstly, that market will contain names you recognize (Marks & Spencer, Unilever, BP, etc.). Secondly, when you invest in your domestic market you do so in your own currency, so you have no currency risk. When you invest abroad you are not only taking a risk with regard to the investment itself, you also make a judgement about how the currency of the country in question will perform against your own currency over the period for which you hold the investment. In these circumstances, a notional gain in a foreign market (in foreign-currency terms) can be turned into an actual loss in your own pocket as a result of currency fluctuations – though the reverse is also true. In addition, there are also the effects of different taxation regimes to consider. Investing abroad is therefore more complex than investing at home.

With the above in mind it is prudent to invest about 60% of equity investment in one's home market with 30% going to other mature markets, principally the USA and Europe, but also the Pacific area (which includes Japan). The other 10% could be invested in the more esoteric areas: in emerging countries, for example, or in specialized types of investment such as (with extreme caution) minerals or other commodities. If the values of equity markets around the world are compared, that of the US is worth some £2.4 to £3 trillion; Japan's £2 trillion; the UK's £750 billion; then those of Germany and France with £250 to £300 billion. In percentage terms that means the USA accounts for nearly 40% of the world's markets; Japan 25–30%; the UK 10% and Germany and France another 10% between them. In theory, it is possible to invest according to a global weighting, so that you invest proportionally to the overall market values (capitalization); this would suggest investing six times more in the US than the UK, for example. However, this is rarely a satisfactory way to proceed in practice, due to differences in reporting, financial structures and tax regulations, as well as currency considerations.

Over 85% of the world stock-market capitalization is concentrated in five countries, which are neither the largest nor the most populous. This value has arisen largely since 1900, which highlights the vast wealth created in the twentieth century. In the USA the equity market represents about 30% of total investment – a further 25% is in deposits and cash, 10% in mutual funds (unit trusts), 10% in government securities and the remaining 25% in different types of bonds, money market instruments and municipal bonds (local authority loans). In addition, probably ten times the money invested in equities (£30 trillion) is in property, and foreign investments account for £1.5 trillion. The total net worth of the US might be (conservatively) £40 to £50 trillion; Japan is probably worth half that amount, so the UK is probably worth £10 trillion.

Brokers can be instructed to have discretion in what they buy (they make the choice), or they can be asked to provide suggestions for investment, which the client agrees to or not as the case may be. The final permutation is that the client selects the investment himself, and simply instructs the broker to buy or sell on his behalf. (This self-selection operation is also something that is available for Personal Equity Plans and specialized personal pension plans.) Often the choice between these approaches is dictated by the circumstances of the client. If the client has both the time and the knowledge he may well wish to make his own selections. However, mindful of the broker's superior access to information through research and statistical records on computer, he may feel the broker is in a better position to make recommendations. Where portfolios are particularly substantial, and where the client has neither the time nor the knowledge to run the portfolio himself, a full discretionary basis of action may be appropriate. The charge for running a discretionary portfolio is higher than for a non-discretionary one – perhaps 1% of value, against 0.75%, charged quarterly or half-yearly. The greater the discretion given to the broker, the more potential risk is placed in his hands.

Where discretion is granted, strict written limits should be given to the broker; these should include a stated maximum percentage of a portfolio that can be invested in one stock (normally 5% to 10%) and should also prohibit investment in unduly risky stocks, such as unquoted shares or shares of only limited marketability. There may also be personal prohibitions – for instance a bias towards 'environmentally friendly' companies, or a ban on all investment involving tobacco or military hardware. One should however be cautious about placing too many restrictions on the broker, since political correctness is by no means a guarantee of investment success.

Rules of Engagement in Equities

Many books have been written solely on how to make a fortune from equity investments. These are often written at second or third-hand, and any genuinely successful investor is unlikely to want to share his knowledge except by way of generalities. However, even such generalities have value because they illuminate the philosophy underlying successful equity investment. Warren Buffet is probably the world's most successful living investor, having built up a net worth in excess of $10 billion from a standing start (second only, in *Forbes* 1995 listing to Bill Gates of Microsoft, who achieved $13 billion at the age of 39, again from a standing start). He is a legendary US investment figure and has been much quoted and idolized by investment gurus. His story (*see* Hangstrom, *The Warren Buffet Way*) is one of caution, care and values, always going for the long-term gain. Intelligent but with the investment savvy to take opportunities as they arose without undue risk, he learnt from the experience of Jesse Livermore (recounted, semi-fictionally, in Lefevre, *Reminiscences of a Stock Operator*) in the early twentieth century and from Benjamin Graham (author of the US investment classics *The Intelligent Investor* and *Security Analysis*, the latter with Dodd), with whom he worked. Buffet, his predecessors and followers derive their investment strengths from their clarity of vision, analytical skill, individuality and independence. To succeed on the scale of Buffet you need exceptional talent and opportunity. His successors and contemporaries – such as Paul Cabot, Philip Fisher, Benjamin Graham, T. Rowe Price and John Templeton (among others) – have all tended to operate from certain common investment theories.

Investment Strategies

Although there are as many theoretical investment strategies as investors, they tend to break down into five groupings:

Growth: This approach emphasizes investing in companies that the investor predicts will have high growth over a period of time, and on moving in and out of shares demonstrating the highest growth potential.

Value: A value investor concentrates on stocks that he believes are undervalued by the market for particular reasons – for instance, because the company concerned has just announced unexpectedly poor results, or because the market as a whole is depressed. Provided the stock is otherwise sound, the value investor will buy as others sell. His aim is to acquire stock cheap: below net asset value per share, if possible.

Technology: A technology investor buys shares that are infants in new but fast-developing technology – e.g. computers, multimedia, the Internet – always seeking out a fledgling company with phenomenal growth prospects (a Microsoft in the making). Foreseeing market leaders for a future technological niche, he will buy at a very low price when probably no one else realizes what the company does.

Speciality: This strategy focuses solely on shares in a specific market sector or market: e.g. banks, Australia. Such an investor will restrict his research to the field he is interested in, hoping to gain over his rivals through his expertise and thorough knowledge of that field.

Hunch: A hunch, or gut, investor will be a speculator, making short-term investments often, and relying on an uncanny knack for predicting change to move in and out of a market or stock at the right time. Where other investors are guided more by analysis and research, this type of operator has a shaman-type attitude, perilously close to recklessness at times.

The hunch investor is personified by George Soros, now in his sixties, who in 1995 had some $11 billion under management in his Quantum Fund. If you had invested $100,000 in the Quantum Fund in 1969 (when it started), your investment would be worth over $200 million to-day. At his peak in 1993 Soros was paid $1.1 billion, much of which he gave away through his Soros Foundation formed to assist in educational and social projects principally in Eastern Europe. One of his key coups was in 1992, when he made $1 billion in what turned out to be a one-sided bet against the British government's support of sterling in the Exchange Rate Mechanism. Yet Soros can also lose spectacularly; apparently he lost $600 million betting against the yen in 1994. Some 30% of his funds are directed towards emerging and just-emerged markets, where overall investment almost doubled from 1991 to 1993 to $94 billion. His influence is considerable (in 1994 his move into gold changed the world gold price), and indeed he is genuinely concerned that the size of his funds, of itself, changes investment patterns. Despite his speculative nature, Soros' techniques (which he has written about in considerable detail) are highly complex and are not easily followed. Political criticism of such individuals is unlikely to be effective, since their international base and vast resources make them difficult to control; they exist in a supra-governmental world that multinational companies also inhabit. They are the modern-day equivalents of the Rothschilds, Vanderbilts, Carnegies and Morgans of previous centuries.

Many highly successful investors combine characteristics of all the types we have listed. To succeed, they combine analysis and prediction, design and opportunity, controlled greed and fascination with investment, patience and independence, intelligence and knowledge, flexibility and value. This combination is rare in itself but, when allied to capital, creates very considerable fortunes for the few individuals concerned. Often they are unknown to the larger world, belonging to an exclusive club of highly-motivated multi-millionaires or billionaires who have happily allied intelligent investment to cautious opportunism over a large number of years.

Characteristics of Good Investments

Perhaps surprisingly, the most successful investors agree to a large extent on the common characteristics of a good long-term investment. These can be summarized as follows:

The expectation of above-average returns on capital from businesses with modest gearing and consistent and conventional accounting policies.
Businesses that are readily understandable and demonstrate a strong character or franchise, and so are relatively price insensitive (for instance, Coca Cola).
Strong, adept, mature management without strong egotism; businesses *not* run by geniuses or whizz kids, where management is owner/shareholder-orientated.
Companies with a strong link between profit and cash – where there is a high return on current assets (such as stock), a high turnover of current assets and modest capitalization.
Ideally, businesses where earnings are guaranteed by others' work: royalty companies, advertising, media generally.
Undervalued companies, where the quoted market price is at a discount to net asset value per share. This occurs when stocks are out of favour or in a recession.
Companies that do not have the above characteristics should be avoided.
Businesses that are highly regulated or unusually subject to political risk, such as utilities (water, gas, electricity) or railways, should also be avoided.

In general, these criteria imply a high degree of successful conservatism, the avoidance of highly indebted or highly capitalized businesses, and an investment portfolio that minimizes political risk and economic cyclical impact. Successful investors who look for these common characteristics avoid high-profile one-man bands, eschew all 'flavour-of-the-month' stocks, ignore brokers' recommendations, discard forecasts as meaningless and concentrate entirely on whether the actual performance of the company meets their essential standards. They can be wrong, but they are more often right.

One of the more endearing qualities of many of these investors is that they see investment as a part-time occupation, and believe that only by relaxing for the rest of the time can you concentrate properly on investments again! In fifty years such investors have turned $100,000 into $100 million or more. Two-thirds of brokers fail to beat the market index, but even through recessions, these investors can average 10% to 20% returns every year: double the market return. US investor John Neff returned 13% per annum for 30 years; Walter Schloss 20% a year for 39 years! These are mavericks who, for instance, disregard fixed assets (such as buildings) in making their analyses – regarding them not as assets but liabilities, in the sense that they require money spent on them once they are up, consuming rather than earning money. They are non-conventional men with an underlying distrust of both politicians and economists. In the US many of the current breed are in their late thirties, managing 100 to 200 clients, with funds under management of $50 to $100 million.

One of the qualities of these investors is that they keep a close eye on their investments. Prices move up or down, but, provided their underlying criteria are being met, they continue to hold the investments. However, if a change takes place in a company, then they will buy or sell according to whether, judged by their criteria, the change is positive or negative. If there is a mistake (as Buffet perhaps made in buying US Air or Salomon Brothers) they admit it and take steps to rectify it. These investors stick almost exclusively to shares or high-grade (high-quality) bonds, rarely if ever buying or selling warrants, options or commodities, and they aim for a consistent annual return 10% above their main market index. Although their rules for selling vary, they could be:

Sell when the stock has gained 30% to 50% on cost
Sell after two years
Sell if a dividend is missed
Sell where earnings per share are 50% higher than cost

These are rather constrained criteria, and an investor will often allow his gain to run well beyond the two-year limit (after all, any realized gain will be subject to tax), provided he is satisfied that there are no better buys.

This highlights the underlying reason for selling an investment: identifying a better long-term home for your funds. Patience and control is absolutely essential to avoid costly misanalysis. Buffet uses a benchmark of testing ten years' assets against inflation, to see if the real value of a company has been sustained without calling on additional capital. This is the key issue – maintain at least the real value of your investment.

Explicit Measures

When investment experts make their choices they emphasize

certain ratios that they use as yardsticks. Often up to forty ratios can be used to evaluate an individual stock, but with so many measures you can quietly get muddled. The maximum realistic number that have practical application is probably twenty, of which about half will be more important than the rest. So what are these measures?

Price-Earnings Ratio (P/E)

This relates the price of a company's stock to its earnings. P/E ratios vary between different countries, different market sectors and different points in the economic cycle, but they are generally regarded as one fundamental measure of value. If there are 40 million shares in a company that makes an annual profit of £20 million, the earnings are £0.50 per share; and, if the share price is £5, dividing the price per share by the earnings per share gives a P/E ratio of 10. A P/E of 10 also lets you know that the earnings yield on the share (the annual earnings as a percentage of the price) is 10% – a P/E of 20 implies a yield of 5%, and so on. It is normal for P/E ratios to vary between 10 and 25 in the UK; anything outside these norms is extraordinary – either 'cheap' or 'expensive'. Beware an unusual P/E: it usually betrays either a poorly performing stock or a 'glamour' stock, either of which could prove short-lived in terms of value. P/E comparisons should not be confined to equities in isolation – look at what you would earn elsewhere, from bonds, for instance.

Over the cycle from the top of a market to the bottom P/E ratios can average from below 10 to above 20 times earnings; in other words 10 to 20 years' purchase. In the USA P/E ratios peaked in 1992 at 25 and have since fallen to 17 – similar to the UK's 16. Prices are over three times book value in the US, which is a quarter higher than normal (both P/Es and multiples of book value tend to be higher in the US than in the UK). These measures indicate a market near or at its peak. That doesn't necessarily mean you have to wait until the market falls before you buy, but it does give opportunities for profit-taking and action if a 'correction' takes place – that is, if the market falls. Also, different market sectors peak and trough at different times in the economic cycle.

Return on Capital (ROC)

Of all investment measures ROC is given most prominence by the major individual investors. It measures annual profit against total shareholders' funds. Although it can be expressed in a number of ways it is perhaps most commonly calculated as:

$$\frac{\text{Net income + minority interest + tax-adjusted interest}}{\text{Tangible assets less short-term liabilities}}$$

This enables a more direct comparison of earnings performance than other ratios. The level of ROC can vary, but, provided it exceeds the level of return from alternative investments it indicates an outperformance of equities over other forms of investment. ROC can be used (in a modulated form) to calculate returns on non-equity investments. Comparisons of ROC between companies, particularly those in the same sector can help in the choice of investment; this measure also enables investments to be focused on high-return shares. Consistency of ROC is an indicator of stability, so an equity investor is looking for a consistently high ROC.

Earnings per Share (EPS) and Dividends per Share (DPS)

If ROC is an indicator of growth in expectations from capital, EPS and DPS measure income expectations. EPS is calculated as:

$$\frac{\text{Earnings for ordinary shareholders}}{\text{Weighted average number of ordinary shares in issue}}$$

DPS is calculated thus:

$$\frac{\text{Dividends for ordinary shareholders}}{\text{Weighted average number of ordinary shares in issue}}$$

These represent the return on each share in terms of earnings and dividends respectively. It is an important measure of value that the income from shares should be at least sustained and, ideally, rise with inflation. Since dividends normally represent some 40% to 60% of earnings, the two measures are linked.

Earnings Yield and Dividend Yield

Earnings Yield and Dividend Yield are expressed as

$$\frac{\text{EPS}}{\text{Price per share}} \quad \text{and} \quad \frac{\text{DPS}}{\text{Price per share}}$$

respectively. They extend the EPS and DPS measures to allow a comparison of percentage returns from different shares. Yields quoted in the *Financial Times* (FT) represent dividend yields net of basic-rate (20%) tax; these vary from nil (where no dividends are paid) to 10%, with an average yield of 3% to 4%. Non-equity holdings, usually Convertible Unsecured Loan Stock (CULS), have higher yields (8% to 10%) than most equities, due to the lower opportunity for gains and the longer-term nature of the commitment. Earnings and dividends per share and earnings and dividend yields assist in comparing income from different equity holdings. This is particularly important where a portfolio emphasizes income over gains; brokers emphasize growth in EPS and DPS in making their investment choices – in a robust market growth in dividends and income can exceed 10%. Again, different market sectors will reflect quite different figures, depending on their position in the economic cycle and their specific results.

Dividends have particular importance for investors, since they represent the present value of the flow of funds arising from an investment. If you assume rates of inflation over a period of time, deducting the initial cost of an investment from a discounted cash flow for the dividends it is expected to generate will give you a net present value for that investment; if positive, this indicates a real return (after inflation). Comparing different rates of real return will indicate the best choice of investment from an income point of view. Of course, assumptions about dividend rates and inflation will be critical to the figures – which is why serious investors tend to work on ten years' historic figures, rather than the five years sometimes reported in published accounts. Ten years is considered a long enough period to underpin valid assumptions about the future, since it will certainly cover the whole of at least one economic cycle.

Book Value Per Share

When buying a share you should be aware of the relationship between the share price and value of the underlying assets. This is measured by:

$$\frac{\text{Book value per ordinary share less goodwill less intangibles}}{\text{Ordinary shares in issue}}$$

What this calculation does is to strip out of the book value per share the intangibles and goodwill, which represent assets not immediately realizable (such as brands) that may be intrinsic to the business but (probably) cannot be separately valued. An investor is always hoping for good value, where the share price represents a 'fair' multiple of book value. Most shares represent 2–4 times book value and therefore imply the market's expectation of the shares' value doubling or quadrupling over time; bargains can usually be indicated where book value is close to share price (or even at a discount), and where the price is a high multiple of book value this indicates a speculative share. Bargains in shares rarely exist, so low book values per share should be subject to close scrutiny. Is there a particular reason for a low price? Will the circumstances improve or deteriorate? Unusually low share prices invariably indicate something is wrong. The greatest relevance of book value to share price is during a bear (falling) market, when sound companies are being exaggeratedly undervalued due to overall economic/political uncertainties or generalized gloom: this indicates a buying opportunity.

Current Ratio and Quick Ratio

When assessing the stability of a business the Current Ratio and Quick Ratio are often used:

$$\frac{\text{Current Assets}}{\text{Current Liabilities}} \quad \text{and} \quad \frac{\text{Current Assets less Stocks}}{\text{Current Liabilities}}$$

Both these ratios ignore long-term fixed and tangible assets (such as equipment, vehicles and property) and concentrate on current items – those payable or receivable within the next year. For banking purposes these ratios are immediate indicators of liquidity. A current ratio of 2 and a quick ratio of 1 are normal. Ratios higher than this indicate non-productive assets (e.g. too much cash – a criticism levelled at GEC in recent years); lower ratios imply potential liquidity problems that would require longer-term borrowing arrangements or increased share capital.

The above ratios (and other permutations thereof) are analytical tools, not theoretical exercises in arithmetic. They have a value if used for critical appraisal of a company and for comparing it to other companies. Obviously all such ratios need to be updated with new figures from interim (half-year) or final (full-year) results as they are released.

It underlies the broking process that the brokers' analysts provide them with this information, critically appraised and neatly packaged into Sell, Buy or Hold recommendations, and the extensive use of computers in broking has meant that this analytical process (and much else besides) is becoming increasingly homogeneous. This can create a herd instinct – something that has a tendency to generate stampedes. Ideally, an individual investor should appraise shares for *himself*, in the context of his own requirements *only*. The lone-wolf approach, intelligently applied, is likely to produce investment kills that the brokers have missed. It also enables a much more sanguine approach to time and change in pursuit of the slow but sure buck.

Investment in Unit or Investment Trusts

As we have seen, the incidence of transaction charges means that direct investment in equities requires relatively substantial amounts of money in order to make the investment in single stocks cost-effective. This creates a difficulty for smaller investors, and as a result new products have been created since the 1960s, to enable the smallest of equity investors to make regular monthly payments, or lump-sum annual payments, to buy equities through the medium of investment or unit trusts. Such trusts aggregate these small sums with many other similarly small sums to create a large investment fund. As time has gone on brokers have created an immense diversity of different types of investment and unit trusts to cater for all investment tastes. These funds can focus on a particular stock market, or a particular sector within a stock market, or can, quite literally, be global. The more general the fund, the more likely it is to achieve results that reflect overall market conditions. As with stocks themselves the shares or units in these funds are quoted in financial pages of newspapers, but caution should be applied when taking a valuation from this source, since the prices quoted exclude selling costs.

Investors should take care when choosing investment or unit trust funds to ensure that they meet their personal investment requirements. Certain funds emphasize growth, while others have income as the objective, and new funds are being created all the time by brokers to take advantage of changes in stock-market structures or to invest in a 'flavour-of-the-month' investment sector. Performances of investment and unit trusts vary widely, as might be expected, since they simply reflect the underlying performance of the individual investments that make up the trust's portfolio. Brokers or fund managers should, at the very least, provide their investors with annual statements showing the number of units invested for their payments and their value. The number of units purchased will vary according to the prices on the day when the funds are in the broker's hands – so an investor making regular monthly payments will find that the number of units acquired differs from month to month.

Up to 1994 six million UK individuals had invested nearly £140 billion in unit or investment trusts: over £90 billion in unit trusts and half that sum in investment trusts (ITs). Overall there are about 1,500 different unit trusts and 300 investment trusts. Unit trusts can offer an unlimited number of units (so are 'open-ended'), but there are restrictions on how they can invest, and they are not allowed to borrow money to invest. ITs can borrow to make leveraged investments, but the number of shares they can issue is restricted (so they are 'closed ended'). Over time ITs have tended to perform slightly better than unit trusts, probably reflecting their less restricted operation; unit trusts, on the other hand, are less risky, due to those same investment restrictions.

Initial fees on ITs and unit trusts are usually 5%, followed by annual management charges of 1% (similar to most managed funds). Special offers on rates are often used to encourage initial investment, particularly as investment competition has grown. The difference between the buying and selling price can be up to 7%. To qualify for tax relief, investment in unit trusts has to be for a minimum period of time, usually five years, and many investment plans are for ten years. They are therefore intended to be a long-term savings vehicle and would not suit short-term funds.

As with other forms of equity investment it is important not to lose sight of general market conditions, and all plans will generally allow a switch to be made each year between the various funds managed by the same investment house. This enables investors to make changes in the balance of their investment, so that, where a market has fundamentally changed, disadvantages are minimized. There are normally penalties if more than one switch is made in any one year.

Investment in unit trusts has been encouraged by governments as a way of channelling small investors into equities in a relatively safe way and of encouraging regular savings – this is why there are tax incentives for making such investments – and some 80% of unit trust investors subscribe monthly. In most of these trusts income is 'rolled up' and re-invested, so that the impetus for growth is in gains and not in income. Provided the investment is maintained throughout the stipulated period, the funds are normally tax-free on maturity, when they are returned to the investor at the prevailing market value.

Unit and investment trusts are often used as a way of investing in more specialized markets, to reduce risk. For instance the investment brokers Gartmore are known as specialists in Far East markets, and often a Gartmore investment trust is chosen to cover this area of the investment world; this is a relatively cheap way of hiring their expertise, since, due to the large number of small investors, the funds in their control are large. The disadvantage of such trusts is that (apart from the annual opportunity to switch), once you are invested you are pretty well stuck with the investment; a long-term view of the likely market performance is therefore important. Where markets are immature or particularly sensitive to external factors, unit or investment trusts are therefore less suitable to invest in.

Unit trusts of over 20 different types are listed in the FT: from UK General, to International Balanced, to Financial and Property. In a year a unit trust can gain or lose 20% of the value put in; after three years it would be expected to have made a gain of at least 15%, though the figure could be much higher or much lower (the best performer at the time of writing had gained 270%; the worst had lost over 15%). Performance tables for unit trusts (possibly invented, so cynics say, to support claims of historically outstanding performance, and so encourage new investment) are generally based on a three-year performance record. Most unit trusts have been around for five years, but not so many have been around for ten. Current ten-year performance records show a top gain of over seven times (a technology UT), but only 50% at the bottom end (in commodities and energy); over five years technology is again top (gaining nearly 500%) while Japan is at the bottom (a small loss). It is wasted effort to predict how future unit trust performance will shape up. For a ten-year period, with such a plethora of choice, it is difficult at the outset to advise anything other than a spread of investment types. It is perhaps true to say that, over a very long period, every investment dog will have its day.

To make a similar comparison for investment trusts, there are again over 20 different classifications, covering different parts of the globe, different market sectors, and different aims and emphases regarding capital and income – high-income, split (income-and-capital), zero-dividend. Here, too, technology has been a great gainer in recent years, while Latin America has reflected the worst general performance in ITs, as opposed to Japan in UTs. Overall results show greater gains over three years in ITs (for example, 600%, compared to the best unit trust performer's 400%). However, both IT and UT results assume that income is reinvested and mid-prices are used (halfway between buy and sell prices) – a basis that gives an advantage to ITs – so there is no real direct comparison. History also tells us that the best-performing sector one year could be the worst next year (after all, if we knew the future then our investment strategy would be simple). It is important to retain an IT or UT investment throughout its normal life to give it a chance to perform; often a panic decision to sell when performance is poor simply means surrendering future gains and maximizing the cost involved.

Personal Equity Plans

As part of the Conservative government's strategy to encourage equity investment and savings generally, Personal Equity Plans (PEPs) were introduced in 1986 by Chancellor Lawson to encourage small investors to place annual amounts directly in equity funds. Neither any gains arising nor the income would be taxed, provided the plan was retained throughout the required five-year period of the investment. Currently the maximum that any individual may put into a PEP is £6,000 per annum in a general plan and £3,000 in a single-company investment, and the funds have to be invested by 5 April in each year.

This deadline creates very considerable hype in the personal equity market around the end of the tax year, and, although the hype is aimed at all investors, PEPs are, generally speaking, really only relevant for higher rate taxpayers who are already making full use of their tax-free capital gains allowance (currently £6,000 per annum). If an investor has realized gains of less than this limit they will not be taxed anyway, even if he doesn't have a PEP, and for a basic-rate taxpayer the tax advantage of dividend income from a PEP (likely to be very small anyway, given that yields are 3–4% currently) can be cancelled out by the broker's charges for running the plan: up to 3% initially, plus 1% per annum management fee.

PEPs are therefore not necessarily suitable for many investors and, despite increased competition on charges, many PEPs have not performed that well. Historically, they have also been restricted to UK equities (although this is changing), so recent market conditions (except 1995) have made for relatively dull performance. Moreover, the manner in which investors are encouraged into PEPs means that brokers are unlikely to stress how slim the advantages (if there are any) are for some investors, and the government, out of deference to a multi-billion-pound industry, is unlikely to point out the relative neutrality of such investment: what you gain on the 'tax break' you lose on the charges.

However, higher-rate taxpayers, who took advantage of a PEP

from day one could now have invested something approaching £60,000 tax-free, or £120,000 in the case of married couples. This would have provided a potential tax saving of 40% on PEP income, and of 100% on realised gains (in excess of the tax-free limit) throughout the period.

Most unit-trust PEPs have increased in value: by 7% over the past year, by 50% over three years, and by 80% over five years; the best have increased by nearly 250% in five years. This performance is rather below that of UTs and also of ITs. This may well reflect the relatively high charges associated with PEPs, the fact that they may be a poor relation of more direct forms of investment, or that they are simply more risk-averse, and therefore mean a lower return. These figures suggest that the value of a unit trust PEP is really in the tax relief – but this would be available in a ten-year unit trust anyway, so why invest in a unit trust PEP?

Pensions

The provision of pensions for private individuals has expanded enormously since the 1960s. Individuals can make pension contributions either through their employer or on their own, or both. The idea behind a pension is that when you retire funds available through your pension plan will enable you to maintain your personal standard of living, or at least maintain a better standard of living than would be possible through the state scheme. Moreover, demographic changes in recent years have meant that the possibility of the State providing anything like a living pension on retirement in the twenty-first century is nigh on zero, so the government has therefore been at pains to encourage pensions for all employees and self-employed people through tax incentives, making premiums allowable against tax up to certain maximum amounts per annum. Current average earnings are £23,000 a year for a non-manual male worker, £15,000 for a non-manual female worker, £15,000 for a manual male worker and £10,000 for a manual female worker, and it is now estimated that, for an average non-manual male UK earner to retire at sixty-five and live a further twenty years without reducing his standard of living, would require a pension fund of quarter of a million pounds. (This assumes that the tax system is the same and that the mortgage is repaid.) It is therefore likely that most of those retiring in the twenty-first century will be poorer in real terms than those retiring at any time since before World War II. Very few people appreciate how much money is required to maintain their personal income, net of tax, for the future.

In the USA vast amounts of money have been concentrated on this problem, and employees begin saving in their early twenties – in the UK few people make any serious provision before their mid-thirties at the earliest. Against the background of increasingly uncertain employment, and with career spans shrinking, the real possibility of enforced redundancy/retirement at the age of fifty-five in the future means that earners will save for only twenty years before a retirement that might then last for thirty years. Even the most optimistic investment adviser would have to admit that in such circumstances income from savings could not even begin to support previous standards of living in retirement (even assuming that the individual maintained good health throughout retirement, and so made no calls on capital to support invalid care). Where the major assets of most families is a single freehold property, even the sale of that could not plug the gap likely to arise on retirement income.

Against this rather depressing background, investors should make positive decisions about their pension requirements and seek to take advantage of all the tax breaks possible to ensure that, as far as possible, their pension is secure. It is highly unlikely that the state benefit will increase consistently in real terms over the next 20 years, and, given its relatively low value (currently £56 per week), it can probably be safely ignored for investment purposes. Whatever you invest for a pension, the same criteria as for any other form of investment apply, but with greater emphasis on a conservative, low-risk approach, since this money is to be what you will live off in (many) later years.

A large number of different policies are available for pensions, and specialist advice should be sought from an independent source in order to wade through the complex plans an offer. Most of them require a regular amount to be saved monthly, which builds up to a capital sum on retirement at a specified date. This amount can be taken either as a lump sum plus a small annual income, or as an annual income. The choice of the date of retirement should be made in the context of all other capital and income available at that point, since it may be advisable to defer taking the pension if other resources are available. This is because the pension fund is a tax-free fund, with neither income nor capital subject to tax while they remain in the fund; income is fully taxable once it is taken when the fund matures. It is advisable to make pension investments with a number of different pension companies, with a minimum of two and a maximum of five, to ensure that the risk in the underlying investments is spread.

As earnings increase, new plans can be considered or old plans can be adapted to meet current circumstances. Pension companies have taken considerable pains to make their products more flexible through time, and investors should regularly review their policies to update them; each year the pension company will produce annual statements of value for the fund, and these should be used as a means of evaluating current and future pension needs. In practice, this is rarely done, so that individuals are stuck with plans that have become old-fashioned and are relatively inflexible. It is important not to oversubscribe to any particular plan in early years, to enable maximum flexibility to be maintained to ensure the risk of being locked into an 'old' plan is minimized. If pressed to do so, most pension providers will change terms to best current practice – something most investors are unaware of.

Since there are tax advantages to paying money into a pension, it makes sense to make additional contributions, if there is cash available, by way of a single premium on an annual basis to maintain the maximum pension investment allowed. Most people make their pension contributions through a scheme run by a large life assurance/investment company, which purchases underlying investment units on the pension holder's behalf, but it is also possible to run an independent scheme that will enable individuals to create their own fund. These funds are often linked to a business, enabling the directors of the company to benefit from this executive pension scheme. Where the funds are relatively substantial (£100,000 or more), the advantage of such a scheme is that it enables a more flexible approach to investment to be adopted, and it can be used to cover different retirement circumstances, with the benefits based on the earning capacity of the individual members of the scheme on retirement. Normally these schemes aim for a payment of up to two-thirds of final salary at the age of retirement, which can be from the age of fifty-five onwards; as with other schemes, a lump sum can be taken tax-free at the time of retirement. Due to the advantages to be gained from these corporate schemes by a relatively small minority, the government has in recent years curtailed the level of contributions allowed in the company for tax purposes, so as to limit the unfair advantage to high earners who could 'shelter' their income through their pension-fund contributions. Such funds also have the advantage that they can be used to make loans to the beneficiaries before retirement. The Inland Revenue will only allow payments to such schemes where they meet specific criteria, and the Superannuation Funds Office must specifically approve such schemes before they can be effective.

The demographics of pension provision are stark. The dependency ratio (those aged 15–64 in relation to those of 65 or more) is presently about 20% but will double by the year 2040. UK pension funds have about £500 billion invested (of which 75% is in equities, a proportion that has grown steadily), or 80% of the UK Gross Domestic Product (GDP) – a proportion which is one of the highest in Europe (significantly, and perhaps surprisingly, the Germans have one of the lowest ratios, at less than 10% of GDP). Since there are approximately 20 million employees in Britain, the average per employee is £25,000 – well short of the estimate of £250,000 needed for an average non-manual worker to retire without reducing living standards. (This simplistic calculation does not take into account the cumulative total of past workers, now retired, nor the unemployed or never- or part-employed.) The numbers will simply not add up unless there is a strong incentive to save, reminiscent of an earlier age; not many of us will win the National Lottery. Now consider that the UK has one-third of the entire pension fund saving in the EC, which makes us among the most prudent of pension providers in Europe.

In 1994 it emerged that most of the best-known investment companies in the UK had been stimulating savings in their own schemes by encouraging many public-sector workers to opt out of the comparatively generous state scheme (SERPS) and join their schemes on the basis of a better product and greater value. This proved to have been a disingenuous front to earn maximum commissions, and in the process largely diminish the value of the employee's pension fund. As a result the companies concerned will have to set aside approximately £2.5 billion to compensate for pensions mis-sold by 'trained consultants' who had been given half a day's pep-talk about the industry and a telephone directory and told to get on with it. Provisions for this in 1994 alone amounted to some £400 million: Allied Dunbar provided £103 million, Lloyds Abbey Life £80 million, Barclays Life £58 million, and so on through a comprehensive list of life and pension companies. A subsequent programme of apparently rigorous retraining has meant that pension 'consultants' are once more fit to consult with, though it could be said that there are now simply different ways to earn a commission. The watchword, therefore, is still *caveat emptor*. But how is a buyer to beware when some of the most trusted names on the investment map give bad advice? The simple answer is try to be independent: ask around, ask people who actually know, who have no axe to grind and have their own successful history to demonstrate. Get different quotes from different sources; spread the risk; do not commit until you have talked it over with a sensible third party. If you aren't sure, don't do it.

If something does go wrong, complain to the pension company first. If this fails to get results, then complain to the Occupational Pensions Advisory Service, and if that produces negative results move on to the Pensions Ombudsman. You have to complain within three years of the event you are complaining about, but there is no maximum to the compensation that can be awarded. As in all financial matters, keep copies of all correspondence and documentation somewhere secure – where the dog and children can't chew it or otherwise reduce it to pulp. The actual policy documents should be kept particularly safe; if you can't trust yourself, deposit the documents with your bank for safe-keeping. If considering a major complaint get professional advice from an accountant and solicitor; in the long-term this should save considerable time and trouble in formulating a clear, well-argued and convincing claim.

3 Non-traditional Direct Investment

Commodities

Commodities is the collective name given to real or nominal mineral or agricultural goods in bulk. These goods are traded on commodity markets, for which the prices are published on a summary daily basis, as with stocks and shares. The first Commodities Exchange was established in Chicago in 1850, to cover trade in grain, and Liverpool's exchange for the grain trade opened shortly afterwards. The commodity market now covers a whole range of agricultural products, crops and minerals, and is divided into two broad sectors. Tin, lead, zinc, copper, nickel, silver and other minerals are termed hard commodities; soft commodities cover agricultural products such as sugar, coffee, cocoa, rubber and soya beans. Separate markets exist for grain, potatoes and petroleum (oil).

Commodity exchanges deal not only in the physical goods, but also in futures contracts. These contracts involve a binding commitment from a party to buy or sell identified amounts of goods within a specified period at a specified price. To open such a trade and enter the futures market only about 10% of the contract value has to be deposited with a specialist commodity broker. It is usually the broker who executes the order on the relevant commodity exchange. A detailed contract covers the quantity, delivery, date and price at which the commodity has been bought or sold. In due course the transaction is open (i.e. an account has been opened with the commodity broker) unless the client wants to take physical possession of the commodity. At the appropriate due date, the commodity will show a loss or profit. The client sells and receives payment less commission. Where the commodity shows a loss of over 5% of the original 10% deposit, the broker is likely to request the 'position' to be closed, to prevent further loss, or the client may provide further funds to maintain the 10% deposit (the latter action is known as a 'margin call').

For strategic reasons, much of the trade in commodities is undertaken by international agreement at prices arranged between the producer and consumer countries. Thus it becomes necessary to examine commodities on a worldwide basis, and research should include geography, climate, technology and usage (especially in the case of metals). An investor in commodities may choose to rely entirely on the feel of the market, but some reliable independent source of information is recommended. Among the leading journals for commodities are *Metal Bulletin* and *Petroleum Today*. Each of the commodities does have its own trade journal and substantial annual statistical sources, such as BP's statistical review of world energy, which details data on oil production worldwide. The impact of external factors on commodity markets in recent years illustrates their extraordinary volatility. Frost had a substantial impact on the coffee market in both 1984 and 1994 (in March 1984 the coffee price in London rose from £1,800 to £4,000 a tonne in 10 minutes!), while platinum prices since 1988 have been affected by the widespread introduction of catalytic converters for cars, and bauxite has been affected by the introduction of synthetic alternatives.

There have been occasional attempts to 'corner' commodity markets – tin, silver and soya beans have all been targets in the past twenty years. Among the best known efforts was that by the Texan oil billionaires, Bunker Hunt and his brother Herbert, to corner the silver market. They began buying silver in 1973 and, unusually, took physical delivery of the commodity. In August 1979 they moved up in scale when they arranged purchases with the offshore International Metals Investment company. The silver price moved from $9.60 to $52.50 an ounce in both Chicago and New York, and this caused the Chicago exchange to change its rules, allowing only sales. Locked into their forward commitments, the Hunts were cornered, and in February and March 1980 they were forced to borrow heavily to meet their commitments, taking out the staggering equivalent of 12.9% of all new loans in the USA in those two months. On 27 March 'Silver Thursday' the price plummeted, and the Hunts were left with debts of about $1,825 million – which inspired Bunker Hunt's classic remark, 'A billion dollars isn't what it used to be'. Fearful of the consequences of default, the international banks arranged a loan to the Hunts, conditional on their substantial personal assets being mortgaged.

Risks in Commodity Investment

The 'locked-in' nature of futures contracts creates the well-known high-risk nature of commodity investment, and investors require considerable amounts of both nerve and funds. Commodity prices are subject to a vast range of variables at local, national and international levels, which can relate to circumstances as diverse as strikes, tropical storms, war or disease. There is a consensus that sales should be made where there are locally declining or stable prices, low inflation or hyper-inflation, but it appears that only experience can deliver informed judgements on optimum times to buy or sell. Quotes for commodity prices are tabulated in the financial media for specific periods, ranging from one month ahead to eight months ahead for agricultural products (such as rubber) and twelve months for gas and oil. There is no limit on the daily trade in metals, including gold, coffee and grain (wheat and barley). Leading companies worldwide have sought to use all future markets, including those for commodities, to 'hedge' or ride out fluctuations in the values of currencies.

Derivatives

One of the means by which 'hedging' may be undertaken – derivatives – has attracted enormous publicity, more for its consequences than for its action. Derivatives are options (the right to buy or sell), rather than futures (which are obligations to buy and sell a specific commodity), a step or sometimes two removed from an actual investment. However, options are also given on stock indexes, currency, interest rates, even on futures contracts. It was the case of foreign exchange which brought down the British bank Barings in 1995, when Nick Leeson bet on a substantial rise in the Japanese stock market over three months (a decision, it appears, partly influenced by the consequences of the Kobe earthquake). As it happened, the market fell, speculators who sold the Japanese Index forward made substantial profits and Barings suffered a crippling loss. Another form of derivatives which attracted attention was the currency swap, giving a fixed rate on one currency against rising rates on others. Local councils in Britain sought to use such swaps by issuing bonds from the late 1980s, and it appears that the vast majority lost on such gambles – although courts ruled such swaps were illegal and (controversially) that the debts thereby incurred were void. The British company Allied Domecq (formerly Allied Lyons) lost millions on such swaps, which also cut the 1994 pre-tax profits of the US company Air Products and Chemicals by $122 million. In December 1994 Orange County, California, filed for bankruptcy after admitting it had lost nearly $1 billion through derivative trading.

Another form of dealing in derivatives is the foreign exchange forward contract, an agreement made to buy a foreign currency in the future at a price specified now. This form of derivative is, perhaps unknowingly, used by millions every year when buying foreign currency from tour operators for their holidays. Tour operators require such forward purchases to function in worldwide competitive markets, and these arrangements can cover not only currencies, but also fuel (as in the case of charter flights) and accommodation. The most familiar consequences of such forward contracts for the tourist are either surcharges or discounts. A third type of common derivative is the inverse floater. In this instance the option becomes a hedge for contrary movements in the markets, not unlike an each-way bet. The value of this type of contract will increase where the option for purchase is against the run of the market concerned.

The reputation of derivatives may seem to suggest that the world's financial markets are a casino, and hedging more akin to a game of chance than a professional skill. Nevertheless, such contracts are both widespread and a necessary investment tool for the larger concern in the late twentieth century. They are also essential in some areas for the smooth running of trade where demand fluctuates but supply is relatively constant; such 'normal' use of derivatives applies to corn, oil, gold and other commodities in daily use, where supply is determined by available resources and natural conditions.

Lloyd's of London Insurance

Lloyd's of London is a society of underwriters in the insurance market, incorporated by Acts of Parliament dating from 1871. It provides an internal market for a broad range of insurance. The specialist underwriters accept insurance risks on behalf of members (the 'Names') grouped into syndicates that are identified by number and title. These syndicates specialize in particular types of insurance business – marine, motor, and so on. Each underwriting agent requires approval by the Council of Lloyd's. The Council consists of 28 members: 8 nominated subject to confirmation by the Governor of the Bank of England, 12 elected from within Lloyd's, and 8 drawn from external underwriters. Although Lloyd's is controlled by Acts of Parliament, most of the regulation of its affairs remains internal, and it is therefore said to be 'self-regulated'. Lloyd's syndicates have no direct contact with the public.

Up to 1994, any individual with sufficient 'unpledged' assets (a minimum figure varying from syndicate to syndicate between £100,000 and £250,000) could become a 'Name'. Names are recommended to join a series of syndicates, undertake to lodge a deposit (in the form of approved securities or other liquid financial assets) determined at 30% of their agreed annual underwriting limit, and accept unlimited liability for the risks insured in their name. Lloyd's operates on a three-year accounting period, so the record loss of £1.373 billion declared in 1989 actually related to the year 1986 (the reason for such a long delay is to enable all claims to be settled, which may take a considerable time).

It was this record loss that exposed the scale of unlimited liability shouldered by the Names and prompted the first of a series of court actions by 2,000 of them (some 10% of the total membership). Many of these actions alleged negligence by the underwriting agents in the syndicates, the diversion of losses to mitigate the effect on 'inside' Names at Lloyd's and, by extension, collusion in the process of 'churning' liabilities from one syndicate to another – allegedly a process of 'pass the parcel', with each syndicate charging a fee for reinsurance of the liability, until the buck appeared to stop with the external Names. This was the so-called London market excess-of-loss business (also termed the 'reinsurance spiral'), in which the same insurance risks were passed round the same syndicates, enriching the underwriters through commission.

The process of redressing these liabilities in the British courts has not been a simple matter for the 'injured' Names. A large number of members of the British judiciary were themselves Names, so only a limited number of judges with no involvement in Lloyds, and hence impartial, were available to preside over the court actions. In effect this caused cases to be delayed or spread over an unusually long period. All the while, the liabilities of the Names concerned grew as a result of the retrospective nature of the liabilities. Lloyd's Council was pressured to establish a hardship fund and instigate reform of the market from 1991, not least as a result of questions in Parliament. Certain of these reforms were put to the vote of members.

It became apparent that for a number of Names their commitment to Lloyd's went beyond all normal financial prudence, and consequently was ruinous. On the balance of evidence, some should not have been nominated in the first instance, given that their assets were illiquid. It also became apparent that the general 'can't lose' euphoria of the 1980s might have encouraged some Lloyd's agents to attract new Names by indicating that underwriting losses, relieved of top-rate tax, would at the very least be counteracted by investment gains and income. How wrong they were! By the end of 1995 – although Lloyd's had introduced reforms, opened itself to corporate interests from 1994, sought multi-million pound settlements with syndicates (such as Gooda Walker) and agreed limits to 'calls' on the Names to enable them to meet their debts without descending into complete penury – the whole affair had inflicted substantial damage to the name of Lloyd's of London.

Though certain observers and monitors of the market, notably Chartstat, suggested that Lloyd's faced imminent demise, there were prospects for recovery by 1995, despite the fact that almost half the Names had left the market (by November 1994 the number of Names had fallen to 16,000 from 32,000 in 1988). Among the principal reforms was a scheme that allowed ongoing Names to transfer from unlimited to limited liability. Under the proposals, Names would establish an incorporated company that would reinsure their previous underwriting commitments; in return each Name would have to pay a premium. Under the plan Lloyd's cut the minimum unencumbered net tangible assets and funds required from a Name from £1.5 million to £100,000.

The Spread of Risk in Lloyd's

One of the principal reasons for the survival of Lloyd's derived from its diversity. Lloyd's has four main markets: Marine, which covers all aspects of shipping and maritime insurance (best reflected in the ringing of the Lutine Bell when a ship or other marine entity – such as an oil rig – is lost at sea); Aviation, covering aircraft and aerospace; Motors, covering the motorist; and Non-Marine, which includes cover for natural disasters, burglary and other risks. It was from the Non-Marine sector that the Lloyd's problems stemmed. During the 1970s and 1980s there was imprudent underwriting of risk related to toxic waste sites, and unforeseen damages claims for asbestosis arose as a result of debilitating respiratory conditions caused by breathing dust from the mineral asbestos, widely used in buildings since the 1940s. Disaster underwriting, covering *inter alia* earthquakes and hurricane damage, had also given rise to unprecedented claims stemming from a series of storms in the late 1980s and from the *Exxon Valdez* oil-spill in Alaska. The scale of the potential loss to property and casualty insurers in the USA was reflected in the 1994 report of A.M. Best, the US insurance ratings group, which suggested the clean-up of asbestos contamination and other environmental threats would cost such insurers about $132 billion over 25 years.

With much attention given to the losses from disaster underwriting and US legal liability claims, the profitability of the underwriting of aviation, shipping and motor insurance through the 1990s tended to be overlooked. By one Name's estimate in 1995, the average return from an (unencumbered) syndicate in the years 1975 to 1995 averaged about 8% a year. Thus, there still exist opportunities for profitable returns by Lloyd's Names and, from 1994, the possibility of membership at one remove, through investment in new corporate members.

Restructuring Lloyd's

Among the aims of the reconstitution of Lloyd's was a clean break with the past in order to maximize long-term returns. In February 1996 Lloyd's ended the hardship fund and sought to split itself into two. One element, Equitas, was to be established to cover the past liabilities. The second element was the introduction of a 'new' Lloyd's, geared towards corporate or collective membership of syndicates. It was accepted that the new corporate members would contribute towards the £460 million estimated cost of reconstruction.

The corporate membership is of two types. First, those investors who, as trusts, invest in a wide range of Lloyd's syndicates, thereby spreading the risk, and in addition seek advice from specialist advisers to propose potential high-return underwriting sectors. The second type of corporate member seeks to invest in syndicates run by one Lloyd's managing agency. To date, the latter type is seen to offer better returns and lower costs, where investors can choose their own syndicates. By February 1996 there were 25 Lloyd's Investment Trusts, the largest being LIMIT (London Insurance Market Investment Trust) and the second-largest CLM Insurance.

4 The Question of Balance

The aim of many investors is to provide both income and capital gains (an increase over the original investment) and to lay-off their risk and take a long term view. If this is your aim it is essential that you order your financial affairs so as to achieve, as far as possible, a common-sense balance between different assets and liabilities, but a balance that is sufficiently flexible for appropriate changes to be made, as economic constraints and personal circumstances change.

Most people will find that they have no means of dealing with capital before the age of twenty-five, because they haven't got any (there are exceptional individuals who have made their money before this age, but they are extremely rare). As for inherited capital, few parents will anticipate their children being able to benefit before the age of twenty-five even though the legal minimum age for ownership of most assets is eighteen. This is because, being parents, they consider their offspring entirely irresponsible until age shall bring them a certain level of maturity (and even this is not guaranteed!). We shall assume therefore, that major asset purchases will not take place until the age of twenty-five.

An individual's first major asset acquisition is usually a house or flat. This is followed by investment policies designed to protect the holder from financial consequences of ill-health, death and mortgage debt – in other words permanent health insurance, life assurance and probably an endowment policy together with a mortgage protection policy – and often these risks are linked. At this stage most individuals will have little capital since a large proportion of their net income is taken up in meeting loan commitments, policy payments and day-to-day living. Between the ages of twenty-five and forty-five most individuals are likely to enter into some form of permanent relationship, which often results in children adding to the financial burden. Whereas up to the age of twenty-five all their spare money may have been spent on themselves, from then until the age of forty-five it is spent on their children and home. It is therefore unusual for even an astute and careful earner and consumer to have any significant funds to invest before he is forty-five, unless he inherits wealth or enjoys a sudden windfall, such as a major lottery or premium-bond win. (There are, of course many exceptions to this: entrepreneurial individuals, or those working in youth industries – such as fashion, music, film and TV – who have to accumulate most of their wealth before they are considered 'past it'.) Even those who survive in their business with some success into their forties find that it is only then that they have managed to repay their borrowings and build up even a modicum of investable capital; and yet this can be swept away through divorce or separation, which can further delay any investment of savings for years. The reality is that for most people it is only on repayment of their mortgage at around the age of fifty that any break-through in their domestic economics will actually arise – by which time they may have been working for thirty years. This explains the maturity of most investors.

The potential for comparatively high rewards in sport, where by definition the emphasis is on youth, is rarely carried through into the post-sport part of people's lives, but there are examples. In the 1980s the footballer Francis Lee, formerly of Manchester City, Derby and England, sold his soft-tissue business for £8 million and has probably doubled that value since. Another footballer, David Whelan of Blackburn Rovers, sold his JJB Sports chain, Europe's largest independent, for £50 million. Similar success stories have come from George Walker (the boxer, since knocked out of Brent Walker amid continuing acrimony and court cases), Alan Pascoe (hurdling gold medallist who created Alan Pascoe Associates), Phil Edmonds (Middlesex and England cricketer with a variety of business interests that have made him a millionaire). Most recently David Lloyd has sold the sport and leisure clubs named after him to brewer Whitbread, grossing up to £20 million. British sporting earnings generally pale into insignificance against those of Americans; basketball legend Michael Jordan reputedly earns $30 million a year just from endorsements, and tennis star André Agassi attracted over $80 million in backing from Nike over a decade, ten times his earnings from tennis itself. Boom can also turn to bust, though. Both Bjorn Borg and Steffi Graf learnt that ignorance of financial matters is no protector of a fortune earned from sponsorship and sporting acumen. On the world stage perhaps Tony O'Reilly, former Irish rugby union player, is the most successful sporting businessman, with an estimated personal fortune of £250 million derived from his directorship of food company Heinz; in 1991 alone his remuneration totalled $75 million.

Income Versus Growth

The portfolio mix will be determined by whether the emphasis is put on income or on capital growth. Where insufficient funds are available from employment or other savings, income is likely to be the main requirement from investment. Conversely, where income is sustained and sufficient the investment portfolio will emphasize capital growth. Since any income-producing investment is linked with a capital value anyway, it is usual for income and capital to arise together, and if income is not required it is reinvested as it arises. Where the earnings have been reinvested, however, share portfolio valuations can often distort the true performance of a portfolio. Since the return (yield) on a share by way of dividend is likely to be 3–4% in any given year, this percentage should be taken into account in measuring the true performance of the portfolio in capital terms.

There are assets such as the family home which do not produce income, and these should be seen as part of a balance of assets, each of which has a different emphasis in the overall pattern of net worth. It is important to ensure that non-income-producing assets are not given too much prominence in a portfolio mix. Where no income arises, the entire emphasis must be on capital growth, and this is often more difficult to achieve consistently in non-income-producing assets. An example of this type of investment is gold, which is often retained as an investment of last resort – 'when the bomb drops' it will still (perhaps) have a value. Western investors have tended to shy away from gold in this context over the last ten to fifteen years, so that it is now seen more as an industrial asset used in manufacturing than as a true investment. The gold price, at some $380, has not varied significantly for some time.

The investor's age is also a determinant of whether the investment emphasis is on income or capital growth. On retirement it is often the case that a switch is made to income-producing assets, rather than those intended to generate capital growth, since income from employment has probably ceased and the time scale for obtaining capital growth during the investor's lifetime is reducing. This is why annuities are popular as a form of retirement investment, since they guarantee a certain annual income over a period of time through retirement. Before retirement, emphasis is likely to be on growth, since, assuming one is living within one's means, there is no need to take capital to subsidize living expenses while income is arising from employment. Nonetheless, however the portfolio is constituted, there should always be a plan, and this plan should be adhered to unless a radical change in circumstances makes its targets impossible to achieve. The plan itself should be flexible, so as to deal with changes in circumstances on a regular (say, quarterly) basis.

Most investors do not actually have plans, and most brokers do not have specific targets in value terms which they have to meet year on year. Objectives tend to be linked to inflation and to the general performance of the domestic market. In other words, most investments are dealt with on the basis that they have to maintain their real worth (beat inflation) and should aim to at least match the performance of a relevant index, such as the FT100 or the FT All-Share Index. To some extent such an approach is bound to be self-fulfilling, since if investments are made largely in (blue-chip) FT100 stocks, which tend to be relatively low-risk, then achieving the required result should be within the capabilities of any competent investor. The most successful investors tend to use information provided by companies themselves (such as the fully detailed versions of annual reports) or by stock brokers and make their own evaluations, ignoring the herd instinct that most investors follow. In this way they can achieve results well beyond those achieved by the average investor, but this requires intelligence, diligence and nerve. Virtually no private investors are able to follow the example of these 'masters of the universe', since they have neither the time nor the skills required. In the USA many private investors seek to achieve a return of 10% above inflation on their investments each year; on this basis most brokers in the UK would have no clients. The performance of UK brokers is prompted by the fact that the majority of their clients are institutional investors, such as pension funds and life-assurance companies, who wield very considerable power in investments and thereby tend to influence brokers into safe, well-known situations. There are examples of spectacular mismanagement of such funds, such as the Maxwell pension fund, but these are comparatively rare, since security is a major factor with most investors. For most brokers, therefore, growth performance is likely to follow the pattern of the market generally, and it follows that over a period of time they will not achieve results that consistently outperform the market.

When investments are offered for sale – in new funds, via a prospectus, or through the relaunch of an existing fund – the statistics used are very often selective. If one believes such advertisements, every fund in Britain is one of the top five performers in their sector – which is, of course, impossible. In fact it is a selective choice of best performance that enables such advertisements to claim that the funds they relate to have consistently done better than their rivals. One should therefore take a fairly cynical approach when choosing funds; no decision should be made on the basis of the advertisement alone, and further information should be sought on the past history of the fund, other funds under the same management, the charges levied, and the risks attached to the investments. A competent investment adviser should be able to produce this information in a readily accessible and understandable manner.

Income from investments theoretically reflects the future value of the assets underlying the investment. A price/earnings ratio, measuring the value of the stock against its earnings, will determine its comparative worth or expense. A P/E ratio of 20 implies that a stock is attributed a value twice that of one with a P/E of 10. Stock markets divide their quoted stocks into convenient sectors (there are about thirty sectors quoted on the London Stock Exchange), and each sector tends to have a different P/E ratio. Where stocks within a given sector have a P/E ratio at variance with the sector average this normally means that they are under- or over-valued (relatively cheap or expensive) compared to their competitors. There may be reasons for this: for instance, Marks & Spencer has always tended to have a premium rating, to reflect the consistency of its earnings and the stability of its business. P/E ratios are therefore one indication of value of an investment. Other important measures have also been detailed in the preceding chapter.

Risk And Security

One of the primary reasons for making any investment is security. It has always been a human trait to try and make the future secure, even though it is unknown. Forecasts and projections are made on financial assets all the time, and often without the person involved realizing it. For instance, when you take out a mortgage you commit yourself twenty-five years into the future, and yet at the time you do so you may only be looking ahead to the next few months. Similarly, life-assurance policies, endowment policies and pensions all have a time horizon that extends many years into the future.

Most investors assume a level of security when making an investment that is simply a reflection of the faith and trust they show in the company or agent with whom they place their money. Despite a very long history of investments and investment companies turning out to be not quite what they seemed, it is a rare investor who makes any personal enquiries about his investment or looks beyond the literature and sales patter provided by the company and its agents. We assume security, but we almost never check it. This is a strange attitude to take towards investment, since we would never buy a house or a car with so little enquiry.

In addition, very few investors make a conscious effort regularly to update their investment position, and to check that the performance being achieved measures up to their defined expectations. Substantial investors pay financial experts to do regular updating and discuss strategy, but very often this is not the case where the investments are relatively few and concentrated in only one or two areas. And yet this concentration alone can diminish security, and so increase risk. There is an underlying presumption that investment is a form of gambling – that there is no difference between investment and speculation. In fact investment implies a calculated assessment of an expected net benefit, while speculation assumes no assessment, merely chance.

What is an acceptable level of security? This is a personal choice and tends to alter with age. The younger you are, the less security-conscious you will be; the older you are, the more likely you will be to concentrate on high levels of security in your investments. Traditionally the highest level of security is obtained through government stocks, since it is considered that the UK government, for instance, is exceptionally unlikely to default on any of its obligations. Government stocks and bonds, such as Treasury or Exchequer stocks, give a defined percentage of income return (which depends on which stock issue is bought) and are repaid on the maturity date specified for that issue at par (100% of the face value). Of course, this level of certainty means that the variation in value over the life of the stock and the percentage return may be unlikely to match those from an equity investment over the same period – though this is not always the case, since in times of recession, when the stock market is bearish (going down), government securities might well outperform the equities market. If you were totally committed to safety you would perhaps pick five short-dated (up to five years to maturity) or medium-dated (five to fifteen years) gilts to invest in, which would give you an annual yield of between 4% and 5% after tax, together with the possibility for a tax-free capital gain.

Another form of absolute certainty is to keep your money in a bank or building society. There is currently a profusion of accounts at different rates. The problem with such accounts is that rarely does the interest rate paid protect the capital value against the effects of inflation consistently over a period of time. In other words, the actual money you have may appear to be increasing, but in real terms its value in purchasing power has decreased. Banks' and building societies' 'investments' are therefore highly unlikely to sustain the real value of the capital invested, and therefore are inappropriate for the long-term investor. Similarly, life-assurance companies over recent years have produced a number of bond (fixed-interest) investments that guarantee a high return on capital, usually over a fixed period of time. Again, in non-recessionary times these are unlikely to prove capable of maintaining capital in the longer term or competing with the stock market for overall capital growth.

The larger the amount of money you are prepared to invest, and the longer you are ready to invest it for, the better the interest rate is likely to be. Instant-access rates are currently between 0.3% and 0.8% per year lower than notice or term (fixed-period) deposits. Most notice or term deposits require a minimum investment of £1,000, and the longer the notice period the higher the rate. A premium of 0.10% is paid for amounts above £10,000, and rates peak at about 7% gross for a commitment of a year; for longer periods of time, say five years, a 7.5% rate is achievable. This compares to a current bank rate of 6.25% and secured lending rates from banks of 2% to 4% above the current bank rate (it also has to be seen against a background of inflation at 3.5%). Unsecured lending is typically 6% or so higher than this (15% or more), and, credit card borrowing a full 10% higher (19% or more). In fact, credit card borrowing is a full four times the bank rate – immensely profitable for the lender and hugely expensive for the borrower. Wherever possible pay off the amount due by direct debit and have bank borrowings to cover where needs must – it will certainly prove cheaper.

In order to maintain capital on a consistent basis, investment in shares is desirable, if more risky. Shares are often seen as posing a bewildering choice between an ever-increasing number of quoted companies, only a handful of which are known to the general public. Nonetheless, all companies quoted on the Stock Exchange, like other limited company businesses, are required to produce detailed annual accounts, and quoted companies publish this information with an annual report that should provide all the detail required for an investor to determine the recent history of the company and its current position.

In essence, the job that brokers do is to make investment choices for the individual investor, based on their analysis and research, and possibly their projections of future results. Brokers also do this against a background of broader economic policy and conditions, nationally and internationally. Notwithstanding the large number of analysts employed in the City (described as 'scribblers' by former Chancellor Nigel Lawson) and the massive increase in technological assistance provided by computers, most brokers will at best achieve middling results for any individual investor, since they will have neither the time nor the capacity to concentrate all their energies on a single portfolio. If one considers that an average personal portfolio with a broker might be worth at least £250,000, this cannot be compared in importance to a pension fund, which might have £1 billion under investment and may invest £250,000 per day. Private investors should therefore be aware that in the scheme of things they are unlikely to be that important to the broking house, and, despite any personal service they may receive (and be charged for), this will be coloured, at least to some extent, by their position in the pecking order. Brokers operate on a 'buy', 'sell' or 'hold' basis, and, once a policy decision has been made on a particular stock, one of these three alternatives will be implemented (fairly) automatically for all managed personal portfolios, subject only to specific individual instructions. On a very broad scale large 'market-making' brokers wield considerable power – this was particularly evident in the 1987 crash, when major US brokers' computer programs automatically sold stocks when they reached a preordained level.

Although all stock markets are structured differently, the UK market is divided into a number of sectors that generally describe the major activity of the companies within them (engineering, mining, pharmaceuticals, etc.), and every now and then the sectors are re-jigged to give a better overall guide to what is happening. (These sectors are not always helpful in deciding where to invest, though. For instance, technology stocks, which have been 'hot' in the USA for some time, have no specific sector in the UK; the technology companies are spread over various different sectors.) Some sectors have a lot of companies, some, like tobacco, very few. League tables of sector performance average the best and worst performers in a sector and are not weighted by value, so they are at best indicative, as well as being historic (and the historic pattern is unlikely to be a helpful guide to the future). George Soros himself believes that in the stock market there are no rules, only change. Hence he operates a 'twin-track' theory: either A or B can happen, so invest in both, even if they are apparently contradictory. This is why a nation plans for war in peacetime, and *vice versa*.

In June 1995 the total value of the FT All-Share index was about £760 billion. The three biggest categories were General Manufacturers (£147 billion), Consumer Goods (£148 billion) and Services (£150 billion). Then came Financials (£124 billion); Utilities – mainly the result of privatizations (£97 billion) and Mineral Extraction (£68 billion). Finally there was Investment Trusts (£28 billion). This gave a snapshot of British economic activity and its emphasis in mid-1995. It also shows how fatuous is the tabloids' description of a fall in the market as 'billions wiped off shares' is – a blinding statement of the obvious.

Where the question of security is of greater than average importance, the most likely forms of investment (which still may include a capital gain) are bonds or preferred stocks. Bonds are issued by the government or by insurance companies and guarantee a certain level of income, denoted by their percentage rate (e.g. Treasury 6% 1999); they can be issued and traded at face value or at a discount and will be redeemed on maturity at face value (par). Since they are quoted on Stock Exchanges, it is possible to invest in a 100% secure bond, such as a government bond, and at the same time produce higher-than-average income as well as the possibility of a capital gain. They are also flexible since they are saleable at any date prior to maturity and also carry tax advantages. Similarly preferred shares in quoted companies carry a right to a certain fixed percentage income and, at the same time, can also provide the opportunity for a capital gain. Although the number of preferred stocks in issue is relatively small, they can be more valuable as investments than equities in the same company, if the market in the equities is particularly volatile, or if the interest rate paid on a preferred stock is unusually high compared to average market yields. There are also convertible preference shares which allow the owner to change from the preference to ordinary (equity) shares at a pre-determined date and at a given ratio of so many ordinary shares for each preference share held at the relevant date.

It is difficult to analyse risk logically. However, a very safe portfolio would consist only of Government stocks and bonds, maturing in the medium term – in five to fifteen years. If the investor wanted growth and security he would put emphasis on 'blue-chip' investments: perhaps up to two-thirds of the portfolio would go into such companies – Marks & Spencer, ICI, Unilever, etc. – which are marked by quality performance and reliability over the years. As blue chips, they usually attract a premium rating, making them relatively more expensive (a higher P/E ratio) than most shares. The remaining one-third would be divided between high-rate cash deposits, safe overseas investments (Europe and USA), and gilts (government stocks). Both these types of portfolio could be expected at the moment to yield some 4% to 5% annually before tax. In virtually all portfolios it is assumed that income will be reinvested, since this produces a much faster rate than investments where income is not reinvested.

For security of capital, but with no opportunity for capital gain, high rates of interest can be obtained from Local Authority loans or from high-rate building societies or bank investments. These guarantee to return 100% of the capital invested, although most are subject to time limits, either on withdrawal or on maturity, whereby if the deposit is not continued throughout the specified term a penalty is imposed for early withdrawal usually by reducing the interest rate applicable. The problem with interest-only investments is that, although they provide the security and are risk-free, they do not necessarily maintain their capital value when inflation is high. Since the 1970s it has been rare for such investments to give a positive 'real' rate of return (actual rate less inflation), and therefore interest-only investments have tended to diminish the value of the capital. At the other end of the risk spectrum it is possible to 'invest' in warrants or options on equity shares, which act as an accelerator or decelerator, depending on the performance of the underlying stocks themselves. The warrant or option is an opportunity to buy a multiple of shares in a company at a predetermined price at a time in the future, so that if their market price increases your warrants increase in value by a multiple proportion (or decrease similarly, if the market price falls). This makes warrants (and options, which are similar) highly volatile as investments and unlikely to produce a reasonably secure benefit for a longer-term investor. Their specialist nature also makes them unsuitable for anyone who doesn't fully understand their workings.

The ultimate risk in investment is to assume unlimited liability. If someone puts £1 into equity shares and the shares become valueless, the most he can lose is £1, but investing Names in Lloyd's of London were subject to unlimited liability. This meant that they were not only liable for the money they put up as collateral for their investment, they were also liable, without limit, for their proportionate share of the losses of the insurance syndicates in which they had invested. This meant that some Lloyd's investors became responsible for losses literally thousands of times their original investment, and, not surprisingly, in many cases this wiped out their entire capital and produced in them (but not in many casual observers) a sense of outrage at the manner in which these losses had been allowed to arise.

Any Lloyd's Name liable 'down to his cufflinks' should have been totally aware of what unlimited liability meant. In fairness, it is possible that this was not clearly explained to some Names, or that the risks were so played down as to make the explanation deliberately misleading. All the same it is no good after the event protesting that you did not understand what unlimited liability was. It is a crucial principle of investment that you should limit your liability to what you can afford, and anyone who went into Lloyd's without knowing that their funds were completely at risk was either criminally misled or just plain stupid. (It is ironic that some of the Names who have condemned the Lloyd's system so severely should also have been quiet during earlier years, when Lloyd's Names made considerable sums of money through very successful investments and profitable insurance.) It is a folly of human nature that there is an extraordinary desire to latch on to a 'can't lose' type of investment, but one should always remember the old caution *caveat emptor* (buyer beware) when offered a proposal that seems too good to be true – invariably it is!

It seems that there are no risk-free investments. Those who bought property in the UK in the late 1980s are living proof that 'safe as houses' is not always true. Even gold, that investment of last resort, has come in for a hammering since its high in the mid-1980s; in 1995 the trading range of gold for the year was a mere $26 as world-wide production continued to increase. It is essential in any investment approach to balance risk and security, with the overriding aim of maintaining the value of one's capital. There will always be risk and adversity in investment, but the prudent investor will always seek to balance the inevitable losses with rather better profits. Going for security alone is potentially an absolute guarantee that the real value of one's capital will decline; pensioners with fixed-income investments know how inflation has reduced the value of their capital. Yet the apparent attractions of high-rate interest are illusory when inflation exceeds the interest paid net of tax. It is essential to plan and manage investments intelligently and achieve a reasonable balance between risk and security.

Investment Protection

Although the next chapter will deal with the balance that can be operated in portfolios of various sizes between all the types of investments detailed above, it is important to note that all types of investment carry a risk. A shrewd investor will always try to maintain a balance of risk that gives as great a level of certainty as possible compatible with maximizing his overall investment objectives. In other words a risk-averse investor is likely to choose the safest investments but thereby produce, in the longer term, the lowest return; the converse can be true for a risk-taking investor. Part of this choice is a matter of age and part depends on the funds available. Younger people will always tend to take greater risks than older people, and where large funds are available for investment the impact of high-risk strategies on a small proportion of these funds is likely to be low, but the potential pay-off could be high. In all these circumstances one should assume you are dealing with your own money. When you hand your money over to any agent dealing on your behalf, despite the legislation available, it is not safe to presume that the result will be precisely as your agent predicted. There is no substitute for an individual investor checking on his own investments, rather than leaving it to a third party.

The complexity of financial instruments has increased enormously from 1945. However, they are governed by a financial industry whose very existence depends on sales, so there must ultimately be considerable profits for the industry, otherwise it will fail. The inclination for agents to use small print to divert a dissatisfied investor is simply part of the centuries-old tradition that the buyer must be aware of potential pitfalls. None of the institutions you are likely to be dealing with is a charity, so where a higher-than-normal return is offered for a lower-than-normal risk a smell of rodent should be detectable! Otherwise intelligent investors so often seem inclined to be conned in circumstances where even a little common sense should have made them cautious. Perpetrators of fraudulent schemes can be prosecuted and imprisoned, but inevitably there will be other fraudsters coming along after them.

By way of example, Barlow Clowes was set up in 1973 to specialize in 'risk-free' gilt investments (government securities). Peter Clowes' role-model was the 1970s investment rake Bernie Cornfeld whose International Life funds grew to global proportions (with the come-on 'Do you sincerely want to be rich?') before they ultimately collapsed. Clowes' fund, based in Gibraltar, at first met its obligations, and funds under management grew from £4 million in 1982 to £87 million in 1985. However, by 1986, Clowes had diverted two-thirds of the funds into anything but gilts. By the time he was arrested in 1988 up to £100 million had been dispersed, including amounts spent on yachts, villas and hugely speculative ventures. He was able to continue to do this as new funds enabled him to repay dissatisfied existing investors – a very old trick. Convicted of fraud and theft in 1992, he was sentenced to ten years in jail. A number of the 18,000 investors in Barlow Clowes were compensated by the government who had to admit that some of its organs, such as the Bank of England, had had some part in encouraging Barlow Clowes on to government turf. In normal circumstances such investors are compensated under the Investors Compensation Scheme, which covers customers of investment and insurance companies that have gone bust while operating under the Financial Services Act.

All investment protection is ultimately a matter of legislation, and successive governments have made brave, if belated, attempts to enforce best practice on all financial intermediaries. No part of the financial world has escaped from increased legislation on the standards that must be adopted, but laws *per se* will never prevent unforeseen disasters. The recent Barings bank collapse shows how technological change (which has increased the speed of financial transactions phenomenally, while supervision continues at a relative snail's pace) can mean that your investment funds can quite literally disappear in seconds. There is no cost-effective insurance available to investors to protect fully against risk, and the government and industry compensation schemes have relatively low ceilings for serious investors (for instance a maximum pay-out to a Barings depositor would be £100,000). It is said that you have to be rich to sue the rich, and it is an unfortunate aspect of self-regulation that most investors lack the means, technical skill and knowledge to undertake a legal action against an agent that has deprived them of their savings. As Lloyds members found out, if your wealth has been misused by third parties, the sums involved in trying to obtain some form of retribution and restitution are colossal.

In other words, if you are an investor be prepared to lose a proportion of your funds at some time. Spread your risk in well-managed, well-funded and well-respected institutions (so that, even if one of them goes 'belly-up', it is not the end of your investment world); these would include the main high street banks and the biggest stockbroking firms, such as Mercury Asset Management, Schroders, etc. It is astonishing how often individual investors will use just one agent and allow all their funds to come within his orbit; if you cannot trust yourself with your money, why trust anyone else to this extent? Spread your business among several different agents, all highly reputable and solid. Make sure all the confirmations of savings and investments actually have *your* name on them, not that of an intermediary who can subsequently claim ownership. Make sure you get, and *read*, regular updates of performance; have them checked out if you are in doubt about ownership or performance. Always doubt investment blurbs – they are inevitably selective in their use of facts, and thereby economical with the (absolute) truth. Always sign forms yourself if they have your name on them, and always get a copy, countersigned by the agent if necessary. Read the small and tiny print – it is deliberately difficult to read, but must be there for a reason. If anything is unclear have any clarification given to you in writing. Have an independent witness to all important meetings, especially when complaining, and be aware that meetings can be recorded. Never give money to anyone to invest without a legal receipt, dated and signed (legibly).

Go into investments with due cynicism. If it proves to be unjustified, let your financial agent do his job; that's what he's there for – not to spend his time discussing investments, but to actually invest. Finally, remember you get what you pay for, and do not expect a royal service without paying a king's ransom. Expertise will always be expensive, because it is scarce.

Investors may not read important documents ('that is what my agent is there for') and may consider numbers as some form of hieroglyphic from an ancient world, even though they can, at a moment's notice, work out in their heads complex calculations about how much they are charged by others or how much they can earn. This trait can only be put down to British bashfulness (or fashionable boredom) about money; perhaps it is a throw-back to the outdated attitude that money is something only people in 'trade' deal in. Whatever the stupid reason, it has cost some individuals dear to put their trust so completely and unprotectedly in others, without question or effort on their part. Needless to say, these are the same individuals who are dumbstruck when the inevitable happens. If they own a mirror they should take a good look in it to find the root cause of their problem. It is always sensible, where large sums are involved, to have a series of checks and balances to ensure that you are adequately protected from what may simply be your own financial sloth. Ignorance is not a defence before the law, nor should it prevent you from pursuing sound financial policies and procedures. You will not always be fully protected, but make sure you make as few avoidable mistakes as humanly possible.

Where assets are physical, such as property or possessions, it is prudent to minimize risk by insuring these items for their replacement value. With buildings this means re-building value, which is often lower than the apparent value of the property – due to the fact that the land is highly unlikely to disappear! For other assets the insurance value should be the true value of walking into a shop and replacing that asset with something exactly like it. Where antiques are concerned this should not be the auction value, for this often represents only two-thirds of the true value (since someone who buys at auction is likely to be a dealer, and will mark the goods up accordingly); in other words, an item worth £2,000 at auction should be insured for £3,000.

The official inflation measure is unlikely to be an accurate means of revaluing most physical possessions. You will not find your new car increasing in value in line with inflation, because the real world is not like that. The official inflation index is a composite of changes in the cost of a range of items from groceries to mortgages, so is at best only an indication of price changes. It is therefore normal practice for insurers of high-risk items to require written proof of value. Very often the initial receipt is adequate to start with, but there should be periodic revaluations, since the value of possessions often changes in a way that index-linking cannot reflect. For instance, the value of Impressionist paintings at auction halved from 1989 to 1992, because the market was speculative and driven by Japanese money. Index-linking, which adds an inflation amount each year, can be completely inappropriate in such circumstances, and a professional revaluation every three to five years would be more suitable. Most reputable auction houses offer expert valuations, with fees based on value but usually negotiable to a fixed maximum.

Currently UK inflation is about 3% based on consumer prices, 3.5% based on wages and salaries, and 4% based on manufacturing prices. In logical terms (not always in fact) the manufacturing price increase feeds through to the retail/consumer sector, which in turn inflates wages and salaries, which then feed back into manufacturing prices; this *perpetuum mobile* has been one of the most difficult (and possibly most damaging) of twentieth-century phenomena. Inflation creates a price spiral that moves infinitely upward, devaluing all in its path. Whether we have found a means to control it is debatable – have we tamed the lion of inflation or is it merely humouring us until it has digested its last meal? Although the inflation rate has fallen from a peak of 23% in 1975 to 3% to-day, this has been a long process and has brought us back to the inflation rate of the early 1960s. The fall may be more a reflection of suppressed demand, brought about by economic uncertainty after a severe recession, than any real and fundamental change. We can probably safely leave this circular argument to specialists, of whom it is said there are as many opinions as there are economists! But what we should do is learn the lesson of inflation's destructive power over value, and do all we can to guard against it.

Capital Division

In order to do this, an investor should be able to calculate the present distribution of his total net worth between various categories and then adjust them accordingly. Net worth is the value of the sum of all assets less liabilities at open market rates. In most cases individuals have no accurate calculation of their net worth, nor do they know whether its distribution is prudent. Inevitably, part of the balance comes about through personal choice and circumstances – most investors have a proportion of their net worth in property, since their home is normally a major asset. In the latter part of this century there has been considerable emphasis on liquidity (cash availability), which is a very strong factor in ensuring investment success. By this standard, the notion of bricks and mortar as a real investment is questionable, if the investment is unlikely to be realized or, if it were, the sale proceeds would immediately be reinvested in other property. Property creates the illusion of profit where none has been realized, since no sale has taken place. Residential owner-occupied property is therefore not, strictly speaking, an investment – it is simply a possession.

The only exception to this general rule has been when owners have determinedly gone out to trade up as their incomes increase, so that the notional value of their property today is well in excess of the amount they could have afforded using their savings alone. For instance, if you had bought a modest house in London in 1970 for £5,000 and if, as earnings increased, you had moved from the two-bedroom terrace house to a multi-bedroom detached house in a better area, using the maximum borrowings (leverage or margin), your detached house could now be worth something approaching £500,000. The gap of £495,000 would not just be attributable to improved earnings but would be more likely to be attributable to the inflationary effect of house prices outstripping general price increases. This opportunity is unlikely to be repeated in the near future, although, given increases in earnings, there is always a tendency for house prices (which represent a multiple of wages) to increase in line with wages over the longer term. In such circumstances no wealth is actually created – only the monetary illusion of improved prosperity through the manipulation of a particular market, using inflation as the lever (since the loan on the property has diminished as a real liability as its value declined). This is the property 'feel-good factor'.

Generally speaking the ideal division of capital might be 30% in property, 30% in equities, 30% in alternative investments and personal possessions, and 10% in cash or near-cash assets. For the reason given in the preceding paragraph, it could be argued that a 30% proportion in property (stated net of mortgage) is too high in investment terms, and should be closer to 15%. In other words, if your house is worth £75,000 without mortgage, you would look for a total net worth of £500,000. There are few people in Britain who have anything like this proportion. That immediately means that their flexibility in investment is rather restricted, since the emphasis of their wealth is on a non-income-producing asset whose value currently is likely to be static and decreasing after inflation is taken into account.

If 30% of the overall net worth is invested in equities (which would also include equity-type investments, such as bonds and preference shares), these are the core of potential for capital gains and liquidity and therefore form the most important part of an overall investment strategy. The relative amounts invested in fixed-interest securities and equities should vary according to stock-market conditions. Since fixed-interest securities entail less risk they should form a greater proportion of the portfolio where market conditions indicate that equities are high-risk (usually when the market is historically very high or economic conditions are depressed). In normal circumstances the proportion of equities to fixed interest securities should not fall below 75:25; this creates a mechanism for 'automatically' correcting investment decisions which may have proved incorrect in the short term. Since equities and bonds tend to work in opposite directions, when equities fall, bonds rise and vice-versa. There are brokers who always argue for full investment in equities, but, unless there are fixed-interest investments held elsewhere, this seems to expose the investor to too great an equity risk. Conversely it would seem unduly risk-averse to have more than a 50:50 split in bonds favour, even in apparently adverse situations, since bonds have more limited volatility than equities so could take longer to recover.

An individual with a relatively high net worth is likely to have purchased valuable items that might fall under the heading of alternative investments. These are not only personally satisfying but they also form an important counterweight to paper investments, whose general volatility tends to make them unpredictable. It is important to remember that personal possessions are not income producing, and therefore, where net worth is particularly high, they should form a considerably lower proportion than the 30% proposed above. Providing the possessions purchased are of high quality and are maintained securely and in good condition, they should hold their value in the longer term after inflation is taken into account, always assuming that, like equities, they are sold near the top of a cycle (and bought near the bottom) – there is nothing so unwanted as unfashionable items, whatever their pedigree (and this is as true of companies as it is of paintings). It is argued that the problem with possessions, as opposed to investments, is that the cost of buying and selling is considerably higher, since auction-room and dealer commissions tend to be at least 10% of value. Some noteworthy collectors, such as oil magnate Armand Hammer, dispose of their collections by starting up a retail business in that area, thus not only avoiding paying commission to a dealer but actually earning for themselves the commission on selling their own collection! Obviously, most individuals would not have such an opportunity, but it is a thought to bear in mind!

By their very nature, personal possessions and alternative investments are idiosyncratic; to have an intrinsic value a collection must consist of items that, either taken together or individually, are unique. The most successful collectors tend to have been those with a very strong conviction of what represented high quality and value. It is no good buying your antiques in Bond Street at the highest possible price and then having to wait several years before the price you paid can be recovered at auction after paying commission. It is much more prudent, and probably more interesting, to make your purchases through a knowledgeable provincial trading source (dealer), who will charge only fair prices but who can also authenticate what is being bought. Overall, investments in art objects have to be seen as pleasurable, otherwise they are pointless. If you want to create a museum, be like Paul Getty and fund a building for it.

It should be possible to create a balance of quality items across the areas of furniture, pictures, jewellery and specialized collections, so that when the values of one area of collecting go down those in another go up. Personal possessions are perhaps more subject to fashion than other forms of investments, and there are collectors who have waited ten years or more for their particular collections to come back into fashion. However, it is noteworthy that the art market generally lags behind the stock market by six months or so, with prices peaking as the gains on the stocks are reinvested in 'real' items. It is also important to distinguish between a collection and a hobby, between possessions and consumables. A collection implies a long-term, high-quality accumulation of intrinsic value that can also be pleasurable. A hobby is a pastime – the main aim is pleasure. (A hobby can become a collection, but only where the criterion of quality applies.) Possessions have an intrinsic resale value, whereas consumables do not; clothes, for instance, are generally consumables, since they normally have no intrinsic (monetary) value, regardless of how much they cost.

Personal possessions form part of the broader area of alternative investments which are covered in depth in the following chapter 'Collecting and Investment' but they should still be viewed as part of an overall balance of net worth and not considered in isolation from all other types of investment.

The remainder of the portfolio, approximately 10% would be in cash or near-cash assets. These could be any interest-earning deposit in a building society or bank, or could also take the form of National Savings Certificates or short-term bonds. Alternatively, cash could be kept in a foreign currency if, after careful consideration, the expected currency appreciation is deemed to be more beneficial than the rate of interest earned on a deposit. Investors should concentrate only on major currencies – sterling, US dollars, Japanese yen, German marks or Swiss francs. The appreciation of currency is extremely difficult to predict but can give a good return – up to 15% a year before tax. However, this sort of prediction carries inherent risks, linked to interest rates, budget surpluses/deficits and political stability.

The importance of liquidity to a portfolio is that it enables the holder to adjust quickly to changing market conditions – by definition liquidity must be in short-term instruments. It allows for impulse buying that, intelligently done, can allow an investor to snap up a bargain (this is particularly true in the area of alternative investments, where chance plays a greater than normal role in investment opportunities). It is important to adapt the level of liquidity to market conditions. Where interest rates are historically low (as in the mid 1990s), the proportion of net worth in liquid assets is also likely to be low, since the return they can produce is considerably poorer than that from other forms of investment. Nonetheless, it is prudent to maintain at any time a minimum liquid balance of approximately 5% of net worth, with a maximum of perhaps 15%.

It is part of the art of investment to time the sale of assets carefully, so as to accumulate cash at the top of the market before a 'correction' (fall), and subsequently to re-invest once the correction has taken place. It is highly unlikely that any investor can predict the timing of market peaks and troughs with complete success, and a degree of luck is undoubtedly part of an investor's armoury, but it is still necessary to have an opinion on whether markets are high or low, so as to determine the level of liquidity. It is said that Sir James Goldsmith liquidated the bulk of his portfolios before the markets peaked in October 1987, thereby securing a net worth considerably higher than it would have been if he had waited to sell. It has long been a market adage that you should ignore the top eighth of a bull (rising) market and the bottom eighth of a bear (falling) market. In other words, take good gains as you find them, and don't always wait for the next improvement, which may not happen. Similarly, sell on losses; don't allow them to accumulate – there are classic tales of those who waited too long.

Unavoidable Events

Investment can never be undertaken in a vacuum. The conditions of the market and personal circumstances will ultimately determine the vast majority of investment decisions. It has long been a truism that most abrupt changes in investment circumstances arise from the so called 'three Ds': debt, divorce and death. In an earlier age, Mark Twain said that there were only two certainties in life, death and taxes; these are still matters that should concern a prudent investor, but debt and divorce, more common now than in Mark Twain's time, should also be taken into account.

Debt and Debtors

In an investment context, the most publicized form of debt in investment over the last five years has been that of Lloyd's Names. Since these debts arose from unlimited liability on insurance (or re-insurance) policies where the outcome was unknown, they represented an extreme form of investment risk. There are no circumstances where a prudent investor would be prepared to give unlimited liability for anything.

There is, however, a degree of risk in dealing with most trading entities, since it is unsecured creditors who provide their working capital. British companies have a poor record of paying unsecured creditors, and sums owed by trading companies, whether in respect of goods and services supplied or interest or capital payments on loans are often subject to delay in payment with no compensating interest. It is a fact that a small proportion of UK businesses are completely dependant upon unsecured creditors' finance to continue in business.

A prudent investor should not consider making unsecured loans or providing goods or services without being certain of the good faith and ability to pay of the company concerned. In order to do this, financial references should be taken up with a bank or other trade source. (It is appreciated that such references may not ultimately have much value, but at least they should provide an indication of how the company operates.) If the sums involved are large the accounts should be examined by a competent professional to evaluate the risk.

Families of some wealth will quite often provide finance to another family member, or to a company owned by friends, only to find that their personal relationship has nothing to do with the business relationship. Generally speaking, any money transaction has to be evaluated on its own merits and not on the basis of purely personal considerations. Even the most wealthy families in Britain can get caught up in unnecessary debt through imprudent lending to third parties. The sale of some 200 of the treasures from Luton Hoo in 1995 demonstrates the problems that can arise in such circumstances. The heir to this estate, Nicholas Phillips, a cousin of the Queen, committed suicide in 1991 apparently due to the pressure of debts of £20 million incurred through failed business ventures. The Sotheby's sale, which raised £4.4 million, included items from the collection of the great-grandfather of the deceased, the diamond magnate Sir Julius Wernher. The financial genius of the fortune-maker of 1903 (compared in his day to the American billionaires Frick and Mellon) was unfortunately not inherited by the great-grandson.

Divorce

By 1995 nearly 50% of marriages in the UK have ended in divorce. Divorce is emotionally, financially and physically disruptive. Since, in many circumstances it involves personal antagonism, it is highly unlikely that either party can approach with objectivity the financial arrangements that need to be made. While most divorcing couples would agree that both have the interests of any children at heart in making the new arrangements, it is sadly often the case that the children become a lever by means of which one or other parent seeks to gain what they feel is rightly theirs. One of the problems that generally arises is that most couples do not have a clear idea of their individual net worth, and have made no differentiation between assets in their individual names during their marriage; as a result, they end up arguing about ownership. Where any substantial wealth is involved couples should consider carefully how bank accounts and other investments are controlled, so as to avoid the possibility of one party withdrawing funds without mutual consent; the earnings of one party in a deteriorating marriage can be spent or removed elsewhere by the other very quickly and easily. Similarly, it is prudent that all investments should be in the name of the party who actually funded them. This avoids arguments at the time of divorce about who rightly owns what. It is bad enough to deal with the division of personal possessions such as furniture, without becoming involved in details about where the money came from to make investments.

In 1993 there were 182,000 first marriages in the UK and 154,000 divorces, and the rate of first marriage has declined steadily since the early 1970s, when there were over 400,000 first marriages. The current rate of marriage is the lowest since the nineteenth century, when the population was half its present size. Nowadays one in four single women who have never married live with their partner (three times the 1979 number), and nearly one-third of women under fifty live alone or with their children, with the number increasing at double the rate applicable to men. By 1993 56% of men and 59% of women under fifty were married: the lowest proportions since the 1930s. There are therefore a number of indications that the impact of shared property in divorce will become less important, as the number of married couples declines (legal rights over shared property outside marriage are less clear-cut than within it). Against this, the identification of property ownership is generally easier outside marriage than inside it.

Contested divorces, by definition, leave both parties dissatisfied. It is therefore helpful to any couple with substantial assets if as much as possible of their net worth is clearly set out and defined on a regular basis. Property should always be in the name of the person or persons who bought it, as should any loans thereon. Investment can only be dealt with logically where there is a clear line of ownership, decision-making and control, and the most successful investors will always be those who operate alone, since they are not then subject to conflicts that may arise where there is any joint ownership. Divorce law in the UK concentrates on the family home, which is usually considered to be shared (this does not mean it has to be registered in joint names).

The marriage vows indicate that all property is common in a marriage, but this is not necessarily legally enforceable. Divorce courts look at a fair estimation of spouse's entitlements, which is intended to put them back to the position they would have been in if the marriage had not taken place. In other words, despite the commonly held view that divorce means a 50:50 split of net assets, this is unlikely to be the case where a substantial amount of money is involved. When Maureen Starkey, the former wife of Ringo Starr, went to court to redress her divorce settlement (over which she sued her solicitors), she sought to gain access to funds based on the income of her ex-husband, and not on the basis of her actual needs. This was apparently a classic confusion of need versus want. The court decided that Mrs Starkey should be supported by her ex-husband while she remained unmarried and while the children were minors, but only to the extent that she could live a reasonable lifestyle. In other words, if you marry in the UK and marry a multi-millionaire, do not expect by right to be a millionaire yourself when you divorce.

The USA is the undisputed world leader in contested divorces, and prenuptial agreements have become an important part of the marriage ritual (assuming the marriage itself is legally enforceable – some marriages in Las Vegas and the fringes of the US may not be as legal as they at first seem). One of the wealthiest US divorcees is Patricia Kluge, who was married to John Kluge, billionaire owner of Metromedia, which he sold for $5 billion. Under divorce negotiations in the context of a pre-nuptial agreement she received a Virginia mansion set in a 12,000 acre estate, together with a settlement estimated at $15 million flat; in addition her ex-husband pays for the upkeep of the house and grounds, put at $1 million a year. In the UK in 1985 the Thyssen-Bornemisza case was the first that enabled the very wealthy to show they could reach a court settlement, without the full and frank disclosure of assets normally required. This has been taken to imply that anyone with a net worth of £20 million or more can use the 'millionaire's defence'. In general the maximum sum a UK court is likely to consider awarding to a wife where the asset values are high (£5 million or more) is 25% of net worth after a long marriage, having regard to the wife's assets and proven contribution to creating the wealth.

There may be a view that divorce settlements in such circumstances give preference to male high-earners, but the underlying concept is that you cannot marry someone with a considerably higher net worth and then claim that, *ergo*, half of it must be yours; the award will depend on the proven input of the spouse, evaluated neutrally by the court. Obviously individuals of high net worth do not get married in the expectation of divorce, but there is an increasing trend towards premarital agreements, drawn up and signed at the time of marriage, which seek to avoid the worst problems of division of assets if a divorce should take place. Although not foolproof, such documents give a measure of certainty and potential security to both parties. There is generally nothing in life less productive than going to law; it is immensely time-consuming and costly, and the only certainty is that the lawyers will get paid. There are many lawsuits where all the available finance has been consumed by the legal costs, and this should be avoided wherever possible. The question of rights to assets in marriage can also spill over into inheritance.

A recent case in America (it had to be!) involved 26-year-old 'supermodel' Anna Nicole Smith, who married the 89-year-old J. Howard Marshall II in 1994. One year later he died with an estate worth $550 million. Inevitably, Anna was branded a fortune-hunter by the Marshall family, and the testator's son Pierce became temporary guardian of his father's assets, on the grounds of his father's mental incapacity. Anna, a former Playmate of the Year whose large charms had been shown to a wider audience in *Naked Gun 33⅓* (also starring O.J. Simpson, whose own matrimonial experience was the stuff of one of the most notorious recent murder cases), was left with no access to money even after she 'gave up much of my career to sit at his bedside day after day and nurse him'. What she also gave up were hot water, electricity and credit cards, as Pierce refused to fund her; a cheque for nearly $1 million to Harry Winston's, the Beverly Hills jeweller, bounced. With a Hollywood mansion and a Texas ranch as wedding presents Anna also claims possession of her deceased husband's other assets. Since Texas (and seven other American States) permit 'community property', which allows a spouse to claim all assets generated in a marriage, Anna stood to gain at least $50 million.

Divorce can be a messy business, and there is no happy solution where the parties are determined to seek restitution – solicitors have a delicate job in disentangling emotion from law, accountants in determining fiction from fact and completeness from omission. Ultimately the court will decide a contested divorce on the facts as given and the law as it exists. Neither party will come away satisfied, and only time can put such experiences into a better perspective.

Death

The reluctance of many people to consider death at an early age can be disadvantageous. Although the British are not quite as squeamish about the subject as the Americans, it is unusual to find a British person aged under forty who has made a will. Even if your only asset is a simple property that has some equity on it after payment of the mortgage, you should consider where you wish that money to go in the event of your untimely demise.

The legal framework for dealing with the estate of someone who has died without leaving a will (intestate) is very clear, but it is virtually unknown to a layman. If a married person dies and the estate is worth less than £125,000 it goes to the surviving partner. If the estate is worth more than this sum, then the excess is divided between the spouse (who receives a life interest) and any children (in trust). If there are no children, £200,000 goes to the spouse, together with 50% of any excess; the remainder goes to the parents or (if they are dead) the brothers and sisters of the deceased. Only if there are no parents, brothers or sisters does everything go to the spouse.

If an unmarried person dies intestate, the estate goes to the children equally (if they are minors, in trust). Where there are no children, it will go to the deceased's parents if they are alive; if they are dead, it goes to brothers and sisters, or (if they, too, are dead) to more distant relatives, starting with grandparents, then on to uncles and aunts. If none of these relatives are still living, then the estate goes to the Crown (i.e., the government) – although why this should be is beyond our comprehension. Where any of the relevant relatives above have children, they become entitled to their parents' share if the parents are dead.

Whether the deceased was married or unmarried, this method of disposing of their assets may not be at all what they would have wished. That is why it is important to make a will at an early age. Will-making is also important because it allows the person concerned to consider whom they would wish to benefit specifically. Friends, charities or other entities that they have a particular affinity with and would like to see helped in some way – none of these would be covered by the normal intestacy rules. There are also planning considerations, in respect of Inheritance Tax, that should be taken into account when making a will, in order to minimize the amount of tax payable to the government on your demise. It is worth remembering that most people with loans on their property will have a life-assurance policy linked to it through their endowment mortgage, so that on their death the full amount of the loan will be repaid. This potentially leaves a valuable property, the value of which is all part, usually the major part, of that person's estate.

Planning for death is an important piece of investment ritual, since, if the estate is large, it ensures continuity of ownership and clarity of purpose. The wills of very wealthy individuals are generally drawn up in considerable detail to ensure that assets are dealt with in a very specific way. We are all familiar with the Agatha Christie films, where the family solicitor reading the will provokes an uproar; dramatic this may be, but is indicative of the emotive response that bequests can have. The stronger the personality involved the greater the vehemence with which they express their last wishes. John Lennon, for instance, included in his will a clause providing that anyone who disputed it would get nothing; this is one way to ensure your last wishes are carried out to the letter. The basis on which a will should be drawn up is to use a statement of net worth, so that no assets are overlooked in determining the procedure to be followed on death. We do not live in a culture where our worldly goods are buried in the grave with us, so it is sensible to ensure that all loose ends are tied up in advance, to reduce legal costs and arguments. Most people, when pressed, have a very clear view of where they would wish their wealth to go (and there are some very rich pets to prove it!). Will-making is therefore not really conditional on age – indeed the older you are when you make a will, possibly the less likely you are to have clarity of vision.

The case of Doris Duke is an indication of how things can go wrong with wills. Pony-tailed Bernard Lafferty, her Irish-born butler, was removed by the US courts as executor of her $1.2-billion estate (which included a $25-million Boeing 737) after he had managed to race through several hundred thousand dollars after her demise at the age of eighty in 1993. Although she left the bulk of her considerable estate to charity, Mr Lafferty was left $5 million and an annual allowance of $500,000 in the fifth version of her will; this compared to his original salary in 1987 of $500 per week. Her former doctor challenged the will, alleging that Ms Duke was coerced into signing the new will, and in any case was incapacitated by the drugs prescribed by her new doctors. There were further allegations that these doctors had hastened Ms Duke's end through a lethal overdose of morphine (there had been no autopsy). This is a classic case of infirmity and mental decline allowing the influence of personal staff to become too great (the same happened with the legendary US billionaire Howard Hughes). Ms Duke's will also stipulated that her remains be fed to the sharks – one example of eccentricities that had no doubt been indulged ever since she inherited $100 million from her father, the founder of the American Tobacco Company, at the age of thirteen. (Lafferty himself then died, aged 55, in November 1996.)

One should avoid leaving it too late. Howard Hughes' will was never found, and this omission caused considerable expense in identifying the likely beneficiaries. One advantage of making a will relatively young is that tax planning can be done at an early stage. The essence of such plans is to avoid paying inheritance tax (IHT) on the transfer of assets, either during one's lifetime or on death. There are a number of categories of potentially exempt transfers (PETs) that can enable wealthy individuals to transfer part of their wealth without paying tax during their lifetime, provided they survive for seven years from the date of gift. There are substantial exemptions in respect of agricultural land and buildings and businesses, and thought should be given to such matters, so as to maximize the benefit of such gifts to the recipients and minimize the necessity for them to pay inheritance tax. Conservative government policy has generally been focused on easing the inheritance tax regime in order to promote continuity of ownership and to emphasize the principle that taxes should concentrate on income and not on capital. Indeed, it is the Conservatives' published aim to abolish IHT (and capital gains tax). This is a policy unlikely to be endorsed in the same way by a future Labour government, and this could have a substantial impact on families where the wealth is concentrated in only one or two areas that are currently dealt with leniently by existing tax law.

If a will has been made and inheritance tax planning carried out, it is likely that there will be planned disposals of net worth during the testator's lifetime, so as to reduce to a minimum IHT payable after death. There are restrictions where a benefit is retained, even though the asset has been given away (for instance where parents have passed a house on to the children but still reside in it), but a deliberate policy of disposal of assets before death can be advantageous to save IHT to accomplish the desires of the owners and to prevent argument or misinterpretation on death itself. It is not uncommon for grandparents to set up trusts to benefit their grandchildren, missing out their children, and this is a tax-effective structure, though it can sometimes lead to the grandchildren being considerably more wealthy than their parents, who may have to rely on their children for support! In most circumstances parents will wish to leave the bulk of their estate in the first instance to their spouse and thereafter equally to their children. In some historic British families there is a right of primogeniture, under which the eldest male automatically inherits everything; when the Marquis of Bath died recently the whole of his estate went to his eldest son, formerly Lord Weymouth, who subsequently evicted his brother from the estate! In circumstances where this is a tradition it is sometimes necessary to revoke an inheritance if a child is likely to deal recklessly with any property that comes into its hands. A recent instance of this involved Jamie Blandford, heir to the Duke of Marlborough. In another case, that of the Marquis of Bristol, drug addiction has ended any chance of an old family's wealth surviving intact into the next century.

There is therefore a need to keep any arrangement flexible enough to ensure that any beneficiary of a trust who would waste the trust's assets can be prevented from doing so. This is normally achieved by giving the trustees the power to restrict any distribution to beneficiaries on reasonable grounds and by stipulating a minimum age before which children cannot fully inherit. In UK law this cannot be less than eighteen, but twenty-one or twenty-five are often stipulated, so that the children can acquire sufficient maturity before they come into their inheritance. A successful series of trusts can ensure that continuity of ownership of primary assets is maintained and that there is an in-built protection against a spendthrift in the family. This concentration of control in the hands of third-party trustees, such as the family solicitor, can often ensure that a dynasty is maintained intact, and many very wealthy American families, such as the Rockefellers and the Gettys, have successfully used such structures for many years. In the UK this type of arrangement has tended to be confined to landed gentry, although the recent case in the Palumbo family, where the children sued their father over his management of their inheritance, indicates that 'new' money is starting to be maintained in a similar way.

There are circumstances where normal financial planning becomes redundant, with tragic consequences for the family. The Frasers of Lovat suffered three deaths in the family in quick succession, which forced the sale of historic Beaufort House, together with its 19,500 acres and contents in 1995, thus ending a tradition of ownership dating back to at least the early 1500s. In 1994 the youngest son Andrew was gored to death by a buffalo in Tanzania, and a few days later his brother Simon died of a heart attack, having accumulated debts of over £7 million; the following year their father, Lord Lovat, died aged 83. Despite the fact that the estate had been in trust since 1965, and that there was an heir (18 year-old Simon), the personal debts could not be satisfied except through the sale of the Beaufort estate. This ended a continuity of family ownership of nearly 500 years, being interrupted only in 1745, when the English government confiscated the estate in retaliation for the Lovats' support for Bonnie Prince Charlie's rebellion (the then Lord Lovat became the last peer to be executed in the Tower). No amount of prudent fiscal planning can counter such unexpected events.

Changes in Asset Structure over Time

When considering net worth it is important to realize that not only are market conditions continually changing, but your own personal perceptions will also change. The degree of risk that you would accept when young will be very different from that acceptable when you are retired; at the age of twenty a twenty-five year commitment will seem acceptable, but this will patently not be so at the age of sixty-five. And the process of youth giving way to maturity and subsequent decline is just as true of investments as it is of people. All companies have a natural lifespan and can only be rejuvenated if there is a continual process of introducing new products, new directions and new management. The historic stock-market cycle lasts about five years between a recession and a recovery, and most companies will find that their products can survive unchanged through only three cycles or so. Technological and demographic changes ensure that most products need constant revision if they are to continue to compete in consumer markets. There are industries, such as oil and gas, where the time-scale for exploiting the product is considerably longer than for consumer commodities, but even here companies need continually to seek out new reserves and exploit opportunities throughout the world to maintain their profitability. When looking at investments one has therefore to be conscious that just as you change, so does the investment.

The most important objective is to maintain the real value of your capital throughout the period of investment – in other words to match inflation – since this will maintain the true value of your assets. You should therefore choose as an investment adviser someone who understands what your time horizon is, so that the investments you make are appropriate to your age and expectations; it is unlikely that a very young broker will suit a retired person, since the clash of expectations will be too great. As one gets older, and the desire to reduce risk becomes greater, the proportion of investments in fixed-interest-type products will increase, for these offer more certainty as to the return they provide, both in terms of amount and time. It is rare for investors to maintain a high and consistent level of interest in their portfolio throughout their life – there will be times when they will be unable or unwilling to focus on it, and times when they are exceptionally interested. Particularly where net worth is high, there is a tendency to leave the investments to look after themselves, which they won't; a supervisory role is always required to review and interpret portfolio performance. Very wealthy individuals hire professional specialists to interpret and make new recommendations on investment performance.

The timing of investment transactions is also important. To buy at the top of the cycle means that you are paying a relatively high P/E ratio, and the stocks are therefore expensive. When a recession occurs there is a tendency for stocks to fall across the board, and P/E ratios decline accordingly; this means there is an opportunity to buy cheaply, when the general economic conditions are penalizing even well-performing companies. There are also differences of timing within the overall cycle (the expression 'cyclical stocks' describes those that are most sensitive to the stage the cycle has reached). For instance, in recessions people tend not to move so often, so you would expect property and building-materials stocks to fall further than those that suffer less in recession, such as oil stocks or media stocks. The reverse is also true. One sign of positive sentiment is an improvement in house prices, since renewed demand increases values, and building companies again become active. New-car registrations are also another indicator of general economic activity and the place in the cycle. An intelligent investor will look at the big (macro-economic) picture as well as the detail (micro-economic); both offer opportunities: the former general, the latter specific.

In the UK the recession of 1980–81 hit manufacturing hardest, concentrating on the Midlands and the North. The subsequent recovery (and boom), which tended to favour service-industry stocks, was suddenly halted by the 'crash' of 1987, when stocks fell rapidly and unexpectedly. With a major easing of monetary policy under Chancellor Lawson, there was a recovery, leading again to a recession – that of 1990–1, which this time fell hardest on the service industries, particularly in London and the south-east. Recovery then followed once more, tentative and export-led. The example of the last fifteen years leads to the conclusion that predicting the next cycle, either in terms of timing or emphasis, has to be rather more guesswork than fact. Certainly there are indicators in these matters, but they are unlikely to be strong enough for accurate predictions to be derived from them. Chartists, investors who use historical charts based on past cycles and performance to guide investment decisions, are likely to be actually formalizing guesswork, not making accurate predictions. There are too many changes to make the prediction of markets possible: driven by geographic, demographic, economic, liquidity, political and global issues amongst others. George Soros is therefore likely to be right – there are no rules in investment, only changes.

5 Collecting and Investment

Previous chapters have considered what might be termed 'conventional' investments: residential property, equities and other finance-derived products. These are traditional areas that have given individual investors considerable success over the last half century. However, as increased wealth benefits a growing minority of individuals and families in the UK and other countries, it is noticeable longer-term markets are emerging in non-traditional areas. Investors attracted to such alternatives feel they have enough of their wealth in conventional areas and are looking for other uses for their money that are more individualistic and personal, and sometimes more representative of 'new' money rather than 'old'. This is an area where value is not always measurable by simple monetary yardsticks, but also by character, vibrancy, usefulness, status and other qualities that mere cash lacks. When there are so many millionaires, money is no longer the sole measure of perceived wealth.

One of the possible 'alternative' homes for investment money, collecting, is examined in this chapter and the next, while Chapters 6–7 look at some other less usual possibilities.

From 1945 to the 1960s the major auction houses, principally Christie's and Sotheby's, concentrated their auctions on a few areas that were representative of 'old' money. In effect they acted as agents for needful ancient families, and sales (which were virtually black-tie affairs, with furs and tiaras worn at major sales) were conducted in an aura of polite reverence. To meet death duties and relinquish unwanted heirlooms, the British aristocracy used the auction houses to sell large quantities of antiques, which generated brisk demand from the then 'new-money' generation of ship-owners, television magnates, film stars and property developers. Prices rose in line with demand, and the auction houses expanded their sale venues beyond London to New York and Geneva.

The objects that were sold were restricted to paintings (principally Old Masters), classic furniture (such as Chippendale, Hepplewhite, Sheraton) from country houses, silver, jewellery and ceramics. As the decades progressed the paintings category expanded to include nineteenth-century and early twentieth-century masters, including the Impressionists, Post-Impressionists and moderns, such as Picasso and Braque, and for the first time the work of living artists was sold at a 'serious' auction. As demand for oil paintings outstripped supply, etchings, drawings, lithographs, sculpture and other artefacts came to be sold at 'secondary' sales. What had been considered comparatively worthless sketches came to be valuable – a few pounds could turn into hundreds, even thousands.

Part of the reason for widening the range of sales was the irreversible decrease in the material available for auction as international museums competed for items that, once acquired by them, would never come back to the market. In addition, tastes changed, with more modern pictures becoming fashionable and saleable, and of these there was a comparatively large supply. By the 1970s work by pop artists such as Andy Warhol, Roy Lichtenstein, Robert Rauschenberg and Jim Dine was being auctioned, not least because their very commerciality ensured a continuing supply of their works. (There was also the advantage that living artists could add considerably to the publicity and hype surrounding what were then quite controversial sales; indeed Warhol's jokey persona made him famous for much longer than his allotted 'fifteen minutes'.) Other sale areas declined in popularity. Silver and gold items, for instance, declined as it became more difficult to protect them against theft, and as their usefulness declined in a society that was becoming less formal – also, there were no craftsmen producing new items in these materials to match the work of a Benvenuto Cellini.

In the 1970s and the 1980s the major auction houses continued to expand their activities, assisted by the increase in general economic well-being. In the 1990s there has been some retrenchment as recession has hit markets around the world. Despite the historic time-lag between stock market peaks and auction peaks it has become apparent that even wealthy individuals are disinclined to buy when general circumstances are poor. This may offer buying opportunities for the discerning collector, but it means that the 'big' money stays away. Consequently auction markets have tended to settle down into a more predictable pattern. The highest-priced items continue to be

Old Master paintings, with certain very particular items of furniture, jewellery and pottery not far behind. Few items achieve prices in excess of $1 million, and most are more likely to fetch between $5,000 and $50,000. The latter make up the bread-and-butter market, where lesser specimens of furniture, silver, watercolours, etchings, jewellery, books and manuscripts, antiquities, ceramics and general collectables provide the auctioneer with a steady stream of income from both seller's and buyer's premiums at 15%. For auctioneers (as for dealers) the biggest problem currently is to find a collection of sufficient quality or notoriety to capture the public's imagination and thereby generate prices that exceed estimates.

Background

A brief, even cursory, examination of the record of the art and antiques market before the 1960s reveals a foundation of 'old-money' values. Its constituents were Old Masters from the eighteenth and earlier centuries (oils, watercolours and prints), pre-Victorian furniture, silver, decorative jewellery, ceramics, books and manuscripts, and antiquities. This largely reflected both the contents of the western aristocratic residence from the early eighteenth century onwards and an ideal, promoted by many generations of collectors and those who dealt for them, that also dated back to the eighteenth century and Sir John Soane, whose collection formed an early forerunner of the British Museum. It mirrored a patrician heritage, owing much to scholarship and derived from aristocratic collections of long pedigree, that was imitated with remarkable flair by the aristocrats' industrialist successors. The auction market was not entirely averse to modern masters, such as the Impressionists, Picasso or other inheritors of the western artistic tradition, but it remained reluctant to reflect some of the newer influences permeating the retail market. Within a decade, a new generation of dealers and art impresarios, especially in the United States, made substantial inroads into this old-world collector's arena, not least by encouraging a new breed of professional for whom works of art became an expression of contemporary culture wedded to an investment opportunity.

This change in the configuration of the market did not displace or exclude the older values of good taste. It simply added to them, opening up a wider market in terms of both items seen as collectable and prices. By the 1990s not only had the areas for potential collectors become a great deal broader than they were in the 1950s, so, too, had the appreciation of a collective heritage, both nationally and internationally. Throughout these years, by a process of chance combined with language, historical precedent and innate instinct, Britons remain among the world's leading wealth creators in the sphere of art and antiques.

The core of this wealth lies in the difference between purchase price (adjusted for inflation) and the amount realized on subsequent sale over a period of time and the reinvestment of the resulting profit in the next wave of saleable/collectable pieces. Entrepreneur collectors of this sort include not only the accumulator of items by chance, but also a wide range of creators and connoisseurs of artistic properties and their heirs. In the contemporary British market, the vast bulk of the items sold are still in those 'old-money' areas familiar to the buyers of the early 1950s, and for these areas there exist many specialist publications that detail each segment of the market. However, the potential areas of investment in art and antiques is now extremely broad, and the next chapter examines three new markets that have matured from about 1980 and reflect the interests of a wide age range across an international spectrum: Photographs, Pop and Entertainment Memorabilia, and Classic Cars.

Collecting

Collecting appears to be a natural part of the human condition. During the twentieth century the process has even become the subject of psychological analysis, especially where collecting extends to mania or obsession. Psychologists determine collecting as an extension of self, and it is an extraordinarily widespread activity – in June 1995, for example, it was estimated that at least one in three Americans was a collector.

Anything is collectable, but not everything can be an investment. Some of the more bizarre collectors were the natives of Sarawak who, up to the 1930s, collected the smoked heads of their rivals and enemies. Few would claim that such a collection would have monetary value (even though the Ripley Museum in San Francisco has purchased such grotesque items). An equally bizarre collection item was the bones of Virginia Clem, Edgar Allan Poe's first wife. Poe's biographer acquired them, when the New York graveyard in which she was interred was deconsecrated, and stored the relics in a box under his bed, periodically showing them to other fans of the poet. Such cases are unusual, since general good taste is normally one of the criteria for selecting an object, especially in the West, for investment in a collection. Value is subjective, but, there has been general acceptance of a set of investment criteria for fine collections for almost three hundred years. The yardsticks for evaluating the status of any given item can be summed up as quality, association, significance and purpose.

The value of a work of art or antique derives from information and the interpretation put on that information. Assessment is fluid, relying on scholarship, instinct, and more indefinable aspects such as added value and utility. Rarity or unique status is often overplayed. A field that is too limited cannot sustain a market (seventeenth-century English newsletters are a good example), or one that depends on a small number of persistent and regular collectors (as with classic cars), which can cause a significant distortion of values and lead to a bubble market. The most common fields for collectors in the late 20th century appear to be stamps and coins. The vast expansion of 'museum culture', which led to the creation of a museum a day in Britain in 1988, has caused further distortion of the market, as a combination of institutional, charity and taxpayers' money has sidelined the more modest, yet perceptive, private collector.

Private collectors have been classified in several categories. The British ceramics expert and dealer Henry Sandon simply defines collectors as 'magpie' or 'real'. The distinction is appropriate. The magpie collector tends to accumulate items without any particular purpose or specialization (at their most acquisitive John Paul Getty and William Randolph Hearst were extreme examples of this trait, but many public institutions, ranging from universities to museums, incline to this catch-all approach). The real collector, often with specialist assistance, will set out on a familiar (or untrodden) path of collecting with a closely defined purpose, the limits of which can be as varied as the personalities of collectors, confining his collection, say, to depictions of a particular theme, or to objects of a particular era, school or type.

The genuine ('serious') collector falls into one of two categories: connoisseur or speculator. The short-term advantage may appear to lie with the speculator, but the best collectors will always be connoisseurs, who with due diligence, select and pursue a subject in which they are interested. One of the basic features of any collection is the collector's emotional affinity with the material – best summed up by the twentieth-century French collector of images Gerard Levy: 'In collecting, everything done without love is lost, because there is no spark and there is no life'. The choice of subject for a collection can be made for all manner of reasons, and indeed can be changed over the years by broadening the area of interest, narrowing it, or moving into a different area altogether. Occasionally the choice can be pure accident. One of the finest collections of contemporary art in the 1950s resulted from an American company commissioning paintings for use in advertising campaigns.

A speculator, by contrast, is attracted by short-term results alone. As an individual, he has the difficulty of trying to absorb a mass of appropriate information within a short time, much of which will not be drawn from experience, and is unlikely to preserve, let alone increase the sums he invests. In 1995 some speculators in the markets of the late 1980s turned to British courts for financial redress against the dealers from whom they had bought, claiming that they had been misled as to the value of the items they purchased. Such cases were dismissed.

To be effective in the longer term, the speculator can invest in a business involved in a specific market. There are a small number of publicly quoted companies in Britain in which such investments can be made – for example Partridge Fine Art or Mallett's (which became a plc in 1985), both of which have showrooms in central London. There are also companies that designate funds for investment in the field of art, antiques and related collections – Camellia Investments, a publicly quoted company, being one of the more notable. Through such businesses the risk is spread on an international basis, and dividends are payable, as with any other business. They may exist as dealers in the traditional sense or be holders of a variety of investments, where art and antiques form only part of the portfolio. Investment possibilities also extend to the auctioneers themselves, chiefly Sotheby's and Christie's. The US owner of Sotheby's, Alfred Taubman, bought the company in 1983 for £80 million and capitalized on his investment five years later by selling 2.6 million shares for some £30 million – just over 10% of the company by 1988 stock issue records.

Investment can also be made in a wide range of private businesses, many of which are sustained by sleeping partners. Here the advantage lies partially in anonymity and partially in having ready access to a source from which a private collection can also be built; both the area of interest and the returns from the business depend on the dealer or dealers concerned. This approach has even been adopted by the auction houses – Sotheby's purchase of the estate of Pierre Matisse (the son of the painter Henri) in 1990 included the inventory of his gallery: some 2,300 works by modern artists. It is recognized that a percentage of a major auctioneer's assets may lie in such 'intangibles' (which may also include images of items), and these are listed as such in annual reports. Detailed information on many antiques and fine arts dealers in the UK is available through the annual Business Audit Ratio report, which details the turnover, profit, shareholding and status of a range of such businesses both in the UK and abroad.

Once an area of interest has been decided upon, an investor/collector will define the parameters of the purchases to be made. Knowledge of the price ranges within the area is a primary consideration, for it remains true that the price paid for an item concentrates the mind. A wide selection of literature available in libraries will give a good idea of the likely current prices. In addition to articles in broadsheet newspapers, a weekly summary of the issues and trends in the marketplace is provided by the *Art Newspaper*, and specialist magazines such as *ArtNews*, the *Antique Collector* and *Apollo* provide in-depth examination of particular spheres.

Many of the best collectors with limited means, realizing from the outset that being able to afford the best of what they would like may lie beyond them to begin with, have begun by seeking to obtain the best they can afford. Then, over time and as their collection grows, they often seek to upgrade the material, selling off duplicates or the more common or lesser items, so as to secure better or finer examples. This will obviously involve a certain amount of money, though it does not need to be an absolute sum and can very often be a broad sum put aside for the purpose of buying, and also to provide for the storage and presentation of the material. In most spheres of art and antiques the latter involves costs that must be considered, and specialist articles, books and dealers will offer advice on the care of collections. Any documentation or information relating to material collected should be retained safely, since this has a value in its own right.

For the more scrupulous or parsimonious collector there remain avenues for collecting which are cheap. The most common is to build a specific collection from scratch at minimal expense. In recent years collectors of, for example, comics, toys, film and pop memorabilia, records and posters have shown that merely keeping material, which may have involved minimal outlay, over a period of two decades can provide rich rewards. The supposition that such opportunities are unrepeatable is erroneous. In many spheres it is still possible to assemble a representative collection, sometimes of the highest quality, through sheer doggedness and an open-minded approach, or simply through swapping with other collectors; it is often said that today's rubbish is tomorrow's collectable.

By 1995 the claims for certain types of collectables attracted criticism from long-term collectors and dealers in the USA. This was levelled particularly at the pronounced increase in 'manufactured' collectibles, ranging from limited-edition promotions to 'special-edition' artefacts that had little prospect, historically, of maintaining their initial purchase price. In effect, the term 'collectable' was being applied inappropriately as a selling point and could entrap the unwary. As with other activities, collectors will make mistakes, and it becomes a matter of experience as to how to pace the building of a collection.

Where a collection is being built, certain proprietary rights will arise as a result of the item being acquired – reproduction rights, for example. There are limitations on reproductions under copyright law, and works should not be purchased just because the collector thinks there is a likelihood of exploiting such rights as a source of income, but the potential for secondary income should now increasingly be borne in mind. The means of exploitation might take the form of producing and selling physical copies or of selling rights to reproduce the work, as can be the case for paintings and other images. Photographs are useful for security purposes, but they can also provide the basis for copies and may be extensively used on a fee basis – as is the case with the Bridgeman Art Library. It is, of course, necessary for such photographs to be of a high professional standard.

Awareness of proprietary rights in works of art and antiques have long been recognized. Some of the finest Western artists, from the Renaissance master Andrea Mantegna onwards, have used reproductions or prints of their work as a combined means of promoting themselves and generating income. In the nineteenth century the British artists J.M.W. Turner and Sir Edwin Landseer were acutely aware of the importance of reproduction fees and generated substantial income from them when mass-market printing came into vogue. Among the more unusual recent examples has been that of the UK lottery millionaire who acquired the additional limited-edition rights to reproduce a set number of prints of a painting bought with some of his winnings which, by due calculation and expedient sale, subsequently generated more than the original work cost. Large-scale exploitation of proprietary rights, which crosses into the area of intellectual property, is now endemic. Among the more remarkable success stories has been that of the Metropolitan Museum of Art in New York, which now generates from such rights profits that enable it to meet the cost of mounting major exhibitions.

The Market

The British market for art and antiques is made up of three different sources: private collectors who deal, auction houses and retail outlets – specialist, general dealers and those who deal via catalogues or other published information (which may now be electronic). It is not uncommon for an item to pass through all these sources (thereby still remaining in the trade) until it eventually finds a home in a private or public collection.

Private collectors who deal

The private collector will, by and large, sell only periodically, from home or even at car boot sales or the occasional fair. Such private sales may on occasion be conducted to raise funds for organizations such as charities, political parties or churches. The quality, quantity and price of the material on offer from this source can vary enormously.

The British phenomenon of the boot fair, similar to the flea markets of Europe and garage sales of North America, has given tremendous pleasure and impetus to the informed collector. Indeed, there have been a number of instances since 1989 where items purchased from boot fairs or local sales have resulted in extraordinary gains, some of which have made national headlines. Christie's, New York, sold for £67,226 a painting of a humming-bird, *Ruby Throat with Apple Blossoms* by the early US natural history master painter Martin Johnson Heade, bought at a car boot sale near Bristol for £5 in 1989, while a work by L.S. Lowry, bought for £9 at a local Midlands sale in 1990, was valued at £2,000 by Sotheby's later the same year.

In 1994 the British government sought to curtail the likelihood of such sales including stolen or forged items, and, among other steps to assist protection of the consumer, abolished the ancient 'market ouvert' right dating from 1189. Market ouvert had allowed ownership of an item to pass without hindrance ('no questions asked') between the hours of sunrise and sunset within a very specific area of London. It applied to the Caledonian market until, as a result of the Blitz, the regulation was extended to Bermondsey market.

Auction Houses

The auction market remains the most regularly publicized sphere for the buying and selling of art and antiques. The market in Britain is dominated by Christie's, Sotheby's, Phillips and Bonham's, along with local subsidiaries. Details of their forthcoming sales, specialist departments, and prices realized are covered in the broadsheet press regularly. In addition to the majors, there are a host of smaller, local auction houses throughout Britain, and the most readily available listing of these is in the *Yellow Pages*. Many specialist collectors' publications, such as the *Bookdealer*, or the *Antique Collector* now list forthcoming sales. For an overview of sales across the country, there is a small-format booklet published monthly, the *Antiques Gazette*, which lists a host of sales. Auctions and auctioneers are variable, some efficient, some less so, some more aware of what they are selling than others.

The catalogues produced for auctions can vary enormously in quality and usefulness to the buyer unable to attend the sale in person. Catalogues can run from a few photocopied pages at a price of up to £2 to a fully illustrated de luxe production. (The latter have always been collectable in their own right, not least for reference, and broad-based collections of such catalogues now command prices from the hundreds to thousands.) Catalogues may be picked up in person or ordered by post, and a subscription for catalogues covering a particular area of interest may be obtained, which allows a discount of 10–15% on the annual price – there will often be a form for this purpose in the back of current catalogues. The notion of subsequent catalogue discount (one-third off the annual subscription cost), so prevalent in the USA, has only recently been introduced to the UK by Bonham's. Sample past catalogues and prices realized will generally also be available from auctioneers.

Besides detailing the items to be sold, the catalogue will set out time, date and location of the auction and the conditions of sale or purchase. The conditions are statutory, but repeat customers will find that there is considerable variation in approach. What cannot be avoided is charges. These were introduced in the 1980s by most auctioneers, at a rate of between 10% and 15% of the price realized for both buyers and sellers (since 1995 there has been some variation among auctioneers regarding buyers' and sellers' premium relating to price realized). In addition, value-added tax is charged for services in association with the purchase (packaging and the like), and some lots are sold inclusive of VAT (these lots will be notified at the auction).

A lot may vary substantially; it may be a single item, a set, or a mixed bag of completely different objects – just as the sales themselves may cover a single area or a range of areas. For the more substantial lots, auctioneers will caution 'owner collects' for items that are too bulky to post or too costly to insure for transit at the auctioneers' expense. For many auction sales in Britain you can request 'prices realized', if you cannot attend the sale in person; this is a record of the prices (with or without the buyer's premium, as the case may be) realized by each lot. Certain items may be withdrawn from sale, for a variety of reasons, and corrections to catalogue descriptions will be announced just before the sale starts.

It is preferable to attend a sale in person (not least because the lots can be viewed personally and matched against catalogue description), but this is increasingly not possible. Commonly a representative is asked to bid on a buyer's behalf; this may be a relative, a friend or a representative of a commercial organization. This physical presence is particularly valuable for enabling one to gauge the way the bidding for a lot is moving, and has secured many a good lot. Certain methods of conducting an auction are laid down by regulation. Predetermined prices can only be levied for those items that have been given a reserve (minimum selling price), and this reserve cannot be changed during sale to pursue a higher price. Concerted rings of bidders are illegal, and the pursuit of imaginary bids – especially under the guise of bids 'on the book' (sent in by fax, telephone or letter by bidders who cannot attend in person) – to try to raise the price is also discouraged.

The introduction of bids by telephone and fax has some importance, especially at local sales. A telephone bidder is often expected by those in the room to be more determined, and this can often affect the price to the telephone bidder's advantage. Such a bid is made by prior arrangement with the auctioneer; the bidder is required to give lot number and a phone line on which he or she can be contacted, though if the saleroom cannot establish contact (for instance, because the bidder's phone line is engaged) the opportunity is lost. The introduction of fax and telephone bids has also made international buying more common, especially in a market where the dominant language is English.

Bids in person require a certain stamina, patience and nerve. Stamina is required because not all auction houses are fully fitted with modern conveniences, patience, because the progress of a sale can be slow and the bidder will need to concentrate on the lot or lots in which they are interested whilst avoiding boredom, and nerve because the vast majority of people, unless bidding by sheer whim, become very nervous as the lot number approaches. After a while experience will expose familiar bidders and their interests. Collectors who attend auctions regularly will develop an eye for the lots on sale and a sense of the atmosphere and interest; such sensitivity gives rise to an instinctive knowledge of what to look for, or when to stop bidding. Once items are sold, lot prices should be noted and both lot numbers and prices checked against invoice, paid receipt and the actual item itself. The vast majority of auctioneers now allow payment by credit card, which is especially useful where currency conversion is involved and, despite the charges, can be beneficial. There are rules and regulations regarding the import and export of works of art to and from the UK; information about these is available from the leading auctioneers and from H.M. Customs and Excise.

The Retail Market

The retail market, at its most professional, is governed by a number of official bodies or watchdogs ensuring propriety in the industry. Among these are the British Antique Dealers Association, whose numbers are certified and subject to inspection, and the Antiquarian Booksellers Association, which covers the book trade. Regulatory bodies lay down conditions of sale, the information to be provided (such as the source of the item, known as provenance) and also provide a trade information service. In Britain the vast majority of dealers are defined as small businesses. They will charge VAT on most sales and services, generally aim for a mark up of 30% or more on items for sale and offer only limited credit terms beyond standard bank or credit guarantees. Transactions 'within the trade' do offer discounts, but the private buyer may enquire (and usually obtain) some discount for quantity, cash or regularity of custom.

The majority of retail dealers in Britain offer a range of stock (equivalent to the auctioneer's 'mixed sale'). Objects may be reserved by paying a deposit (equivalent to about 10% to 15% of the price), but the investor should be aware that the stock may not all be for sale. This approach may be frustrating but is not uncommon. It reached its extreme in the 1980s with the Cheltenham dealer Summerfield, who sold only a minute proportion of his vast stock in his later years. On his death his hoard of antiques, antiquarian books and pictures was sold in a series of sales in Cheltenham and London that brought high prices, since much of the material had not appeared in the market for almost half a century! As it happened, among the lots sold was a drawing that was reattributed to the nineteenth-century French artist Jean Augusta Dominique Ingres in November 1990.

A specialist dealer might be expected to have both more specialist knowledge and a defined stock, but this may not always be the case. Some areas, such as collectables, remain very broad, particularly in such cases as ephemera or stamps. By and large, neither a name nor directory entry alone will clearly define the specialist nature of such outlets. Apart from making personal visits, some of the best ways to discover likely specialists in a given area are to look at the trade paper the *Antiques Gazette*, the *Antique Collector* or to scan the regular articles published by the broadsheet newspapers, notably *The Times*, the *Daily Telegraph* and the *Financial Times*. One recent application of new technology has been the introduction of the Thesaurus Index, by which, for a fee, collectors can be notified of all the items specific to their sphere coming up for auction in the majority of British auction houses.

Over the past decade, the resources and items for sale through catalogues has burgeoned, in common with a general trend towards home shopping. Many retailers, especially in traditional postal areas such as books or stamps, offer catalogues on a regular basis, most of which are circulated free of charge to a list of past, present or potential customers. Where charge is made for catalogues, the US practice of offering discounts for subscription or waiving subscription charges if purchases are made is now becoming more common in Britain. Many public libraries will carry specialist art and antiques trade journals from which the names of dealers who offer catalogues can be obtained, and a number of retail magazines, such as the *Record Collector*, the *Book and Magazine Collector* or *Stamp Monthly* will contain regular listings of dealers offering catalogues. The quality and content of catalogues can vary enormously. A highly illustrated production, equivalent to those from the major auction houses, remains a rarity in Britain, though in a number of cases, such as the catalogues issued by the postal auctioneer Messengers (who auction ephemera and printed collectable matter via the post) or by the doyen of book dealers Quaritch, the quality of content and attention to design and appropriate illustration is exceptional. Many catalogues remain little more than photocopied lists but, despite their appearance, the majority are highly informative.

Two approaches are taken to pricing in such lists. The first is an estimate price (standard for postal auctioneers) which may be compared to a standard listed price; stamps, for example, are priced against the 'catalogue' price in Stanley Gibbons' publication of stamp values. Bidders are required to submit a price that is a near equivalent to this range within a defined time scale. Some postal auctioneers will follow the practice of retail auctioneers and work to reserves for items. The second approach to pricing is by fixed price–purchase made on a first-come, first-served basis. Purchase from catalogues relies on the information given, and, while inadequate or misleading information invalidates a sale, the burden of evaluation is with the buyer – in other words *caveat emptor*.

Depending on the scale of the operation, sales by catalogue may require payment of VAT on bid prices or items, and additional postage and packaging costs. Such costs will be listed in the catalogue, or covered by a broad phrase or two. In many cases it will be important to demand delivery by registered post if this is not already part of the service. Delivery may be made by a COR (cash on receipt) or COD (cash on delivery) basis. An increasing number of sales may be made by credit card, debit card, bank transfer or bank draft (credit card purchases may require consideration of the current interest rate to avoid extended charges). A number of catalogue dealers will now hold items for a period after purchase and make personal delivery without charge when they are in the buyer's home area (this is especially the case for residents of large towns or cities).

One of the notable, but often overlooked, advantages of dealing regularly with catalogue sales derives from the 'nature of the beast'. The compiler draws up catalogues from a selection of his stock, and he may have further unlisted items of similar nature that are not included in the current catalogue. Additionally, compilers have greater flexibility to travel and more time to investigate likely leads for new stock, and in the process it is not uncommon for them to act on behalf of regular customers as near-voluntary agents, seeking to satisfy very particular requests. Such interest is, more often than not, mutual, and can result in close association: *84 Charing Cross Road*, which told the story of the relationship between a London book dealer and an American collector, probably remains the most famous example.

Selling

The balance between buying and selling is a matter of experience. There are dealers and collectors who are adamant that perceptive buying is far more important than a judicious sale, since good items can sell themselves. A good sale hinges on those points that make an item alluring to a buyer. The most common are quality and international appeal, authenticity (is the item what it purports to be), and provenance and history.

Although allowances against tax on important works of art (in-lieu agreements) and a variety of other schemes exist to curtail the increase in the export of works of art of national importance, many sellers have chosen to put works up for auction in the 1990s. There is advantage in selling at auction and paying the necessary capital gains on profits above the £6,000 (index-linked) allowance, because the prices realized at auction have often exceeded the sums offered by the Treasury for private treaty sales. (The Treasury, however, maintains that it accommodates this differential by offering a 'special price' which exceeds that of the open market.) There are also cases where works of art offered to the Treasury have been refused, and then 'saved' for the nation at greater cost, after appearing at public auction. One of the most publicized sales in the past decade has been that of Canova's statue of the *Three Graces*, for which the difference between the price at which it was offered to the nation and that at which it was subsequently 'rescued' amounted to several million pounds.

There is a second scheme for works of art, detailed by the Office of Arts and Libraries document *Works of Art*. This covers works on which conditional 'in lieu' tax exemption is offered for works that would otherwise be covered by inheritance tax or capital gains tax. The conditions are complex and the regulations extensive, and all this is reflected in the take up of the scheme – in lieu allowances fell by almost 80% between 1991 and 1992. A third scheme which allows owners to retain items of notable quality *in situ*: so long as the work is accessible (in a suitable environment), is conserved and is covered fully by security and insurance, it can be held by a new owner without tax liability for the transfer of ownership. In effect this scheme, dating from 1984, has allowed major works to be kept in private collections. Once again, the process is cumbersome and takes some months to complete, but spread over years, the tax exemption can be substantial, and the scheme does allow owners to sell a work on the open market at a provident moment.

Where the items are to become part of normal household goods, albeit insured separately, provisions for duty-free transport across borders is widespread. Where items are purchased from overseas auctioneers, UK customs duty and/or VAT will be payable on import – a charge reclaimable for those registered for VAT.

In the main, items bought at auction cost at least 30% or so less than the retail purchase of a similar item. The auction market is particularly attractive for being amenable. In many cases items in excess of the collector's wants can be readily resold; indeed, it is recognized that it is possible to cover the entire costs of a purchase by reselling excess material in a lot.

Quality

For the seller, a number of markets (from diamonds to cinema posters) operate international grading scales, with each piece allocated an appropriate grade that identifies and recognizes its quality. In most spheres of collecting, however, quality can be largely subjective, influenced by change in taste and perception of condition. Knowledge and experience of museum pieces, items illustrated in auction catalogues and the terms used in descriptions will help in identifying those elements of condition that will be reflected in values.

Maintenance of condition is one of the inevitable responsibilities of a collector, who, over time, becomes something closer to a custodian. It is now recognized that collectors do make substantial contributions to the maintenance of a collective heritage. Since 1945 there has been an increase in the number of businesses that maintain the skills necessary to keep works of art in premium condition, and, despite the not infrequent occasions when experts choose to differ over picture restoration or the refurbishment of furniture, the general state of collections in the UK is very high. If restoration or advice on maintenance is needed, lists of recommended experts in specialist fields are obtainable from major museums, such as the British Museum (in some cases a small charge will be made for full details of such services). Where partial reconstruction is necessary, as in the rebinding of books, more than one museum expert or dealer should be consulted (such advice is often free of charge), and more than one restorer or expert should then be approached. The cost of the work will obviously depend on the item being dealt with, but some indication of likely costs may be obtained from professional restoration bodies, the details of which are obtainable from major museums and galleries and from professional associations, such as LAPADA (London and Provincial Antique Dealers Association).

The importance of international appeal has grown in the past two decades and now applies as much to ceramics and sports memorabilia as it always has to schools of painting. Not only does internationalism literally expand the potential market, it also allows for a seller to choose where, and in what currency, he will sell. For objects with wide-ranging appeal, this can bring substantial gains, especially in fields where there is no language barrier.

The development of new markets has tended to go hand in hand with economic development. Thus, by the beginning of the 1990s, works relating to South Korea, the Philippines, Malaysia and other emerging economies began to attract buyers on a scale which had not been seen before. There is an apparently strong and natural tendency for countries to seek to recover and repossess their heritage when economic means allow. A good French example was the repatriation of a work by the French painter Bernard Buffet. Sold in London for £240,000 in 1989, it was resold in Lyons for £550,000 in 1990.

Authenticity

This can be a point of contention. There have been several well-documented cases where auction houses or dealers have had to pay substantial damages to sellers and buyers for errors deemed unprofessional. The 1995 case brought by a Swiss buyer over a painting sold through Christie's as by Egon Schiele, but proved in court to have been substantially repainted, led to a £500,000 damages award. In November 1991 substantial damages were awarded to an American vintage car collector over the sale of a fake 1913 Rolls-Royce Silver Ghost bought in Britain in 1983, and the provincial auctioneer Messenger May Baverstock won, on appeal, a widely publicized case over two paintings later attributed to Stubbs. One of the more notable cases involved competition between the two main auction houses, Christie's and Sotheby's. A painting of Clement VII was originally sold for £197 in 1987 by Sotheby's, Chester, as a nineteenth-century copy after the Italian painter Sebastiano del Pombo, but a year later was sold by Christie's, as an original, for £418,000; Sotheby's made up the difference to the original owner. In cases of doubt, the opinion of at least two independent experts should be sought.

It has to be acknowledged, though, that expertise remains

subjective, and a judgement stands only for the time it was made. Among the most famous post-war instances of subjective judgement are the cases of works attributed to Rembrandt, the authenticity of which remain in dispute, and of the forgeries by Han van Meegeren, which some art historians and experts sought to confirm as the works of the Dutch master Jan Vermeer, but which were proven to be forgeries in a famous 1940s court case. Later instances have included the case of the British artist Tom Keating in the 1970s, whose fakes of the work of Samuel Palmer deceived the art world for almost a decade.

In most realms of art and antiques forgeries, fakes and facsimiles exist. But only one is the result of a criminal act: the forgery. A forgery is produced with the intent to deceive or commit a fraud by securing the acceptance of the item as genuine; at its most blatant, the addition of a copy signature or mark intended to bestow authenticity on a 'work of art' is common. In certain cases of potential forgery substantial proof of intent is required to overcome the defence that the object is a pastiche, produced 'in the manner of' a well-known artist. It is the act of committing a forgery that is criminal, and, under English law, it appears from a 1990 case that no redress for forgery is possible where its perpetrator or perpetrators are deceased – no claim can be made on the deceased's estate.

A facsimile, by contrast, is an exact copy or reproduction. Facsimiles are an area where scholarship is important, given that there exist many works that are genuine but were produced in multiples by the same artist or artisan (as with edition prints or photographs); here confirmation of sequence of production may be required. Traditionally one of the most common methods of preventing re-editioning has been the scoring of plates by artists at the end of a limited-edition print run, or the destruction of the original surface or material from which the multiple was made (as in the case of a lithographic stone or photo negative).

Provenance

The provenance or history of an item usually provides documentary support for its authenticity. Such documents can be faked, amended or indeed be spurious (there is a case where a first edition of Allen Ginsberg's poetry was dedicated at the author's signing session to a buyer who claimed his name was 'T.S. Eliot'). In extreme cases substantial scientific analysis would need to be undertaken to confirm the originality of support documents. The case of the Hitler diaries is among the most notorious such cases in recent years. In the early 1980s German journalist Gerd Heidemann came forward with a source of what he claimed were the diaries of Adolf Hitler. The diaries were bought for publication by the *Sunday Times*, beginning in April 1983, backed by an original judgement by Lord Dacre that they were genuine. Other experts denounced the whole event as a hoax; only a short time later Lord Dacre withdrew his attribution, and the diaries were confirmed to be a hoax perpetrated by a German forger.

Provenance covers the past history of an item. This would normally cover records of the previous ownership and location of an item, its past progress through collections or sales, or where it was originally made or bought. In many cases this material is in published sources. Only recently have such sources begun to be transferred to digital systems, which can allow for rapid and expedient identification of provenance. In Britain the leading auctioneers will answer enquiries by telephone, and provide details of prices realized in recent sales (though it is important that such enquiries be specific). Though the history of an item can overlap with its provenance, it is often distinct. History covers the status of the item in the body of historical knowledge or research, including, where appropriate, its exhibition, its relation to the life and work of the maker and its relation to items of similar nature.

The scholarship involved in establishing provenance, history and authenticity is a selling point and has a substantial value. Many dealers' and auctioneers' catalogues make reference to such scholarship. There have, however, been rare incidents where such expert scholarship has subsequently been exposed as having been pursued for financial gain. Though the matter is still subject to some dispute in detail, there is now sufficient evidence to prove collusion for financial gain between the expert on the early Italian masters, Bernard Berenson, and the dealer Lord Duveen through the 1920s and 1930s, with attributions given in exchange for money. In the case of antiquities, scholarship has, to all intents and purposes, created a market, and this has encouraged looting of archaeological sites, notably in South America and Italy. There are also cases where the origin of the material becomes a matter of international dispute. Among the best documented of recent cases has been the gold hoard, known as the 'Seveso Treasure', acquired by Lord Northampton; this collection of Roman gold was the subject of court cases brought by both Lebanon and the former Yugoslavia in attempts to prove title.

Misattribution can be an expensive experience. In 1978 a marble bust of Pope Gregory XV was sold for £65 by Christie's and was later resold by a Clapham book-dealer for £240; later attributed to Bernini, it was sold by Sotheby's in 1981 for £120,000. A considerable body of case law now exists to enable sellers to bring cases for compensation for such misattribution under certain conditions.

Art and Antiques

As with stocks and shares, investment in the broad field of art and antiques is cyclical and subject to the amount of money available in the market as a whole. Each decade through the 20th century has been marked by peaks and troughs. The most recent low was in 1990, when the average fall in auction sale turnover was 20%, but there has since been a steady recovery in the majority of markets, most notably in the United States Fall (Autumn) sales of Impressionist and Modern Master paintings.

From 1946 London was established as a key market for art and antique sales by means of specific promotions, particularly by the then wholly British auctioneers Sotheby's and Christie's, who later extended their coverage by taking over other established houses in Europe and the United States. These two auction houses acted as wholesalers or clearers for works from Europe to the burgeoning US market, where huge savings had accumulated during World War II. The supply of material for auction was then, and largely remains, dependent on the three Ds – Death, Divorce and Debts.

A number of British auction houses published regular results of their sales, supplemented by yearbooks from 1958, but the first attempts to quantify the returns on art and antiques as an investment were made in 1966, with the publication of the Sotheby's Index, an annual review of price movements in the areas most popular with buyers and sellers. It initially proved inadequate and in 1975 was rebased on a notional 100 for contemporary prices. This allowed comparisons with other indexes, such as those for stocks, but fluctuations in capital gains and other taxes, the depredations of inflation and increased charges for handling works at auction were not readily accommodated by the Index; in effect, its 'gains' tended to reflect optimum returns. Thus, the figure of 512 for December 1987, or that of 1038 for Decemer 1989, had to be viewed with some caution. Even the fall to 983 by December 1990 appeared at odds with reality, and from 1991 the Sotheby's Index no longer operated in Europe. Meanwhile, from the late 1960s, a number of specialist investment or financial companies, typified by the US concern Salomon Brothers, produced tables of compound annual rate of return from investments in art and antiques, and the Telegraph newspaper group in Britain introduced in 1980 its own subscription index of prices realized, which remains current. (As historical background, and for an indication of the relations between taste and prices for pictures, Gerald Reitlinger's *Economics of Taste*, which charts the rise and fall of picture prices from 1760 to 1960, is an illuminating work for any long-term student of investment in paintings.)

Where currencies were floated from 1972, the conditions for the market changed, with more items sold in markets where there were locally declining prices. The policy of transferring sales to those regions which had stronger currencies became commonplace. This was also true where inflation rates rose rapidly. More items came on to the market, and this was one of the reasons for the increase in the range of items put up for sale. The combination of declining prices, inflationary conditions and wider markets led to an uneven distortion of the Art Index, suggesting greater gains than were actually the case, because the value of money had declined substantially.

At the top end of the market the corporate investor and immensely wealthy individual began to buy through the auction houses in the 1970s, challenging the institutions, such as museums. Such corporate collections included those of IBM (the pioneer of such collecting), Armand Hammer's Occidental Petroleum in the US, the Peter Stuyvesant Foundation in Holland (begun in 1962) and a number of smaller collections, such as that of Robert Fleming, the British merchant bank. Wealthy individual collectors included Walter Annenberg, the Bunker Hunts, Baron Thyssen, the Ortiz family of Bolivia and the Ludwigs of Germany. One substantial long-term investor in the field was the British Rail Pension Fund, which had secured an adjusted annual return of over 10% by the time its collections were resold in the mid-1990s. By 1980 the cumulative effect of the arrival of the heavyweight buyers was to reduce the number of potential purchasers at the top of the market to a mere handful. These were joined by the Japanese, who, as a result of tax advantages for ownership of works of art and salesmanship by the auction houses and dealers, invested many billions in the market until the recession of 1989. The scale of the Japanese investment was stupendous. From 1984 to 1990 imports to Japan of paintings alone grew from a value of

$223 million to $3.65 billion, and in 1990 the UK exports of works of art to Japan rose 42% with those of pictures as a whole rising by 91% to £433 million.

By 1995 this 'clearing-house' effect was so notable in balance of trade figures (especially for Switzerland, which, to all intents and purposes, serves as the staging post for the international trade) that specific reference was made to it in government statistics. In reaction to the opening market in works of art governments introduced incentive schemes, designed to aid the retention of works of significance, and rules to prevent the export of works of art. The British government established the committee for the Export of Works of Art in 1966, and in 1974 the first British legislation covering in lieu settlements against Inheritance Tax (previously known as Estate Duty) was introduced.

The cyclical nature of the markets was amply demonstrated during the last recession, which first took effect early in 1990 (about a year after the recession began to be felt in other spheres of investment). The years 1991 and 1992 saw a capital reduction in their turnover of up to 50% for the majority of the auction houses. At the top end of the market the Japanese withdrew almost entirely, while in the remainder of the market purchases funded by borrowing, augmented by lines of credit offered to clients by the auction houses themselves, evaporated. (Sotheby's offered such a service through its Sotheby's Financial Services subsidiary.) The most highly publicized of these credit deals, revealed only in 1990, was that negotiated by the Australian tycoon Alan Bond, who bought Van Gogh's *Irises* at Sotheby's in 1989. Bond had, it appears, borrowed $27 million of the $53.9 million sale price from Sotheby's, and, being subsequently unable to repay the sum, was forced to sell the picture on to the J. Paul Getty Museum, in Malibu, California, for an undisclosed price. Such internal supports for the market by the major auctioneers are not so recent a phenomenon. Sotheby's made its first offer of a guaranteed price for Poussin's *Nativity* painting in 1956. The introduction of buyers' and sellers' premiums of up to 15%, the imposition of VAT on the premium, and service costs all increased the direct costs to buyers and sellers alike from the 1980s (though some adjustment in the scale of buyers' and sellers' premiums has now been made in the market). The nature of the market also shifted west, with New York accounting for almost 40% of the world art market turnover by 1992, against London's 24%.

6 Some Newer Areas of Collecting

There are 40- to 50-year-olds operating in 'new-money' areas of the economy who have wealth-creation abilities equal to anything that 'old' money has produced – well-established film stars, pop stars, technology whizzes and some financiers, for instance. Unstuffy, laid-back, easy-going (up to a point) – casual, even – they often have 'anti-establishment' views and values. When such people turn to collecting they look for fields that correspond more closely to their lives and interests than 'traditional' areas of collecting and are not necessarily shaped by previous generations' views of what constitutes value.

Since the late 1970s the advent of such buyers has broadened the range of fields for collecting well beyond the traditional 'old-money' areas. Here we shall look at just three of the many new markets that have opened up over the last twenty-five years: photographs, pop and film memorabilia, and classic cars.

Photographs

Establishment of and interest in the photography market as an area for collecting derived from a series of coincidental events of the late 1960s in North America and Europe, and the market has performed exceptionally over the past quarter of a century. A mass commercial market in photographs had existed from the inception of photography in 1840 by Louis Daguerre and Joseph Niepce in France and William Henry Fox Talbot in the UK. Many photographers and retailers made their fortunes out of the explosion of demand for contemporary images in the subsequent decade. In the 1850s and 1860s photographers, photo-essayists and photo-artists such as Francis Frith and Julia Margaret Cameron in the UK and Matthew Brady and Thomas Eakins in the USA came to be recognized as both pioneers and masters of their 'art'. A number of photographers received considerable patronage during the Victorian era, but this interest had dissipated by 1900, for no obvious reason, and, beyond commercial use, the works of individual master photographers became known to only a small circle until the beginning of a revival in the 1950s. The fall from grace of such photographers was typified by the remark in the 1960s by Helmut Gernsheim who dismissed the work of the English photographer Roger Fenton as 'Victorian trash' (in 1978, however, Fenton's photograph of a Nubian model sold for a record price for a British photograph of £5,400). Modern photographers, from the American Alfred Stieglitz on, received widespread attention and commissions from a number of major sponsors, including governments, while their forebears were lost in the shadows.

A consistent market in art photography, pursued by the artists Edgar Degas and Pierre Bonnard, meanwhile continued with the Surrealists, who saw the photograph as a work of art. The invention of the photomontage brought further recognition, with the works of Man Ray and Francis Picabia coming to the fore. A range of leading twentieth-century artists, from Marcel Duchamp to Pablo Picasso, from Robert Rauschenberg to Andy Warhol, produced original photographs as artworks. The best known contemporary photographer-painter is probably the Englishman David Hockney.

The Market Emerges

Re-appraisal of the nineteenth- and early twentieth-century pioneers was initiated by a small number of individual collectors and institutions. Those of note included Stieglitz himself, the American collector Sam Wagstaff, the Metropolitan Museum of Art in New York, Jane Armstrong of the Photographer's Gallery in London, the Art Institute of Chicago and the Victoria and Albert Museum in London. The first specialist dealers, including Wagstaff, drew on the works of major collectors, such as the Frenchman Georges Sirot, and researchers, notably the German-born Briton, Helmut Gernsheim, who produced the first authoritative reference work the *History of Photography* in 1955 (he also rediscovered the world's first photograph, in an attic in England). This work was followed by, among others, the source work (*The Directory of Photographic Collections*) by the Royal Photographic Society of 1974 and the *Dictionary of Photography* of 1979, published by Macmillan. By the mid 1970s institutions had formed photograph collections – those of the Kodak Museum in Rochester, NY, the Getty Museum in Malibu, CA, the University of Texas in Austin and the British National Museum of Photography, funded by Kodak, in Bradford being of particular note. The Getty Museum has made the single largest purchase, acquiring the accumulated collections of Arnold Crane and Sam Wagstaff for over £14 million in 1984.

Periodic re-discoveries of collections, such as those of Matthew Brady, found in the national archives in Washington DC, gave further impetus to recognition of the range and quality of the work of early photographers. Some collectors were already sensitive to the quality of Brady's work, among them the film director George Stephens, who collected it avidly. Photographs appeared in general and book-dealer's sales from an early date, often for their autographic, rather than photographic, merit. In March 1985 the American publisher Malcolm Forbes bought an 1864 photograph by Anthony Berger of Abraham Lincoln and his son Tad, signed by Lincoln, for $104,500 at Sotheby's, New York.

The first sales of photographs by the leading auction houses, Sotheby's and Christie's, took place in 1974, although the US firm of Parke Bernet (later taken over by Sotheby's) had been holding specialist photographic sales from 1971. Values increased rapidly, and this led to some remarkable discoveries, including unique or near-unique portraits of such nineteenth-century figures as Lincoln, Billy the Kid and the Duke of Wellington, as well as reviving the standing of photographers such as Matthew Brady and Alvin Langdon Coburn. Photographs are sold in various forms – as multiple prints (ranging from cabinet and carte de visite to landscape images); as negatives (glass-plate or film-negative); as unique prints, such as Man Ray's 'Rayographs' (sold for a mere £110 each in 1971); or as limited-edition prints, each of which will have fine variations. Premiums exist for prints signed by the photographer, the subject or both, which can command exceptional prices as works of art or historical documents; in 1986 Sotheby's, London, sold an inscribed portrait by Marilyn Monroe by William Walling, who was also her lover, for £16,000.

There is one area where caution is advised – that of limited-edition or later prints of classic photographs. During the late 1970s and 1980s many such prints were produced for the collectors' market, and the edition sizes (and, hence, the value of the images) vary substantially. Enquiries should be made about prints of famous images by name photographers to determine the probable date of reprinting and the edition quantity. Prices of similar reprintings (which may be gathered in portfolios) should be sought.

Investor Opportunities

Opportunities for the investor in the field remain, even though it is estimated that over 75% of all Victorian-era photographs in Britain have been destroyed. The vast majority of collections are thematic – centred on personalities, landscapes or events – for few, if any, aspects of human activity have been overlooked by the camera. Outlay can range from the extremely modest (pennies per image) through to sums that require the means of a multi-millionaire. Somewhat unusually, the collector's opportunity is limited not by quantity but rather by quality. A specific interest in photographs may be sparked from a very early age; the English rock stars Graham Nash and Brian May began collecting as children. There are a small number of specialist dealers in Britain, but many images can still be purchased from junk and charity shops, car boot sales and privately. The subject of negatives can remain completely unknown, especially in the case of glass plates, until a print is made, which adds an uncommon frisson to collecting in the field, especially while documentation or research on photographs and photographers remains limited. The extensive influence of the British Empire, and the large number of Britons who travelled widely from the time of the invention of photography, makes the UK a primary source market. In specific colonies and dominions, such as India, ambitious programmes to record the local populace, scenes and customs were undertaken at an official or semi-official level.

Even allowing for the introduction of the machine print (a multicopy commercial process), photography retains the potential for continual renewal, much as fine art does. The durability of the image is now proven, and, while colour photographs are subject to fading, the stability of the black-and-white image assures it a long-term future. Since the invention of photography a variety of processes has been used – the callotype, daguerreotype, and so on and these are specifically defined in reference works on photography (amongst the best is the two-volume *Focal Encyclopedia of Photography*, published by Caxton in 1958). The type of photograph is often described in catalogue entries, along with plate size and other details. In modern times, the most common process type encountered is the silver print: the standard black-and-white image. With daguerreotypes it is common for the appropriate originals to be sold with integral frames, which are often elaborate silver productions. The best of these pairings of original image and frame will carry a premium.

Excepting a handful of limited-edition sales, the photograph market has not been subject to specific investment promotions, nor to new technologies that can distort the market. The prospects for profitable sale and realization of investment is proven, even over a short time scale (days or weeks). Among the earlier instances of a rapid rise in price, was the sale of a print by US master photographer Ansel Adams, bought for $150 in 1971, which had risen in value to $22,000 by the end of the decade. One avenue for the collector is to buy from provincial auctions and resell through the international auctioneers (now including Phillips and Bonham's). Private sales on an international basis are frequent; probably the highest price paid for a single collection was the Japanese purchase for over £1 million of a suite by Julia Margaret Cameron.

Status and Sources of Photographs

Specialist publications, such as *Camera*, the *Antiques Collector* and the *Photographer's Yearbook*, publish details of specialist dealers and informative articles on the subject. When selling in the international market, including sales to institutions, there is a legal obligation to declare any photograph estimated to be over £1,000 in value and over a hundred years old, since the area is now covered by international agreement on the sale of works of art (certain countries have stringent restrictions on works over 75 years old). Sweden catalogues photographs as works of art, and many are considered to be of national significance. Due to currency fluctuations in the 1990s, sales in Germany, Switzerland and the USA will, on average, give a better return than sales in the UK, even allowing for exchange rates.

At both auction and private sale, photographs are sold as either individual items, as collections (frequently in book or portfolio form) and as miscellaneous lots. In many sales a number of works will remain uncatalogued as regards image, date or photographer; any additional information and provenance (past collections, sources, exhibitions and so on) that can be gathered give added value to images, and is therefore of importance to the investor when he comes to resell. VAT normally applies to auction commissions, and capital gains tax can also be payable on high-value or high-volume sales.

To date few photographic collections have been accepted by the British government in lieu of estate taxes, as works of national cultural or historic importance, though certain images from the collection of the critic Kenneth Tynan were acquired by the British Library as part of his archive in 1994. This infrequency is, however, likely to change as the number of significant collections in private hands in the UK diminishes and the potential of the long-term rights exploitation of such images becomes realizable.

The purchase of the major US photographic collection, the Bettman archive, by Bill Gates of Microsoft in 1995, or the focus of the private Getty Foundation on a UK photo library suggests the interest in rights in the late 1990s. Evidence of such exploitation, which crosses over into the field of intellectual property, is abundant. It ranges from gallery and museum reproductions, through posters, books and special editions of works (such as those of the American photographer Robert Mapplethorpe), to exhibitions for which entrance fees are charged.

Memorabilia

The most widely publicized areas of memorabilia in recent years have been those of film and pop music, covering material of the years from 1910 and from 1955 respectively. The modern market in memorabilia dates back to the nineteenth century, with sales devoted to Nelson, Napoleon and other major figures being prominent. From the turn of the century a wide variety of memorabilia of sportsmen and women, theatrical figures, the notorious (such as the murderer Crippen) and the military came to be featured in both general and specialist sales. Some items had always attracted a substantial premium, buoyed by a collective emotional response to the popularity or sheer heroism of the personality. A number of significant collections of memorabilia amassed by private collectors predate the more recent museums, among them Madame Tussaud's (her great collection of memorabilia of the Napoleonic era was unfortunately destroyed by fire early this century), the American Civil War collection of Frederick Meserve, the Folger Shakespearean collection (for which the Folger Library was built in Washington DC) and Queen Mary's collection of material relating to Napoleon and Wellington.

Film, stage and pop memorabilia are frequently lumped together at auction under the term entertainment, but they remain distinct areas for collectors. From the mid-1980s the basis of cataloguing had rested on leading individuals in specific fields rather than thematic lots, such as *Gone with the Wind* or Sixties Pop. What has distinguished film and pop memorabilia has been their wide appeal, covering three or more generations, their international base and the rapidity with which the market developed. In each area a few individuals can be credited with making this possible. In film, the late British authority John Kobler took exceptional advantage, with little or no capital, to beg, borrow or otherwise acquire a definitive base collection of US and British film memorabilia dating from the earliest years. Not only was his enthusiasm infectious (causing Marlene Dietrich, among other stars, to assist him in his quest), his work helped to preserve and promote the significance of a film industry whose confidence had been badly battered with the arrival of television in the 1950s. Kobler's interest was supplemented by a small band of obsessional fans who collected material, sometimes through fan clubs relating to specific stars or through contact with industry workers who could never bear to throw anything away.

Pop Memorabilia

The first pop memorabilia sales in the 1980s, by Sotheby's and Christie's, relied on a similar spread of historians, fans and professionals in the business. Among the figures who stand out are the collector Geoffrey Giuliano, who from an early age had accumulated memorabilia from primary sources that led to his definitive book *The Beatles*, published in 1986, and formed the basis for the first Sotheby's sales, along with items from the collection of Yoko Ono and the estate of John Lennon. Other notable collectors were Charles Rosenay, an American whose collection began in 1965, and Ric Rann who, concentrating on material by top stars, sought the rarest items from as many direct contacts or relatives of the stars as he could trace. Such sources were augmented by sales by the stars themselves (giving rise to the celebrity auction), most notably those of the vast collections of Elton John, which proved the outstanding success of the 1980s auctions, with particular attention paid to his Art Nouveau and Art Deco collections sold by Sotheby's in September 1988.

The Christie's 1980 sale focused on entertainment, grouping film, stage and pop memorabilia together; Sotheby's followed in 1981 with a pop memorabilia sale. There were already proven collectors of stage and film memorabilia, but the element of pop material was dismissed by most commentators as a marketing ploy. All the same the sales did determine a level of interest, concentrated on the major stars, which continues to the present – with Elvis Presley, The Beatles, The Rolling Stones, Jimi Hendrix and Buddy Holly heading the line-up.

Much of the attention of collectors remains focused on the decades of the 1950s and 1960s. In the 1992 London sales Beatles material accounted for 40% of the items on offer. Part of this demand relies on historical status, a wide variety of material from well-documented and authenticated sources and a continuing uncertainty as to the longevity and international appeal of the stars who came after 1970. From the 1980s, the only major attractions for collectors appear to be Michael Jackson and possibly Madonna, along with events which crossed over into mainstream news or current affairs – notably Live Aid or the Sting/Springsteen/Gabriel *et al.* Amnesty Tour. One group that has not figured at auctions has been Pink Floyd. While it has been an international phenomenon from the late 1960s, very little material relating to the band has ever reached the market.

Two consistent trends have raised both the profile and profitability of pop memorabilia from the mid-1980s. The first was the appearance of corporate or institutional buyers, including the Hard Rock hamburger chain, and museums, such as the Rock 'n' Roll Hall of Fame opened in Cleveland, Ohio in 1995. The second has been the potential for third-party exploitation of rights, ranging from images to recordings. This reproduction element has now become important and can immediately cover the cost of the investment (as it did when Bloomsbury Publishing bought a photographic archive of The Beatles).

Film Memorabilia

In film the sheer internationality of Hollywood and its star system established America as the dominant source of film material. (Historically, the wealth of the US industry attracted an array of craftsmen and artists from Europe and further afield, from Igor Stravinsky to Salvador Dali, from Alfred Hitchcock to Arnold Schwarzenegger). The potential volume of material and the interest in it among collectors was first noted at the series of well-publicized studio sales of the 1970s, when MGM, RKO and Warners disposed of old properties. The major collectable stars became readily identified – James Dean, Marilyn Monroe, Judy Garland, Greta Garbo and Charlie Chaplin, for example. Among the first sales to single out collections of material relating to individual stars were those devoted to Rudolph Valentino (the silent idol, who died prematurely in 1926) and the estate of Marilyn Monroe. In retrospect, the prices realized at these 1970s sales were exceedingly modest.

The type of material offered was consistent with examples from earlier memorabilia collections. The range covered costumes, props, images or artworks and documentary material. The approach of the collector was to be discriminating – to specialize in costumes, letters, props, and so on. In recent years, and especially from 1990, association has become more emphatic in catalogue descriptions; this is notably the case for original photographs, specific costume designs (such as those of Jean-Paul Gaultier or Cecil Beaton) or material collected by a business closely associated with a group of stars or a production. The latter reflects, in part the growth of independent production companies after the breakdown of the Hollywood studio system in the 1950s (or, in terms of pop, the management and production companies responsible for productions, tours and events). One of the most publicized British sales of associative material was Phillips' sale of puppets from the collection of Sylvia Anderson, co-producer of such British TV classics as *Thunderbirds* and *Captain Scarlett* in partnership with her husband Gerry Anderson; the original Lady Penelope puppet realized £34,000.

In about 1988 the film memorabilia sector at auction became fragmented. Posters and animated art became separate specialist sales areas. Each is now backed with substantial histories and comparative reference collections, including those at the Museum of the Moving Image, London and the Victoria and Albert Museum, London.

The field of animated art remains a problematic one. Each major animated film will have entailed the production of up to 200,000 separate images or cels, together with many thousands of preparatory images and backgrounds. The matting of this material, the quality, the veracity and its presentation are all important and, as far as the cels are concerned, there remain particular problems for conservation or suitable presentation. Earlier works, especially those of Disney, command a considerable premium, for only a few of the black-and-white cels were not washed and reused. Examination of catalogues will reveal that colour cels will vary substantially in value according to scene, background and provenance.

From 1989 major studios began to produce reproductions of

images in limited-edition form to meet interest in animated art. It remains questionable whether such products albeit limited and signed by the artist or artists involved, will retain value over the longer term, although they are now widely marketed as 'collectables' by specialist retail outlets worldwide. Past history remains the best guide for the investor, and a collection likely to retain its value will rely on only a small number of classic images rather than a broad sweep or more representative output. The advent of computer-generated animation has effectively brought manual cel production to an end, and this will inevitably increase future values for the better cels.

The Current Investor

For the new investor both film and pop memorabilia may seem to be Johnny-come-lately areas of collecting. Except for the recession fall, from 1990 to 1993, the market remains buoyant at both the top and lower end (largely the £100 to £250 range), though the middle ground (from £250 to £1,000) only appears to retain its value when lots are split and resold as individual items or smaller parcels.

The choice within the field is very wide. Many reference works now exist to help identify areas of interest and prices realized. These include the US House of Collectables series, Miller's *Pop, Rock and Film Memorabilia* price guide, the *Lyles Price Guide to Printed Collectables* and a range of encyclopedic reference works for film and pop published by Guinness, Rolling Stone and mainstream publishers. More detailed listings of prices realized can be found in past auction catalogues, almost all of which have been highly illustrated. Among the highest prices in recent years have been the lyrics for 'I am the Walrus', sold by Sotheby's in July 1993 for £40,000, and the unique tape of the emergent Beatles (The Quarrymen) sold to EMI for £78,400 in September 1994.

Despite the large number of dealers, retailers and specialist auctioneers handling memorabilia, an informed and astute investor can still obtain and track down valuable properties. The most widespread opportunities lie in publications, concert programmes and records. These can still be picked up at market stalls, boot fairs and charity shops for prices ranging from a few pence to a few pounds and, depending on their condition, can provide returns that can vary from twice to over ten times their purchase price. If he has the time, the investor may also pursue liquidations, takeovers and clearouts by individuals or companies in the business. In one such clearout, the sale of a record collection by the DJ Tony Prince in 1994, the first Beatles record played on radio, a copy of 'Love Me Do' was sold at Bonham's to Miguel Barsa from Spain for £10,000. Other sources have included cinemas, concert halls, promoters and retailers. A significant number of items remain in the hands of individuals in the business. One of the more unusual of these was a Jimi Hendrix Stratocaster guitar, which after Hendrix's death was owned successively by Ralph McTell, Paul McCartney, David Bowie and George Michael. It was sold at a London charity auction for a record £200,000 to a private buyer (believed, appropriately, to be Eric Clapton).

Information on such sales or likely opportunities can be gleaned from trade publications (*Screen International, Variety* and *Billboard*), through enquiries to liquidators (such as Buchler & Co) or from advertisements in daily financial newspapers. However, finding a cache can potentially devalue the market. The discovery of printers' archives of film posters (in Argentina and Alaska) or hoards of unsold Beatles goods (at a company that printed Beatles wallpaper, or a US manufacturer of Beatles wigs amongst others) illustrate the risks of releasing large quantities of material on to the market in an uncontrolled fashion. Conversely, memorabilia can also be overstimulated, and the abuse of 'limited editions' has created a disconcerting minefield, not unlike the scandal associated with surrealist painter Salvador Dalí's prints, when he signed sheaves of blank paper. For instance, in 1994, O.J. Simpson approved the certification of 25,000 limited-edition statuettes of himself; the total profit on the production was estimated to be up to $8.5 million!

With over fifty specialist dealers and auctioneers for film and pop memorabilia in the UK, sales outlets provide a wide choice for buying and selling. Auctioneers Phillips, Bonham's, Sotheby's and Christie's hold two to four sales in London a year and also include film and pop lots in their local auctions. Outside London, specialist sales (between five and seven a year) are held by a number of auctioneers, such as T. Vennett-Smith of Nottingham and Acorn of Manchester. At auctions 10% to 15% buyer's and seller's premium applies, on which VAT is charged. Additional deductions from the prices realized may include research and cataloguing or photographic fees (up to £12 an image). A charge is made for unsold lots; this can vary according to the auctioneer and should be checked prior to a sale.

Dealers may be contacted or visited direct. A number place

regular advertisements in local and (more occasionally) national newspapers. A dealer's offer price can generally be assumed to be 50% to 30% below retail prices. Retail prices relate closely to auction prices plus a mark-up of 20% to 50%.

Since memorabilia material tends not to be based on like-for-like in terms of condition, size and history, prices will vary. In the hands of the collector, collectors' items remain chattels, so payment of capital gains tax becomes payable only when more than £6,000 of gain has been made in a year. Careful selling can, therefore, generate some useful tax advantage.

In an international market, there can be considerable advantage in selling to Japan, Hong Kong, the USA or mainland Europe, where prices are generally higher. Prices realized from past sales reveal that prices overseas can be 100% or more higher than those in the UK. Even after the costs of appropriate research, and consideration of the exchange rate, sales in these markets will often result in a price advantage.

The popularity of, and demand for, memorabilia covering the history of film and pop music is assured for the immediate future. It should, however, be borne in mind that even seemingly 'legendary' figures may be subject to substantial reappraisal or fall out of fashion. Music Hall is an example of such a change in attitude. In this case, even where the stars were of undoubted international standing, and where a number were to go on to develop new careers in film (notably Charlie Chaplin, Stan Laurel, Maurice Chevalier and even Cary Grant), interest in Music Hall was rapidly taken over by the new media of film and recording. The prices realized at the turn of the century for items relating to Marie Lloyd or Harry Lauder fell rapidly by the 1920s and have not recovered. Within a decade, it is conceivable that the likes of Led Zeppelin, James Cagney and even Judy Garland (to take a mixed selection) could be less highly rated by future collectors.

The massive development of institutions (extant or planned, commercial or otherwise) devoted to the media is likely to reduce further the material available to the ordinary collector. There are already indications that new areas of memorabilia are being sought and developed. (Among them are subjects which, in the past, have been largely bypassed because of their implications – notably Fascist or Cold War material. This material is now more widely available, in part due to relaxation of laws restricting such trade, and also as a result of the opening of Eastern Europe. It is also being reviewed historically, and certain institutions are now being devoted to the subject.) Within the area of entertainment memorabilia 'outcasts', ranging from Fatty Arbuckle to Chaplin and Ingrid Bergman, are presently being rehabilitated. Among other areas which are under development, and reflect the achievements of the twentieth century, are space and science. Interest in these two sectors is particularly notable in the United States but currently rare in the UK and Europe. Other 'new' subjects in which a broad collectors' interest is fast developing are cookery/kitchenware and fashion.

Classic Cars

One of the best known 'bubble' markets of the late 1980s and early 1990s has been the classic-car market, which became a phenomenon over the decades. The market for older vehicles is divided into three distinct elements. The veteran car is dated from 1894 through to 1914 (or 1924 in the USA). The term 'classic' is used in the USA to cover those cars of merit approved by the Classic Car Club of America dating from 1925 to 1942; in Britain the term 'vintage' is applied to this era. It was the Vintage Sports Car Club in the UK which applied the word 'classic' to what had been termed 'thoroughbred' post-vintage cars: those produced from about 1942 until the near present. With only a handful of exceptions, the classic car is a former production model with a recorded original selling price. In terms of estimation, the marque (maker), coachwork (interior trim and finish), the number produced, the pedigree (history of use and ownership) and an overall critical appraisal are determining factors in pricing.

Background

At the outset of motoring in the 1890s every motor car had status, not least because of its cost. While there was no substantial difference in design, the technological difference between the steam-engined and the petrol-engined automobile was a battle of wills between the production companies and pioneers in the industry. The initial advantage of the steam car quickly faded as the petrol engine developed, and it disappeared into the pages of history (although there were sporadic attempts, by the likes of Howard Hughes, to revive the steam car into the 1930s). Few steam cars survived in running order, and those who began collections of cars concentrated on the new breed of motor car. The first collectors bought cars, kept them in good order, and went on to buy further models as they grew older or were attracted by new models or designs. The second type of collector was the restorer or repairer – not that distant from the bicycle-repairers who were to originate many motor companies in the early days. The third type of collector bought cars with a deliberate eye for the best available, and the collections of early film stars, maharajas and the wealthy were accumulated in this deliberate fashion. Some of these collections were started at an early date; the future King Edward VII purchased his first Daimler, with a Hooper body, in 1900, starting a tradition of Royal Daimlers that continues today. There was also a fourth type of collector, one who happened to acquire cars as gifts – among them Picasso and Hitler, neither of whom could drive, but both of whom were given a range of cars in their lifetimes.

Exceptionally in the twentieth century, recognition of, and general universal consent about, those cars that were first rate was almost immediate. The appearance of the Rolls-Royce in 1904, or the unveiling of the E-Type Jaguar at Geneva in 1961, met with widespread acclaim. This recognition of style has been prone to override some of the more practical aspects of a vehicle – for instance, the paintwork of the E-Type proved notoriously difficult to maintain in excellent order, while the pedal functions of an Aston Martin DB5 left much to be desired.

The early organization of the car industry created the mass market for motoring that remains one of the phenomena of the century. The ability to promote and market a succession of models (epitomized by Alfred P. Sloan at General Motors) drew in a variety of talented individuals across the Americas and Europe, among them the designers Ettore Bugatti and Raymond Loewy, and many of the vehicles produced, from the Dusenberg to the Ferrari, from the Lamborghini to the Porsche, were the products of individual vision. Recognition of the ingredients which made a classic, supplemented by weighty media campaigns (in print, on film and latterly on television) generated a widespread base for car enthusiasts, whose relatively small circle was broadened by increasing coverage of road and track races on television and the promotion of major designers and producers as personalities.

Among the first notable collectors were Major Cunningham and M.L. 'Bud' Cohen of the USA. Major Cunningham, a millionaire, managed to pull off one of his best car deals only late in his career, when he acquired a 1931 Bugatti Type 41 Royale sports coupé and two other Royales from Bugatti's daughter L'Ebe in exchange for cash and two refrigerators! The Royale 41 was sold in November 1987 at Christie's, for a world record £5,575,000. Cohn's Mercedes Benz 500K of 1936 was sold for a world record $400,000 (£210,526) in 1979. In the UK, collectors included the Royal Family, Lord Beaulieu and his heirs (whose collection developed into the National Motor Museum) and Tony Frey, noted for his Rolls Royce collection. Among notable European collectors were the Schlumpf brothers, Hans and Fritz, whose collection was to be classified as an historical monument by the French council of State in 1978.

The auction market for vehicles was originated by Southern Counties Car Auctions, who held a sale at Beaulieu in 1960 (one of the higher prices was £170, paid for an original open-top Rolls). Christie's held their first sale of veteran and vintage motor cars in 1972 at Beaulieu, with Sotheby's following. In the USA, companies such as Wings and Wheels developed the market, while other sales began in Holland, Monaco, Switzerland and Germany.

The Market in the 1980s

By the 1980s the classic-car market had developed a momentum that led to substantial increases in prices across the board; the average growth through the decade was calculated at 30% per year by 1989. However, the leading British dealer, Robert Brooks, formerly of Christie's, pointed to one of the basic problems of the market, when he remarked that 'condition can be bought by anybody who can afford the best restoration.... Nobody can replace originality'. Those models which became fashionable and highly traded, by either individuals or commercial concerns, brought the market rapidly towards an unsustainable peak. Older establishments – such as Coy's of Kensington, Power and Classic Cars in Germany, Mille Miglia of Los Angeles and Munich, Stauffer Classics of Wisconsin or the RCI Corporation in the USA – were joined by a host of new concerns eager to capitalize on the 'investment' potential of classic cars. (In part this interest was kindled by substantial research into the motor car and the classic marques. The status of any vehicle became specific, as chassis numbers, production numbers and history were examined, with the limitations of the production run of particular importance.)

Classic cars came to be used as collateral for loans for future purchases, and, as demand increased, the standard of veracity over source and documentation declined. In a market where a vehicle's history and association was the core of its value unquestionably fraudulent or misleading restorations and parts were reaching the market, and the exposure of some extraordinary remakes caused consternation among genuine enthusiasts. One case concerned a Bugatti Type 54 which, during the 1960s, was remade as three separate vehicles (a group of US enthusiasts bought all three, took them apart and reconstituted the original from the parts). By the end of the 1980s new cars were being 'rediscovered', including Bugattis from a questionable source in East Germany, and premium prices were also being based on doubtful distinctions (a difference of $100,000 between the prices of left-hand and right-hand-drive Daytona models in 1989). In November 1989 it was reported that Supercars International, based in Surrey, had sold one of the 36 Ferrari GTOs produced between 1962 and 1964 to a Japanese buyer for £10 million (the previous owner had bought it for £5,000 in 1972).

The extraordinary rise in the market ended in May 1990, when all three of the major European auctioneers – Christie's, Sotheby's and Brooks – held auctions at the same time in Monaco. Prices tumbled. Among the unsold lots was a 1957 Ferrari 315S, estimated at £5 million. The fall was particularly damaging to Christie's, which had only launched its International Car Department the previous October.

Market Recovery

The fall in the prices in the market was steep – typically, an Aston Martin DB6 selling for £106,000 in 1989 was worth 75% less by 1994 – but the effect among collectors was less widespread than expected. The speculative end of the market suffered most, and by 1995 there had been a number of court cases over frauds (in one instance, exports of classic cars covered by insurance proved to have been entirely bogus), but the longer-term collector was secure. The three criteria for buying remained: good documentation, few owners and low mileage, together with proven pedigree.

Pedigree has become a point of contention in the market. By 1996 there was an influx of replica cars on to the British market, notably examples of the Bentley Blower, complete with 'Moor Park' coachwork. The purist Rolls Royce enthusiasts' club dismissed such replicas as 'not a motor car, a hybrid'. The problem stemmed from the apparent confusion between the demands of the reputable auctioneer and dealer and the seeming contrary regulations of the Vintage Car Club. The Vintage Car Club is essentially a sporting organization overseeing the use of historic cars in racing competition, as opposed to pure pedigree vehicles taken out of everyday use. A racing car, is by nature, a consumable, so the club introduced a three out of five score for original elements for cars in competition, covering chassis, engine, gearbox, bodywork and running gear. Where three of the five elements were considered original, then the car was accepted for competition racing. The novice buyer, without appropriate knowledge, was sometimes deluded by the apparent differential between these regulations and the criteria for a pedigree valued vehicle. By contrast, there were a number of fine restorations which salvaged original vehicles and proved excellent investments. One of those most successful in this area was Simon Robinson, who rescued a number of major cars, including five MGs from a British coachworks; each of the restored MGs was said to have sold for between £15,000 and £25,000.

The basic criteria for investment continue to apply – to new deluxe models, such as limited-edition Jaguars and Bentleys (the Bentley Azure, costing £215,000, was launched in March 1995) as much as to pedigree vehicles. There is also some scope for collecting kit model cars produced in limited quantities, such as the M6 GTR supercar which appeared from the McLaren stable in 1985. Top marques retain their values. A Jaguar V12 roadster sold for £26,000 in 1994, up £3,000 over eight years. Ferraris maintained a value of £80–85,000, whilst Aston Martin price ranges covered a broader spectrum, from £27,000 to £500,000 (for the DB 4GT Zagato). Through 1995 the market continued to recover. At Brooks, Monaco, a rare Toyota 2000GT realized £36,000, while the Maserati 250F, driven by Prince Bira of Siam in his New Zealand Grand Prix victory, sold for £564,000 to a Swiss collector.

Unusually for collectables, classic cars have a potential for everyday use. Such usage covers a wide range of activities, from the personal satisfaction of driving a classic at leisure, through competitive racing (in the London-to-Brighton Rally, or the Mille Miglia or Le Mans races, for example), to exhibition or hire (for films and so on). Such usage requires adequate insurance and the acceptance of high repair charges to maintain the value of the asset while it is used. Specialist owners' clubs and collectors' organizations will provide details of recommended maintenance or restoration companies (or individuals) for leading marques; cost will vary according to the work undertaken.

A number of collectors choose not to use their vehicles at all, but rely on specialist storage companies (such as one in Germany that wraps the car in a vacuum-sealed plastic cover and then packs it into a box) to oversee appropriate maintenance and upkeep in premium conditions. This effectively mothballs the vehicle at a level consistent with museum quality. (This museum approach can be on a large scale; the collection of the Swiss brothers Schlumpf, some 600 vehicles, was maintained in secret, in premium condition, in one of their abandoned textile factories in Mulhouse, France, until discovered in 1976 after their business went bankrupt.) The costs of such maintenance will vary from company to company. Details of such custodians are available from both specialist auctioneers and collectors' organizations.

7 Gold, Diamonds and Jewellery

In terms of acquisition for display and artistry, gold, diamonds and jewellery are arguably the most frequently collected precious items in human history. Though properties of precious materials were recognized early in history, there were cultural circumstances which determined their perceived worth. The Spanish conquistadors in South America, for example, threw away emeralds because they broke when hit with a hammer as they were under the illusion that genuine emeralds were unbreakable. Meanwhile diamonds were readily discarded in South Africa until western exploitation began in the nineteenth century (diamonds were still being picked up in the streets and backyards of Johannesburg up to the 1940s). Stable markets for these commodities have existed since ancient times. For the present-day investor gold and diamonds offer a range of options, given their widespread use in industry, while jewellery remains one of the most readily portable (and attractive) artistic commodities in international markets.

Gold

As an investment, gold has always had substantial allure. It retains three properties that make it the ultimate form of money: it is mobile, international and does not degrade over time. Pure gold coin underpinned the establishment of modern trade, and the virtues of such a stable form of currency led, in 1499, to the acceptance of the first single European currency. Known as the 'Portuguese', it was used across much of the European continent for almost a century.

The Price of Gold

The continued status of gold was evidenced by the public concern when Britain came off the Gold Standard in 1931. The government ceased to back the pound sterling with physical quantities of gold at the then fixed price of £4.25 per troy ounce, and the value of the pound fell from $4.86 to $3.40. At the time the fixed price of gold had remained unchanged for almost three decades, even though the cost of living had risen about 60% over the same period. In effect the real value of gold had fallen by some 40% yet, perversely, it was still rated a worthwhile investment! With the end of the Bretton Woods agreement and the flotation of currencies a fixed price of gold was dropped in 1971, and market forces were left to determine the metal's value – as they had for gold for industrial and ornamental purposes since 1968.

From 1970 to 1985 the value of gold relative to sterling increased by an impressive 1,500%, from £15 to £240 an ounce. However, when compared to the fall in the value of sterling during the same timespan and the relative worth of other commodities (especially from 1974 to 1976), the actual increase in average value was $330, or 123%. But, since cumulative British inflation was 175% over the same period, gold's value had in effect declined.

The price of gold hit a peak of $850 an ounce in 1980. By July 1993 it had dropped to $402.60 an ounce and through 1994 fell 4.6% below $400 an ounce – less than half its peak. By the end of 1995 the gold price had moved little, while the cost of borrowing gold for physical delivery for the bullion dealers in London had risen by nearly 7%. However, by December the spot price for delivery in January 1996 showed signs of an upturn, within a price range of $410 to $420 an ounce – a price confirmed in the open bullion market during January.

An accurate model to enable analysts to predict the price of gold remains elusive. The factors which play a major role in determining the price are production, wholesaling and cultural differences between peoples. Since 1900 gold production has been dominated by South Africa and (at least up to 1990) by the Soviet Union. Through the 1980s both countries increased production. The Soviet production increase was greater, from some 270 tons a year to 500 tons a year, and the frequency of gold auctions conducted by the Soviet Union through the Zurich-based firm of Wochzod Handelsbank, increased. Some of these sales succeeded as a result of gold's 'safe-haven' quality, that, especially in Western countries, leads individuals and institutions alike to increase their purchases of the metal in periods of instability or uncertainty. Thus the gold price reached new high at the time of the Soviet invasion of Afghanistan in 1979. By December 1980, though, it was hit by substantial falls, at one point losing $77 in four days, levelling off at a price of only $573 by the year's end. That year gold hoarding became endemic in Western Europe; French people alone held over 6,000 tonnes, worth over $67 billion. A similar but short-lived switch to gold was touched off by the August 1990 Iraqi invasion of Kuwait or by the Soviet coup of 1991. In January 1990 the then Soviet government increased the price of jewellery and gold by 50% to forestall panic buying as a hedge against inflation. Such reactions tend to be only very short-term and are largely an emotive reaction in which normal investment principles are absent. Indeed the Soviets and individual investors were selling in the market at such high points precisely because they were convinced the price must soon collapse!

In some parts of the world there is a substantial tradition for gold to be used as the representation of wealth, notably in the form of jewellery. This is particularly true of India and Saudi Arabia, which between them have been the largest market for 18-carat gold for almost two decades (the number of parts of gold, or carats, in an alloy is expressed via a 24-point scale – 24-carat gold is the pure element, while 18- and 9-carat gold are alloyed mixes). Western European cultural tradition has become less committed to gold jewellery during the twentieth century, which has given impetus to investment in coin, though there is still a strong tradition of wearing gold, not least in wedding rings, bracelets or necklaces. In some markets the price of gold may be influenced by the performance of other commodities entirely. In 1976 and 1984 demand in Turkey increased in consequence of excellent harvests. Farmers laid out for their daughter's dowries by investing in gold when they could most afford it. More recently, in June 1994, the Serbian government, its currency in sharp decline, bought surplus grain from farmers with gold dinars.

As with other metal commodities (such as platinum), technological change can substantially affect demand, both locally and internationally. The increasing use of gold, albeit in minute individual quantities, in electronic products including computers has considerably broadened demand in the past twenty years. Among the more recent applications has been the use of gold on the elements of domestic kettles or for the world's most expensive wedding dress, made by Amorex from fabric spun with 24-carat gold and embellished with diamonds, which was modelled in Beverly Hills in 1992 with a price tag of £3.6 million! Conversely gold has been superseded in some traditional uses; in dentistry, for instance, it has been replaced by synthetic 'natural' cosmetic compounds.

Other influences on the price of gold remain problematic and inconsistent. The 1970s increase was said to have been linked to the investment of petro-dollars as a bulwark against increasing inflation. A link also appears to exist between the price of gold and US interest rates (minus the rate of inflation), an association reiterated in the annual Gold Fields Mineral Services report of January 1995, which attributed the selling of gold in part to a series of US interest rate increases. Gold performance is at its weakest when US interest rates are high relative to inflation rates, and the standard advice is to sell gold when local prices specifically are declining or when there is stable or low inflation. However, over a long period, even this apparent link reverts to the illogical, as for the 1900–1930 period.

The efficacy of gold as a long-term investment is questionable. The possibility of financial or political instability affects its price in the very short-term but does not seem to do so in the longer term. In July 1992, for example, the gold price in Brazil rose on the news that presidential campaign funds had been embezzled. The gold price was also locally affected by the fall of the Russian rouble in 1990 and the devaluation of the Mexican peso in 1994, and the increase in the USA in December 1995 and January 1996, when gold rose above $400 an ounce, was prompted by the political impasse that caused a Government shutdown when the Congress failed to approve President Clinton's proposed budget. In such circumstances it is in the interests of the international community to defend or revalue currencies with the utmost expediency, and this tends to lead to an early stabilization of the gold price. The experience of the collapse of Communism and the fragmentation of Eastern Europe since 1989 has meant the development of alternative means to correct economic weakness that avoid any potential stampede to gold. This does not rule out investment in physical gold, but such investment remains for the individual a speculative and short-term market.

Gold prices are officially fixed periodically by the fixing market in London and quoted at an international rate in US dollars. This fixed price still reflects par values for currencies, and reference works such as the *Statesman's Yearbook* still list currency value by reference to gold equivalent. The free-market price, on the other hand, is fixed daily by a range of spot markets in the world's capitals. The daily gold price for London is traditionally agreed by three banks, and this price is quoted, in troy ounces in broadsheet newspapers and by other financial information providers (metrication became obligatory in Britain in 1995, but precious metals, still quoted in troy ounces, remain an exception). It will typically reflect a particular dealer quote – Bourne & Co, for example. The percentage rise and fall in price is calculated for each working day and the figures are divided between morning and afternoon. Krugerrands remain the most commonly quoted bullion coin, and again, are given a daily quote in the British broadsheet press and by other financial information providers; the quote excludes VAT.

Gold Coins and Bars

In the 1970s, permission was granted for the individual purchase of gold coins by the US, Japan and the UK. This followed the reopening of the gold market in the USA to individuals (in 1974) for the first time since 1933. Much of the interest centred on the South African krugerrand, introduced in 1967, which is the best known of the bullion coins (and the only one widely quoted daily in the London press). Of various sizes, its weight can vary from one-tenth of an ounce to one ounce. From 1970 to 1978, 194 tons of bullion coins were bought, and the UK government imposed VAT on their purchase in 1982. From 1986 there was a substantial fall in the total sales of krugerrands, from 98.1 tons in 1986 to 75.1 tons in 1990, as the EU and other Western nations imposed a ban on their purchase as part of sanctions against South Africa (this ban was lifted in April 1991).

The krugerrand is only one of a range of past and present national, official gold coins – which include the Russian quarter-ounce Chervonets, the Canadian Maple Leaf, the Taiwanese Panda and the British Britannia and Sovereign – introduced by the industrialized nations, in part as a result of the ban on krugerrands. Issues are limited and various. The Australian Kangaroo-design coins, for example, were limited to 2,000 of the 1-kilogram version and 25,000 of the smaller coins. In this Australian issue, by the Gold Corporation through the Perth Mint, the 1-kilogram 99.99% pure gold coin had a face value of Aus$10,000 (£4,094), with 10-ounce and 2-ounce versions launched in the USA in March 1991.

These coins are widely available from coin dealers and banks. Details of availability, current buying and selling prices and new issues are available from high street banks or published in specialist magazines, such as *Coin Monthly*. Across the range of such bullion issues the purchase value is close to 3% above the melt-down value of the gold content, on top of which VAT (or, in the United States, state taxes) are charged. The physical possession of the coins may be taken personally, or they can be held offshore, where they would not normally attract tax. From January 1995 a change in regulations made VAT payable on second-hand coins (in common with changes applicable to all second-hand goods), but only on the profit margin between buying and selling.

A wide range of gold collectable coins or commemorative medallions (such as those for Olympics or royalty) have been minted and are widely advertised. In December 1995, for example, the Royal Mint advertised proof-quality examples of the gold Half Sovereign of 1994, weight 3.999g, in a limited edition of 5,000 at a price of £79.50. Some caution over purchase is necessary. Examples of older issues, notably the US Double Eagle and British Sovereign, were faked in large quantities outside their country of origin (in Saudi Arabia and the Lebanon, for example) in the 1970s, and some of these fakes require expert identification. Other coins have been determined as fakes by national authorities. The most far-reaching case in recent years concerned the Japanese Chrysanthemum issue of 1988, worth £400 apiece, which was withdrawn by the Japanese authorities in 1990 when 107,000 of the coins were impounded and confiscated; a large proportion of these examples were said to be fake, and they included the stock of a British dealer, worth £12 million. In the USA the promotion of gold medallions and gold coins through the 1970s initially fared badly, not least because their issue price of 10% or more above the gold content value was uncompetitive. In reaction to public disinterest, the US authorities promoted new issues, among them the one-ounce Grant Wood gold medallion of 1980. These new issues had a premium of less than 2% and offered 12-day delivery.

The gold content of an issue can become less important than historic values – genuine gold medals for artistic, military or commercial achievement normally bear a premium as collectable items. Olympic 'gold' medals have been sold (such as that of the Chinese athlete Chiu-Zee in 1993), but these are made of base metal and have no gold content; the same applies to Golden Discs and Oscars among other trophies. Certain historic gold coins are exceptionally rare, such as the Cromwellian Sovereign (only two are known to exist, and they can be valued at up to £90,000), while genuine examples of the American Gold Eagle of 1907 command prices of up to £25,000. Among the highest-priced of all gold coins have been gold dinars. In October 1988 Sotheby's sold a specimen of a 77AH Arabian dated gold dinar for the record price of £165,000.

Gold bars may be purchased from bullion dealers, such as

Johnson Matthey in London. The handling and storage charge usually adds a 10% premium to cost, and appropriate VAT is also chargeable for physical holdings not held 'in bond' (in a tax-free designated holding point). The same conditions apply to gold-dust holdings. Ownership is determined by certification, and the bars and dust are duly identified by unique assay marks or tags. As with bearer bonds, ownership is extremely difficult to prove, and stolen gold (such as that removed from Europe during the Nazi era, or in the Brinks MAT robbery from Heathrow Airport in 1983) becomes nearly untraceable once melted, restamped and put back into circulation. VAT has been charged on bullion from 1979, and its avoidance has been at the root of some well-publicized frauds involving the import and export of bullion; customs control on the movement of gold bullion remains extremely strict. At present there is little demand from the UK small investor for bullion (in 1996 the chairman of the London Bullion Market Association stated that there was, in effect 'no demand'). However, to make such investment more appealing, from 1994 the Union Bank of Switzerland offered gold bars with a money-back guarantee, at a premium of about 2% (i.e. less than inflation). Under the scheme, bars are offered in weights of 100 grammes, 500 grammes and one kilogram, with a guarantee of a repayment at a minimum of $360 per ounce at any time up to the year 2000.

Gold Mining

One long-established way of investing in gold is to buy into its mining. Among the world's leading gold-bearing deposits are those of the Carlin Trend, Nevada, USA, and the Witwatersrand in South Africa. Major corporations, such as RTZ (Rio Tinto Zinc) or Lonrho (formerly London Rhodesia Mining) are well-known quoted vehicles for such investment, and their shares are traded in the usual way. RTZ's offshoots include the very productive Lihir mine in New Guinea, (owned 80% by RTZ, 20% by the local company Niugini). Pure mining stocks are only quoted on the Vancouver exchange in Canada.

The other form of enterprise, scattered across the globe from Brazil to the Philippines, from Australia to the ocean floor, relies on speculative funding, commonly by syndication. Such syndicates may range from small numbers of individuals willing to divide investment and reward to semi-official, international recovery operations, such as the 1981 Anglo-Soviet expedition to recover bullion from the wreck of the World War II cruiser HMS

Edinburgh, scuttled in the Arctic in 1942. The salvage company, under contract to the UK and Soviet governments, worked on a no-find, no-fee basis, and its ten divers operated round the clock. The first gold was found on 15 September and by the end of the operation (which lasted 27 days) 431 of the 465 bars known to have been aboard were recovered. Each bar was worth £148,000, and the total sum realized was £48.7 million (net profit), of which the backers received just over 50%, with the balance being paid to the two national governments.

As with other types of mineral speculation, each attempt to extract or recover gold pits risks against reward. In the majority of cases the rights to the claim must be established, and this is often settled and awarded by a court judgement or the take-up of an official permit or option for exploration. Among the court cases of the 1990s has been that by the Columbus-Discovery group, which was granted title to the reclamation of over $100 million of gold from the wreck of the SS *Central America*. On dry land, such claims are often termed patented land and will often include necessary access rights. Dry-land discoveries have often led to a boom in 'penny-share' companies with claims located close to the source of a major strike, but such peripheral exploitation of gold rushes has produced an extremely small number of winners and a large number of losers. In recent years there has been a tendency for dealings in such shares to lead to charges of insider dealing.

Advertisements inviting participation in gold-extraction ventures, which may or may not indicate the level of investment, do appear in a variety of publications, from *Treasure Hunting* to national daily newspapers. A major report on gold in the British Isles, known as 'The Midas Project', was published by the British Geological Survey in August 1995 and identified all gold bearing prospects in the UK. Given the geological nature of the British Isles, options and rights to claims are limited to certain water courses, rivers and a very small number of onshore mine workings in Cornwall, Dyfed and Gwynfynnyd, Argyllshire, Perthshire and Northern Ireland. Among the best-known in Britain is the Gwynfynydd gold mine in Wales, which provided the gold for the Princess of Wales's wedding ring in 1981, where gold had been discovered in 1844. In 1994 the University of Wales identified new deposits of gold in coal mines being bought by Celtic Energy in Wales, and a Canadian firm began mining at Cononish, Perthshire. Other sites, such as wrecks, require permission from individual owners and/or local authorities. The Royal Geological Society will provide information regarding claims on the quality of gold mined.

Where companies or corporations are involved, reference to the Financial Times Index is useful for appraisals of the status of the markets and production of gold in different areas of the world. In 1994, for example, the overall markets in Australia were down by 30.9% and in North America by 38.9%.

Certain conditions are implicit in the vast majority of gold-mining ventures in the west: legality, environmental protection, discretion (secrecy) about the venture and security. Security can extend beyond protecting against theft to protecting individual claims or knowledge of geological conditions. In one exceptional British case, a bullion wreck off the Cornish coast, the finder was prevented from pursuing his discovery after the National Trust claimed ownership of the relevant area of the seabed; despite pressure, he never did disclose the information to the Trust and took his secret to the grave. Part of the problem with British claims lies in the state's rights under 'Treasure Trove' regulations, revisions to which (proposed in 1995) sought to make the Crown claim even more widespread. Whereas previously the Crown was only able to claim objects *hidden* in the ground, rather than those lost or abandoned, the new regulations sought to allow the Crown the claim to any treasure and thereafter agree compensation for the finder. Critics perceived this change as hardly conducive to honesty.

For the more cautious, investment in established gold-mining concerns can be profitable, especially where biological extraction (cheaper and more ecologically sound) replaces the environmentally and physically damaging use of mercury in the separation or purification process. For the adventurous individual investor, though, risks in the pursuit of gold are likely to outweigh the profits – although, for a fortunate few of those willing to make the personal commitment, the returns can be immense. In 1980 an aboriginal gold prospector, Sydney Barnes, and his partner, having found nuggets in a rabbit hole in Western Australia, sold their stake to a Perth businessman for $35,000. Subsequent investigation revealed a vein of gold estimated to be worth some $32 million. Australia remains a rich resource for the discovery of large nuggets. In May 1993 a 16.1-kg example was found in Western Australia.

Diamonds

It has long been recognized that the major problem with diamonds as an investment is that the market is subject to a near monopoly – that of the Central Selling Organisation (CSO), the marketing arm of the giant De Beers Corporation of South Africa (actually based in Switzerland). It controls over 80% of the world's production. In 1990 it made a concerted effort to bring the newly independent states of the former Soviet Union back on board and also sought to reduce the expansion of independent sales (from Gambia and Brazil, for example) on the international market. The attempt to curtail the Russian independence failed, when it bypassed the CSO in August 1995, depressing the diamond price. From the 1940s gem or decorative diamonds have constituted only 15–20% of the market. The remainder, both man-made and natural, are used in industry.

The gem diamond's appeal relies on the 'four Cs', Cut, Clarity, Carat and Colour. The cut is intended to take advantage of the three optical properties of the stone – refractivity, reflectivity and dispersion. It is this last property (notably demonstrated in De Beers' advertising) which brings out the unique sparkle or fire of the diamond. The early form of cut, which first displayed a diamond's brilliance and fire, was invented by Vincenzio Perruzzi about 1650, and the finest cuts were perfected by Amsterdam jewellers in the eighteenth century. The number of facets and size of diamond cuts has varied according to fashion, but the paramount importance of cut remains.

To the untrained eye one diamond appears much the same as another, even when viewed under the loupe (the ten-times magnifying glass used by the trade). A graduated grading system backed by certification was introduced to record the precise characteristics of each stone, and stones were sealed in transparent plastic cases, accompanied by a microfilm of the certificate, to reduce the possibility of switching. The authorities issuing the certificates include the Gemological Institute of America, Switzerland's Gubelin organization, the Belgian High Diamond Council laboratory and the SSEF of Switzerland. Under the most common system of gradation of clarity, the following initials are used.

F, for flawless (and subsequent gradations of clarity to Z).
VVSI, for very, very small inclusions.
VSI, for very small inclusions.
SI, for small inclusions, and
P, for Pique (meaning pricked or indented)

The three middle categories are further divided on descending scales.

Clarity relates to the passage of light through the stone. The determination of clarity is made under magnification. Since the last four categories of clarity are subdivided, there is some disagreement into which gradation (which runs from F to Z) such stones may fall. The exception is pique (pricked or indented). This indicates a flaw visible to the naked eye.

The accepted unit of weight for diamonds is the carat, equivalent to 0.2 grammes. Values are commonly associated with exact or just-over weights. There is no absolute correlation between weight and value, i.e. two stones of the same weight will not realize the same absolute value. Given that the rarity of diamonds corresponds to their size, the greater the weight the larger the increase in value.

The more unusual, and highly prized, forms of diamonds are the coloured stones. The great value attached to such rarities was demonstrated at the sale of the Red Diamond, sold at auction in 1991 for the equivalent of $131 million an ounce! The yellow form arises from a chemical substitution of nitrogen atoms for carbon atoms. Blue diamonds result from the presence of boron. (The best known blue is probably the 42.52-carat Hope diamond, presented to the Smithsonian Institute, Washington in 1958. In its colourful history it was owned by the one-legged Lord Francis Pelham-Clinton-Hope until 1908, who married the actress May Yohe, to whom he gave the diamond to wear on stage.) A natural green diamond is the result of exposure to radiation (typically from a uranium deposit) and may be the inspiration for Superman's kryptonite. The chemical causes of pink to red diamonds remain a mystery. Technically any diamond not graded D, E or F is a coloured diamond. In the G–Z range, the colours are graded faint, very light and light.

Investment in diamonds (as opposed to diamond jewellery) was widely promoted from 1975. In 1978 a string of diamond investment companies were established in Europe, the USA and Japan, and the appeal of diamonds was widely hyped. Price rises reached an unprecedented 10% a month, and this bubble was further inflated by dealers offering buy-back guarantees. The price of a 1-carat D-flawless rose from $15,000 in 1978 to $64,000 in 1980. In August 1978 De Beers took advantage of this boom and raised prices by 30%. In May 1980 the bubble burst, however, and by July 1986 the index had fallen to 75% below the average 1980 price for a D to H 1-carat, investment-grade stone, from flawless to VS2 in clarity. Such a reversal was inevitable and resulted in significant casualties, including the largest US diamond investment company, the International Diamond Corporation (IDC), which was declared bankrupt in 1982. The Federal Trade Commission and several US States took legal action against the IDC over misrepresentation and issued cautionary warnings of the risks to investors in diamonds. In the UK the market took a similar turn. The CSO's efforts to counter the market fall was reflected in the drop in the company's reserves, from some $2 billion in 1979 to about $200 million by the end of 1980, as it bought up stocks offloaded in the crash.

Despite these cautionary precedents, there remain opportunities for investors in the market for both jewellery and non-jewellery diamonds. Diamonds are untraceable, easily transferred and, in normal circumstances, a stable form of wealth. However, investing in them today requires greater acumen and access to considerable technical knowledge, as a result of technological advances since the late 1970s. It was found that neutrinos could alter the colour of stones, and that lasers could be used to excise minute inclusions, the holes being filled with a substance of the same refractive index. The identification of such alterations is extremely difficult to detect, and they may or may not be revealed to a potential customer (there is no obligation on the seller to make such disclosures). The individual investor needs to be assured that the source is impeccable. These problems of quality and dealing with a wholly genuine article may, however, have been solved by Dr John Watling, an English-born chemist, who in 1994, developed a means to 'fingerprint' diamonds, gold and other precious metals. This 'fingerprint', it is claimed, reveals a signature for the area where the piece was originally formed.

The International Diamond Exchange publishes listings of recommended dealers or sellers, which can include normal retail outlets. Appropriate documentation will be given for such gems. Certification, stating quality and gemmological characteristics, is most commonly encountered at auction. Insurance requirements demand that a second opinion as to value is sought and given in writing. In the case of diamond jewellery, the valuation will be exclusive of the setting, which can substantially alter the overall value. Diamonds may also be purchased at auction. The leading auction houses, notably Christie's and Sotheby's (centred on their outlets in Monaco and New York), will sell stones, of varying colours, carats and values on a regular basis. Inevitably many of these sales are to the trade.

The potential for small investors to back diamond-mining companies is not limited to the large multinational concerns. In 1990 the Argyll diamond 'pipe' was discovered in Western

Australia, largely through the efforts of the niece of the late broadcaster Malcolm Muggeridge. Though commercially exploited by a UK/Malaysian joint venture, it remains open to the private investor. The Argyll stones are noted for their colours and have been regularly auctioned by Christie's in Australia for prices up to $500,000, and the vast majority of the company's output lies in gemstones, rather than diamonds for industrial use. A similar operation was established at the Aredor diamond mine in Guinea, West Africa, which was opened by the Australian company Bridge Oil in 1985. Its finds have been spectacular. In a sale by tender (sealed bid) in March 1989, a 255.61 carat diamond from the mine was sold for a world record price for an uncut diamond of $10,036,000 (£5.8 million). The largest flawless diamond outside the British crown jewels, the Centenary Diamond of 273 carats was found by De Beers in 1988 and is estimated to be worth £50 million. Conditions for leasing exploration sites are similar to those for other minerals. The leading discovery of recent years was made by RTZ at the Crater of Diamonds state park, under a lease granted by the state of Arkansas in 1992. It proved to be the world's largest diamond-bearing rock formation. Both large-scale and specialist small enterprises of this type are recorded by the DTI, and details of their prospectus and the level of investment may be sought.

Jewellery

Jewellery is one of the most common forms of investment, but is unusual in that the purchaser has the option to influence, even dictate, the artistic form of the final object by the choice of stone, setting or form of string. These factors are crucial to the valuation. Through the 1980s the appeal of jewellery fluctuated according to fashion, and many potential collectors, those who might have bought pieces in the £2,000 to £100,000 range moved towards costume jewellery. In the 1990s jewellery has come back into fashion and has wide appeal for a new generation.

The Market in the Twentieth Century

Jewellery from royal houses and aristocratic families underpinned the market from the second decade of the century. By far the major source was the collections of the Russian aristocracy, notably the fabulous collection of the family of Prince

Youssoupoff (the assassin of Rasputin), who was forced into exile after the Russian revolution of 1917. Those jewels which could not be brought out of Russia were seized by the Soviet authorities in the 1920s and were to feature (as in the 1970s) in highly publicized scandals touching members of the Soviet hierarchy, including relatives of the then Soviet head of state Leonid Brezhnev. The Russian crown jewels were sold by Christie's in 1923 (the same year that the Prussian crown jewels were auctioned) but fetched only modest prices: a brooch of Catherine the Great sold for only £350 – though when resold at Christie's, Geneva, in 1975 it realized £10,000, a compound increase of 30% in real value. Many Russian jewels were to find new owners in America, through dealers such as Dr Armand Hammer, or make their way into the collections of relatives of the Russian Imperial family, such as the British Royal family.

The uncertain financial climate of the late 1920s and 1930s coincided with one of the most creative eras of jewellery design. The couturier Paul Poiret, working with the Russian-born designer Erté, produced some of the most striking and impressive Art Deco designs of the 1920s; the major French house of Cartier introduced the baguette cut for precious stones, with characteristic right-angled outlines, while the house of Lalique diversified into a wide range of jewellery, including chokers and bracelets. Through the 1930s the Italian jeweller Bulgari, founded in the 1870s, began a series of modern designs which culminated in the elaborate 'cocktail' jewels of the 1950s (Andy Warhol held Bulgari's products in such high esteem that he called the company 'the most important museum of contemporary art'). Bulgari earned pre-tax profits of £9.6 million in 1995 and had plans to go public. In the United States a new generation of jewellers and dealers came to the fore, among them Harry Winston, who began work at the age of 15 and founded the Premier Diamond company in New York when in his late teens. He was to be among the most influential dealers and designers through to the 1980s – along with Meyer Rosenbaum, founder of the Meyer Jewellery company, Detroit – and went on to acquire a number of famous gems, including the fifteenth-century Moon of Baroda diamond. Major US jewellery companies came to rival the French houses of Cartier and Boucheron, Tiffany (whose work was often signed Tiffany-Schlumberger), Van Cleef & Arpels. In 1939 Louis Arpels and his designer Maurice Du Valet originated sculptural jewellery, including the famous 'Butterfly' and 'Ballerina' series.

In many cases these jewellers would become responsible for

resetting some of the most famous gemstones in history, including the Hope diamond (once stored in a radio for safekeeping) and the Polar Star – a cushion-shaped diamond of 41.285 carats, formerly in the collections of Napoleon's brother Joseph and of Prince Youssoupoff. Reset in a ring by Boucheron, this jewel was resold from the collection of Lady Lydia Deterding for a world record of almost £2 million in 1976.

Among the technical developments in jewellery design were the introduction of platinum, from about 1900, and the use of cultured pearls. The first cultured pearls had been produced by the Japanese Kokicho Mikimoto in 1896, and the technique for their production was perfected in 1915. In 1921 they were first sold in London, and by the 1930s pearls had fallen to 10% of the 1928 price. This new arrival was not universally welcomed; Tiffany and Cartier referred to strings of cultured pearls as 'white beads'. Immediately after World War II the process for making artificial diamonds was perfected and patented in the USA (after the Swedes had inadvertently failed to patent the process), and the identification of coloured diamond variations was also begun.

Market Revival of the 1950s

A market revival began in the 1950s with the 'New Look' and the return of Chanel. Both costume jewellery and pearl strings and ropes (made popular by Grace Kelly) made a considerable comeback. By the 1960s Victorian ornamental jewellery revived in popularity, and a sequence of record-breaking sales, including the collections of Queen Marie Jose of Italy and the Princess Royal, reinvigorated the market and attracted collectors back to important jewels. The sales culminated in the landmark Dodge sale at Christie's, Geneva, in 1970.

From 1970 the jewellery market started to be affected by the extraordinary speculation in the diamond market, and from 1970 to 1980 the compound rate of return on diamonds reached 38.7%, against a compound inflation rate of 7.3%. In May 1970 an emerald-cut diamond reached a European record price of £263,000. A further influence on the market was the dogged work, begun in the 1940s by Dr Gubelin of Geneva, into the mine origins and gemmological characteristics of coloured diamonds. This gave reliable verification for stones for the first time. Buyers from the developing economies of the Middle East and the Far East were increasingly prominent in the market and increased the competition for high-quality jade (where the thicker varieties proved more popular), diamond and gold jewellery. The work of named designers continued to be a profitable investment, especially after revival of interest in Art Nouveau, which brought the works of Tiffany, Lalique and Mucha back to the public eye. By 1979 a Lalique choker had realized a world record price of £48,000. Seven years later, a Lalique glass brooch with aquamarine and diamond sold for £86,000.

A high point in jewellery sales in the 1980s was the Duchess of Windsor sale in March 1987, at Sotheby's, Geneva, held to benefit the Pasteur Institute, France. Making headlines around the world, it was the world's largest jewellery auction and realized a world record £50 million in total. Among the most publicized pieces were the Cartier 'Panther' designs (though this design was first produced by Jeanne Toussant for a vanity case in 1917, it was not until 1948 that the Duke of Windsor ordered the first panther brooch from Cartier).

The Contemporary Market

The present market divides between retailers and auction houses, for private sales of jewellery are exceptional. Many of the leading jewellers, from Garrard (the UK Crown jewellers) to Wartski (which has specialist knowledge of the East European market), from Aspreys in London to Tiffany's in New York, offer a wide selection of past and present works at prices from below £1,000 a piece upwards. Mark-ups for such pieces are generally reckoned to be between 30% and 50%, but it is not unusual for seasonal sales to take place, during which discounts of up to 25% are offered.

Building a jewellery collection is very much a matter of personal taste. The sources of specific information on jewellery are wide. Auctioneers' catalogues and yearbooks are useful for reference, as are a variety of specialist articles (in publications such as the *Antique Collector*), exhibition catalogues and books. In the sphere of design, there is expertise to be found at the major auction houses, but among the most comprehensive reference sources are the libraries and staff of the Victoria and Albert Museum, London, and a number of regional museums (which are detailed in the annual *Museums and Art Galleries Yearbook*).

While brilliants, different gemstones, artificial diamonds and natural diamonds are readily distinguished by testing – just as a gold or silver assay is readily identified – the status of pearls requires further explanation. Natural pearls exist in both salt-water and freshwater varieties, and the preferred colours are rose, cream, white and black. The highest-rated rose- and cream-coloured gem pearls come from the oyster beds of the Persian Gulf. Black pearls are found off the coast of Panama and Mexico and off three Pacific islands; their coloration is due to a combination of mineral salts in the local waters and the plankton on which the oysters feed. Markets can be tightly controlled – production from the island of Marutea, for example, is under exclusive contract to the American Salvador Assael. The more widespread cultured pearl, perfected by the Japanese, derives from a manufactured process in which bead pearls are inserted in the oyster for development. Pearls can be differentiated by means of X-rays. Unlike other jewellery, it is recommended that pearls are restrung every few years.

In 1995 diamonds were considered to be comparatively low-priced in the UK retail market. The revival and spread of the market to a lower age group resulted in an increase in diamond jewellery sales of 25% in Britain during the year. Where buying at auction it is recommended that pieces be viewed, since the main houses often provide very broad descriptions in catalogues; apart from those by leading auctioneers (Sotheby's, Christie's, Bonham's and Phillips), the catalogue descriptions may be both simple and unillustrated. In the main, descriptions may vary from two lines and a broad estimate to a full history. In almost all lots, the cut of stones or their setting (using terms such as cluster or scrolled-bar) is given, as are any markings or the maker's name. Dates may often be general, such as nineteenth or twentieth century, if they are given at all. Since many pieces by leading jewellers remain unsigned, and since jewellery does not readily lend itself to verbal descriptions or comparisons of one piece with another, the most useful method for determining values remains sight, born of experience. Valuation for jewellery does depend on more variables than is common with other investments. There are also exceptional factors for certain stones; opals, for example, can still be given a low valuation because of superstitions about these gems (deriving from accounts of bad luck or tragedy experienced by owners of a number of better-known opals).

In the retail market the renewal of interest in jewellery sparked by the Duchess of Windsor sale has been developed by the established jewellers, such as Tiffany's, Wartski, Asprey and Van Cleef & Arpels. In London leading jewellers are concentrated in or around Bond Street or the Hatton Garden area. The distinction between the raw-material supplier (such as Laurence Graff, the diamond dealer) and the retailer of finished jewellery is now far less distinct than it was two decades ago. Retail outlets for fine jewellery are now widespread, and it is useful to compare prices for pieces of interest, since the variation between values from specialists (such as S.J. Phillips in London, or Ares Rare in New York), or indeed provincial jewellers, can be substantial. The majority of jewellers now offer both contemporary and old pieces, as well as services such as evaluation or resetting. There are also specialists in particular types of jewellery; Young & Stephens in London specialize in estate jewellery with aristocratic provenance. In recent years a number of leading jewellers, among them Chaumet of Paris and Van Cleef & Arpels have opened shops within department stores.

In the wider market, there has been a notable concentration of ownership, arising first in the 1970s, with major jewellers being taken over as part of international groups specializing in luxury goods. This has tended either to limit the range of stock on offer or to lead to the promotion of particular names to the exclusion of others. Auctions focusing on a particular designer (or brand) are only a recent occurrence at auction – Christie's held its first such sale, devoted to Cartier, only in 1992. It remains evident that such leading names continue to provide the best general return for the investor, with fully documented historical pieces, notably those of the Fabergé company of Russia, continuing to dominate the specialist market. However, there are areas of the market that show no increase in value: for instance, demand for tiaras and sets of high Victorian dress jewels remains limited.

Investment in Contemporary Jewellery

Among the opportunities that remain for the collector are jewels designed by leading contemporary or near-contemporary artists and designers. Among these have been Salvador Dalí, Andy Warhol and Paloma Picasso. Paloma Picasso has been designing jewellery for Tiffany's since 1980, and her work is often titled – for example, *Love and Kisses* or *Loving Hearts*. Much of this jewellery was designed for a specific clientele and has a 'pedigree' value. Many pieces remain unique and are likely to be as sought after as the products of the Fabergé factory! Certain designers have only come to public attention in recent years. Chief among these has been the 1930s Sicilian designer Duke Falco di Verdura, who has become known for his characteristic animal or sea-creature designs, among them elephants and shells, based on the natural image. In 1995 his gold starfish with cabochon coral cost about £9,400, while a yellow sea-shell, studded with diamonds and turquoise, cost about £33,800. The attractiveness of his pieces has led to the best of his work now being remade (rather than reproduced) by the American jeweller Ward Landrigan at prices of up to £100,000. Among leading contemporary US designers is Joel Rosenthal, who works only on commission, and whose work is characterized by a silver setting that harks back to sixteenth- and seventeenth-century jewellery design.

In the international market, one of the major areas of growth in the past decade has been platinum jewellery. The demand, which rose by 11% over the year to May 1995, centres on Japan and was instrumental in the rise in the price of platinum from $398 to $420 an ounce in 1995. Japan now accounts for nearly half the world's demand for the metal, and a large proportion is used for hallmarked jewellery. Despite this demand, platinum jewellery has proved a poor investment for the Japanese, because of the substantial rise in the yen against the dollar. Given the dominant role of the Japanese in this market, it is difficult to see how the high price of platinum jewellery can be maintained.

8 Intellectual Property

Intellectual property covers copyrights, patents, inventions and related processes and ideas. Many are intangible, conferring on an individual the right to exploit a property that does not physically exist. The first intellectual property to be recognized in England was the process for making stained glass, granted by Royal assent in the 15th century. In succeeding centuries a huge number of other properties and processes have been accorded copyright or other forms of rights protection. In theory intellectual properties have only a notional value (as base materials, for example, in the case of a film or video) until they are applied, but the potential value of rights can be immense. In the corporate sector the term 'people businesses' has been coined to typify companies that rely heavily on intellectual input. It is only in recent years that attempts have been made to quantify the real value of intellectual property rights more precisely than the traditional notions of 'goodwill' or 'brand' can do.

The legal basis for the ownership of intellectual property rights, while it can be complex in detail, is maintained by a series of national and international agreements. These identify the owner (not necessarily the creator), the term of the rights concerned and the territory to which they apply. From 1989 moves to harmonize both the terms and the effective policing of rights to such properties, not least to prevent widespread counterfeiting or copyright fraud and theft, have been undertaken at inter-governmental level. This process culminated in the conclusion in 1994 of the Uruguay round of GATT (General Agreement on Tariffs and Trade), to which specific agreements on intellectual property (finalized in 1995) were appended. Since the 1970s the revolution in the use of information and the associated intellectual properties from which it derives has been recognized. Its status has been encapsulated in studies, such as Porat's nine-volume *The Information Economy*, published by the US Department of Trade in 1977, and in the establishment of such institutions as the Institute for the Information Society in Japan.

By the 1990s intellectual property had become increasingly important for national balances of trade. The USA counts the income from such property as its second largest export earner, while in Britain (where the figures include income from trade in money, which is a form of intellectual property) it ranks third. Due to the UK's particular success in this area there has been a long-term tendency for the status of such activities to be underrated by both government and commentators. Some indication of the scale (and benefit) of such activity to the UK is given by the fact that in 1992 'invisibles' accounted for 18% of GDP, representing a world market share of over 10%; this percentage exceeds the GDP contribution of all small business put together. Royalties accounted for a surplus of £433 million, while investments as a whole earned a surplus of £11.7 billion. These are significant values. In 1994 the British Academy was one of several institutions that issued studies on the interpretation of the financial value of such properties.

Intellectual Property Agreements

Intellectual property is given legal form in agreements (usually a fully detailed contract between the owner and a potential exploiter of the exclusive rights granted) that can be readily transferred, assigned or relinquished. The British government has not yet sought to ring-fence such transfers – as it has in the areas of gold, art and antiques – nor to offer tax concessions to encourage the retention of such properties in the UK. (The last government review of the subject was undertaken by the National Consumer Council in September 1990.) This remains the case despite examples of the increasing acquisition of innovative British computer software companies, particularly in games software, by overseas interests in the 1990s. The field for the investor therefore remains unusually open and unrestricted, subject to valuation and capacity for exploitation.

The options for an investor to acquire intellectual property rights fall into three categories:

1. Direct investment in the creation of rights by taking a part or whole share in the output, as with theatre 'angels'.
2. The purchase of intellectual properties from owners or assignees.

3. Investment in entities that licence or administer intellectual properties (which may range from film libraries to applied-science concerns) or direct investment in media-related or other rights-owning commercial companies.

In the first category the rights granted to the individual are protected by law to avoid unreasonable exploitation, and unequal or unfair contracts, as in the cases of Elton John, the painter Stephen Conroy and the singer Gilbert O'Sullivan, are now readily overturned by the courts. Any agreement on the purchase of intellectual properties requires both parties to be fully aware of the terms for present and future income generation and the acceptance, usually by contract, of these terms in a legal framework. Patronage of an individual, often at an initially modest level, can take the form of direct financial support. Many painters, for example, receive a regular income from their patron in return for a percentage of works produced, and this type of arrangement can evolve into a business enterprise, as it did in the case of that between the painter David Hockney and his patron Kasmin in the 1960s. It goes without saying that such patronage requires commitment from both sides. The terms of patronage, which have to be openly 'fair' by legal definition, will vary. The contract between the parties will be subject to agreement on a specific price, a specific term and a specific purpose.

The second option transfers ownership of the property to the purchaser from the creator, owner or assignee (who may be a relative or a benefactor under a will). Up to the 1980s such transfer of rights was, in the public mind, largely related to artistic properties, notably films, music, photographs or other images, manuscripts and the like. These properties had tangible, physical elements together with an intangible aspect, such as publishing rights or rights to stage a play. Among the best known examples of an individual transfer is that of Agatha Christie's rights to *The Mousetrap*, whereby all royalty income from the play was made over by the authoress to her grandson Michael. (It included what became unusable film rights, originally sold in 1952, for which options were continually renewed.) What was not known at the time was that *The Mousetrap*, which had cost only £2,803 to stage originally, would prove to be the longest running play in theatrical history (17,723 performances in London were recorded up to 23 June 1995) and generate an income in excess of £22 million. In 1968 the food group Booker bought a 51% stake in the controlling company, Agatha Christie Ltd, in return for an unspecified sum, and by 1974 the Christie company was making profits of £366,000 from assets put at a modest £900,000. The Booker stake had risen to 64% by 1988. By the end of the decade the renewal of paperback rights to Agatha Christie's works in the USA brought in £14 million alone.

Transfers such as these do not, however, have to be of the fixed-term sort protected by national or international agreement, since the vast majority of intellectual properties enter the public domain when their copyright protection runs out. Under present British legislation copyright protection lasts for fifty years from the originator's death (the term is the same in the US, the Commonwealth and other Western territories), although EU legislation now extends this to seventy years, which will be the accepted period in EU states. This protection was extended to photographers in the 1980s, but did not infringe the older tradition of commission, under which the commissioning party obtains rights to properties he has commissioned.

Under certain conditions, and exceptionally, by government legislation, renewal or perpetual extension of copyrights may be granted. The Earl of Clarendon's works were given perpetual copyright in the eighteenth century, so as to underwrite the Oxford University Press (at the time purely a scholastic publisher charged with the printing of the Bible) and to support the establishment of the Clarendon library. J.M. Barrie's *Peter Pan* was granted perpetual copyright in the 1980s in order to provide funds for the Great Ormond Street Hospital for Sick Children in London. Such extensions do, however, apply to only a very small number of properties.

The Theatre Angel

One of the best known types of investor participating in intellectual property in the UK is the theatre 'angel', who pledges a specific sum in return for a shareholding in, or a profit percentage (dividend) from, a stage production. If the show fails to make a profit, the sum pledged is lost. The most famous production of recent years to be funded in this manner was Andrew Lloyd Webber's musical *Cats*. A £100 investment in this show in 1981 was estimated to be worth almost £2 million in 1990, and by January 1996 the worldwide gross of *Cats* was over £2 billion. Not unusually, *Cats* itself relied on the acquisition of third-party intellectual property rights – those in T.S. Eliot's work, which was adapted by Lloyd Webber. The Eliot rights were jointly administered by the poet's widow and his publishing company Faber & Faber.

The initial costs for a production in London's West End are now of the order of £450,000, with 'angels' funding 180 units of £2,500 each. The hoped-for break-even point for a production will be calculated by assumptions about costs, seat occupancy and the potential of ancillary rights, and the division of the income, once the production reaches profit, will be set out before commitment. The costs will include royalties for the author and others (such as the director and stage designer). These amount to about 4% to 6% of costs, and an advance on the royalties is paid, which is subsequently recouped from the show's earnings; the producer usually remains unpaid until profit is reached. About half of all new productions make no profit, one in four break even, and one in four make a substantial profit (though it is currently estimated that only one in six shows will eventually be profitable). *Cats* investors typically make back 80% of their original investment (adjusted for inflation) every year.

The balance of probability for a success relies on several factors:

1. An appropriate vehicle to start with. The incidence of revivals is a reflection of this caution, with a tendency to concentrate on safe areas.
2. A suitable star with a contract of over six months. Experienced hands, ranging from Elaine Paige to Tommy Steele, from Julie Andrews to Glenn Close, are backed for their star quality in a suitable vehicle. If the angel is unsure about the likely star's track record, the Spotlight organization will provide information about the agent from whom details of the actor's work can be obtained.
3. Suitable opening dates. In London's West End, February and November are lean times, but the conditions that encourage an audience or influence its perception remain otherwise unpredictable. Exceptionally warm summers can severely limit audiences for matinée performances, and social events or news events, such as the Gulf War or terrorist threats, can also keep theatre-goers away.
4. The probability of a secure trade – most commonly what is termed the coach audience, which may range from school parties to senior citizens. Such trade is particularly helpful during lean months.
5. Tourist trade. London's theatres can attract up to 10% of their

audiences from tourists from all over the world.

6. The appropriate venue. The relation of the type and complexity of a production to its venue is closely linked to the probability of success. The disaster of show *I*, which never even opened at the Piccadilly Theatre, London, in 1982, is a long-remembered lesson for all 'angels'.
7. The financing. Break-even should not require seat occupancy of over 45%, and when (if) it is reached royalty, production fees and theatre costs should not rise substantially.
8. The prospects for subsidiary rights. Licensed productions, film and television, amateur productions and touring rights should be an element in the equation and can be a crucial source of future income. Authors or composers, such as Lloyd Webber or Bernard Shaw, have made substantial fortunes from such rights, but the return for 'angels' can also be substantial. The British actor-impresario C.B. Cochran reaped consistently good returns from running productions across Europe and the USA for almost five decades.

Information is available to 'angels' through trade publications, but the main source of potential shows will be producers. These are contacted through the Society of London Theatres, Covent Garden, who will add an 'angel' to a list that is sent to producers.

For the ordinary investor this type of investment falls into the category of 'fun money', because of its risk, and it is impresarios who take on this risk, as full-time professionals on behalf of a wide range of backers. In 1990 the government of Nauru which had received millions in compensation from the Australian government and British government after somewhat one-sided exploitation of its phosphate deposits made an extraordinary collective investment in the musical *Leonardo*, which flopped on the London stage in 1991. One of the more unusual government-backed productions was that of *Jesus Christ Superstar* in Seoul, South Korea, in which the Japanese government invested £2 million in 1994. Andrew Lloyd Webber's trading on the assets he has created has brought him considerable wealth. After buying his Really Useful Productions company back into his own hands for £77 million in 1990, he subsequently sold a stake of over 30% to the Philips subsidiary PolyGram for over £78 million the following year. His company is still approachable by potential 'angels', although his productions' success has meant that by December 1995 the minimum investment in a RUG production was £5,000, and there was a waiting list of potential investors.

The *Stage and Television Today* trade newspaper, issued weekly, publishes advertisements from individual producers, performing companies and commercial companies requesting applications for investment in specific productions. Such productions issue a prospectus, and a detailed analysis of the document will reveal the potential for the individual investor. In addition to these purely commercial promotions, the UK Government has encouraged two forms of partnership funding in the arts. The Business Sponsorship for the Arts Scheme, which entails investment in return for concessions, promotion and ancillary financial return, is by definition more suitable for commercial companies, but does not preclude individuals. To cater for individual investment, 50:50 partnership funding by the Business Sponsorship Incentive Scheme (administered by the Office of Arts and Libraries) was introduced from 1984, going nationwide in 1989. This matches personal or commercial investment pound for pound by Government funding through an established arts organization.

Film and Video Investment

One of the most common, but largely overlooked, sectors of intellectual property is film. This includes full-blown feature films or any of the wide variety of material broadcast on television or issued commercially (most usually in video formats). Despite consistent efforts by the film industry, government support for this sector in Britain offers no concessions to outside investors. Through the 1980s individual investment in features in Britain was typified by George Harrison's commitment to Handmade Films and the personal investment by the Monty Python team in individual projects. One of the most publicized investments was that by Channel 4, along with other production entities (notably Polygram), in the feature film *Four Weddings and a Funeral*, which was made at a cost of $5 million and by October 1994 had returned an estimated gross profit of $220 million. In 1989 certain feature-length projects began to be launched under the Business Enterprise Scheme (BES), notably the films produced by Kenneth Branagh's production company Renaissance Films. The usual BES conditions applied in this case, and the return to investors was made by the sale of a percentage of the company to Sony in 1991. A similar BES arrangement for £160,000 was made for the hit British film *Leon the Pig Farmer* of 1992, one of only twelve UK films made that year.

In this area, which is notorious for both its risks and its rewards, the sources of information for interested British investors are limited. Almost no information about investment is available from the trade journals, and for over forty years the British Film Institute has not promoted private investment before project development. Even the apparent benefit of the investment of £70 million of National Lottery money in film development was greeted with scepticism and described as a 'waste' by some of the UK film industry's most experienced commentators in 1995 (one of the side issues to emerge was that, under current legislation, up to 45 pence of each pound spent on film is reclaimed by the Treasury in some form or another). It is acknowledged that in the UK there is neither a natural pool of capital nor the portfolio-management approach to film-making that is seen in the USA, where the lifecycle of a film (about five years) is properly understood and exploited. Though the parliamentary National Heritage Select Committee concluded that simple tax incentives, such as accelerating write offs and changing withholding tax, would assist the industry, its recommendations were not taken up by the government. Investment in film in the UK fell from £435 million in 1984 to £131 million in 1989. It is significant, however, that there was a balance-of-payments surplus of £230 million on film in 1993, against a deficit of £10 million on television material.

One continually successful area of investment in film material in Britain has been that of video, now supplemented by digital networks. With average spending on video in the UK running at about £70 per household per year, the domestic market alone is substantial. Total video sales rose to £643 million in 1994. Outside the mainstream broadcasters and film production companies, the most successful video productions have been based on the characters Thomas the Tank Engine, Postman Pat and Rupert Bear. Such characters are now carefully controlled by rights holding companies, answerable to individual copyright holders. Among the most successful British organizations of this type have been Britt Alcroft Ltd, MPL Communications (the business of Paul and Linda McCartney) and Copyright Promotions Ltd, which was floated on the stockmarket in 1991. A large number of production companies exist in the sector, and the majority are listed in the annual *Music and Video Week Directory* or the so called 'White Book' – the *Knowledge*, produced annually by PA Publishing.

At present almost all major media concerns, from News International to Pearson, have video divisions, and these are now increasingly supplemented by multimedia divisions. The range of material produced is large and can work across a wide range of vehicles, such as TV or computer games. Investment in specific productions is made through public or private shareholding, and in many cases, the companies will seek to reinvest a large proportion of profit. Detail of production is available either from brokers or the individual companies themselves.

The prospects for an investor are very varied. Beyond normal investment interest in a sound business, the criteria for evaluation should include those given for intellectual properties under the appropriate option set out previously in this chapter under the heading Intellectual Property Agreements. Personal interest can be particularly important for character merchandise. In the case of the Dutch characters, the Smurfs, the interest of a US TV executive, sparked off by an unexpected hearing of the Smurf song, led to exposure on a US network, and then to the worldwide Smurf phenomenon. In Britain, the dogged personal interest of Britt Alcroft in the works of the Reverend Awdry has made Thomas the Tank Engine a worldwide success, first on video and TV, and subsequently on a very wide range of merchandise.

Individual Rights

There are numerous pitfalls for those who generate or come into rights to intellectual properties. One of the pitfalls is underselling. In 1972 the US golfer Arnold Palmer signed away all rights in his name to the Pro Group of Tennessee in return for an annual fee of $50,000 a year. By 1991 the annual sales of the Pro Group, largely represented by Palmer material, were some $32 million, and the net profit reached $320,000. After the company was taken over in early 1992 profits turned to losses through 'blundering, scandal and lawsuit' that had reached $10.8 million by 1994 when John 'Jack' Lupton rescued it with an injection of $2.5 million and Palmer, to protect his own interest, invested $400,000. As *Fortune* put it 'Arnie has been a loser every round'. The convoluted story of the sale of the major Beatles songs (vested in ATV Music after the buyout of Northern Songs) eventually revealed what a bargain Michael Jackson had secured when he obtained the catalogue for £29 million in 1986; he re-sold it to Sony, in an exchange of copyright interests, for over £200 million in 1995.

Individual rights, including the likeness of famous persons, were largely overlooked until the 1980s. Then the US trend for protection of an entire persona extended to the UK, when the band The Police began charging fees for photographs. The potential scope for such rights was taken to the extreme with the Doisneau test case, in which two anonymous individuals, Dubliner Jack Costello and his then girlfriend, sought compensation in a Paris court in 1992 for their appearance in one of the French photographer's most famous pictures, *The Kiss* of 1951. They lost the case under a judgement of June 1993.

One of the most notable areas for investment in, and subsequent exploitation of, individual intellectual property rights in recent years in the UK has been that of the estates of deceased people. Under present copyright law the potential can be very broad; copyrights in unpublished works by the long-deceased Jane Austen and R.L. Stevenson and the composer Henry Purcell have been created in recent years. (This potential for exploitation was one of the problems highlighted by the purchase of Winston Churchill's papers for the nation, using National Lottery monies. No copyrights were actually bought, and it was never determined which papers were State property and which were Churchill's personal property.) In America such income is appositely designated 'dead money', and in California a law specific to such personalities (the California Celebrities Act) was passed in 1985, giving a fifty-year title to a likeness and name for commercial purposes; this has given rise to such oddities as the (licenced) 'Always Elvis' sparkling wine launched in Detroit in 1980. In 1996 there was a failed attempt to import this law into the UK in the 'Elvisly Yours' case, in which the heirs to the Presley estate sought income from a specialist UK retailer of Elvis memorabilia.

The intent of individual or corporate investor is to acquire the rights, entire or in part, to such estates is not dissimilar to that of the art trade's 'coffin chasers' or 'knockers'. Underlying this attitude is a view that rights are easier and cheaper to acquire, invent or reinvent when the subject is dead. Recent cases of exploitation of estates have been those of Marilyn Monroe and Andy Warhol; the reported licence fees from the Monroe estate in 1991 were £500,000 a year – from an estate valued after her death in 1962 at £420,000. One of the more controversial British acquisitions was made by the BBC in 1994, when it acquired material relating to the estate of Peter Sellers from the estate of his late wife Lynn Fredericks. It was evident that some of the film rights concerned were arguably owned by Lord Snowdon.

Intellectual property is not limited to the readily apparent rights but can cover concepts and likenesses. Modern technologies, especially in the field of communications, can add a premium to the ownership of intellectual properties in whole or in part. The emergence of compact-disc technology in the 1980s vastly increased the value of popular music rights, allowing 'old' bands' catalogues to be resold to the original audience some years after first issue. However, the scope for new-technology exploitation of past rights shows some signs of consumer resistance as saturation status is reached – the failure of the Digital Audio Tape (DAT) format being an example. Where control is apparently vested in, say, an individual, a single business or a process in its entirety, there can be questions over a monopolistic element. EU Commissioner Sir Leon Brittan highlighted this aspect in June 1991, stating that 'companies cannot unreasonably sit on their intellectual property in order to stifle enterprise', and it remains possible that some form of deregulation by government (as has been suggested for television rights) may be possible in the near future.

Past Product Investment

An investor can seek a return from the creation or exploitation of subsidiary rights in a past product. The product base can be quite diverse, but it can encompass reproduction rights to pictures or photographs, the licensing of film stock in the public domain (even amateur film that has special qualities) and, more rarely, the re-introduction of a scientific discovery or product covered by a new patent or process rights. Professional research into and acquisition of subsidiary rights in intellectual property can produce substantial gains (subject to tax in the normal fashion) and informed usage of such rights has, in certain instances, given returns of up to as much as 40–100 times their cost. However, this type of product cross-over can entail some complications. Certain works by the US Pop or Kitsch artists Andy Warhol and Jeff Koons entailed the reworking of someone else's image and were subject to out-of-court or public-court settlements for infringement of intellectual property rights. The Warhol settlements were made out of court, but those involving Koons were made very public in 1990, when he was sued by a photographer over the unacknowledged use of a photograph of dogs that became the basis for one of his works. In the past decade seeking to pass off a real-life story as fiction without due acknowledgement has become one of the more contested areas, but such claims are not entirely new. Thames TV was reported to have paid some £500,000 in an out-of-court settlement with the female rock band, and its management, that inspired the 1980s hit series *Rock Follies*, while the case of the creation, success and subsequent damages claim over the show *Beatlemania* is well documented.

The opportunity to buy intellectual property is as open as ever, and rights (active or, in the case of 'public domain' material, latent) may be acquired by direct approach to the owner, at auction or through a representative who may also be expert in the field. However, converting latent value into cash, almost without exception, requires tenacity and access to likely markets, as well as the resources to develop the idea into a commercial product. These requirements have made the consolidation of rights into a corporate entity a sensible course of action for a wide range of creative individuals or owners of such properties. This is often reflected in personalized company names – dead-pan, as in Phil Collins Ltd, or more tongue-in-cheek, as with Elton John's company William-A-Bong Ltd or IRS, the tour-management company owned by the management of the band The Police.

The potential for cross-investment in intellectual property is one reason for the premium that has been put on information and expertise in such markets in the 1990s. In contrast to regulated markets, the concept of 'insider trading' does not yet exist in the rights market, and information about properties that may be acquired can come from many sources. In the West, and increasingly in the other leading world markets, rights purchase is covered by standard international agreements. An acquisition will usually involve the payment of a lump sum, often equivalent to 50% of the royalty or fee income projected to be generated over the fixed period. The fixed term for artistic inheritance (now including photographs) within the EC is 50–70 years from the death of the originator, depending on the territory. A July 1995 directive extended the EC copyright period to 70 years after death (though this was subject to implementation by member states) – a period derived from German copyright law, which gave much longer protection because of the early deaths of creators of such properties in World War II. This extension has caused some problems over implementation. It has required certain past acquisitions to be reappraised and, in at least one case in the UK, has caused the closure of a photographic archive because the means for accurate distribution of income to descendants proved impractical.

There are exceptions to the general copyright law in the cases of entirely anonymous works and certain copyrights with shorter duration (such as those for drugs and some recordings), which can be renewable. In the case of anonymous works no rights exist, and the works are deemed to be in the public domain if true authorship cannot reasonably be determined. In short-duration cases copyright is awarded for periods of from 15 to 25 years, varying with the type of application made (by a drug company, for example) and the territory concerned. In the United States, Congress approved a three year-extension to the 14-year patent for major pharmaceutical products in December 1995. Application to copyright lawyers, or reference to intellectual property bodies is recommended for such variable cases. The sum payable for a property is negotiable and relies on the experience on the part of the purchaser or his or her advisers. Many agreements for transfer of rights require a written contract, the key element of which is not the implicit sum involved but the legal ability to acquire control of the property. (This was, for example, one of the absolute tenets of Walt Disney, for whom the ability to control the entire rights to properties was paramount.) Where older rights are concerned the duration of rights acquired cannot always be indefinite. For instance, Disney was successfully sued by Peggy Lee in March 1991 for using the *Lady and the Tramp* soundtrack on video without her prior agreement; the settlement was believed to be of the order of £2 million. A similar case is outstanding over the use of Igor Stravinsky's compositions on the video of *Fantasia*, his music publishing company, Boosey & Hawkes of London, arguing that the film rights were not transferable to the video. This means that past rights are not necessarily transferable to new technologies free of charge.

The advent of new communications technologies, from cable TV to CD-ROM, has caused a substantial review of the wealth-creation potential of intellectual property. The individual investor must view each possible acquisition on specific merit and, where applicable, demand appropriate background figures, such as royalty income, fees payable, liabilities and so on (collectively, this approach is known as 'due diligence'). These figures may usually be obtained from a representative of the owner, such as a literary agent, rather than the owner in person. A great many contracts will include allowance for a 'royalty audit' to determine true figures should there be reason to doubt the earnings information given.

The profile of intellectual property in an international context, especially in historic terms, is of increasing significance. An image is more international than words, and increasingly commands a premium. There are exceptions, however. Images relating to the Nazi era in Germany, including individuals convicted of war crimes, are used on the basis of contract law, since these individuals were deprived of their copyright by the courts. But this does not apply to documents of the era, as was proved in the case of the Goebbels Diaries, published in 1991 and 1992, or the claims of the Bavarian State to the literary estate of Adolf Hitler until the end of 1995. The size and state of the likely primary market must also be considered.

Science-based Intellectual Property

Unlike artistic properties, the potential of which is largely self-evident, scientific properties require a different approach. They cover patents (registered individual ownership of a very specific process, design or object) and rights to reproduce a product that derive from patented technologies (including biotechnology, combinations of processes, such as generic drugs, and computer software). The purchase of scientific properties, or investment in an individual inventor or scientist, can be made without specific scientific knowledge. However, in the majority of cases it is necessary to make appropriate checks with patent agents (registered with the Royal Society and the Patent Office, among others) and with European and US patent offices to clear claims of originality and ownership. Patent infringements or errors in patent registration can be potentially ruinous.

Any owner must also be prepared, directly or indirectly, to take appropriate action to protect the value of his asset. This can include legal action against infringement or theft. In many cases the owner of title to a scientific property is not stranded, and has recourse to a number of bodies, backed by the full weight of the law, to assist in disputes. In Britain these include the MSF union, trade organizations (such as the Authors' Copyright and Licensing Society – ACLS) and police and customs officers. Major corporations, including Hoover (in the Aquamaster case of December 1990, brought by Vax appliances of Droitwich) and Matsushita of Japan have, in recent years, been found guilty of infringing individual rights and have had to make multi-million dollar settlements to the owners of the rights. Among the more entertaining cases was one in 1992, in which a French court ruled that the US toy corporation Hasbro violated Barbie copyright in the doll with its rival Sindy. There was also the failure of Disney to win a case against the underground comic-strip artist who developed a strip based on a naughty twin of Mickey Mouse in the 1960s.

While now less important, state proprietary rights to scientific processes or discoveries made in Britain still exist. There remain occupations in which, by definition, any output of significance by an individual or team may become a property of the state (most commonly, this applies to members of the armed services). Subsequent patent or ownership rights can rest with the State for up to 25 years and can be exploited (or not). Financial compensation is offered to the individuals (and occasionally institutions) concerned as directed by an independent panel answerable to a government department (ranging from the Ministry of Agriculture to the Ministry of Defence). Among the more famous cases in which compensation has been granted, but which gave rise to sour relationships between government and individual, were those of Sir Frank Whittle's jet engine and Sir Christopher Cockerell's hovercraft. Sir Christopher received a payoff of £150,000 for the hovercraft, after a three-year dispute, in 1972. In 1948 Sir Frank Whittle was awarded £100,000, while the inventor of radar, Sir Robert Watson-Watt received only £50,000 in 1952. (Interestingly, the settlement paid to Cockerell was recouped by means of a patent infringement case brought by the British government against the US government in the 1980s.) This rather mealy-mouthed approach is not unique to Britain, and there are instances elsewhere of scientific advances that have been, to all intents and purposes, blocked or terminated by government action. In the United States the concept of the laser was for a long time blocked by official delay and then curtailed by an ordinance that effectively made the proposal a state secret. In some countries payment of royalties or other realistic compensation to an inventor is simply ignored – as was the case with Kalashnikov, the inventor of the assault rifle, in the former USSR.

In recent years the Hotol supersonic engine project was thwarted by the UK government, which classified the project and delayed meaningful development until in 1993 inventor,Alan Bond, having won back his rights, agreed a joint venture for its development with a major Russian company. Any investor in inventions has therefore to be mindful that the possibility of government action remains. In Britain, changes in government policy from 1989, some the result of privatization, have made individual proprietary rights to scientific properties much more widespread. Many of the abuses of rights by government monopoly, classification (as secrets) or the prior claim of the employer without due redress for the employee have been eradicated, making for a much more open (and fair) market for these properties. One recent judgement to open the market for scientific rights was the European Patent Office's ruling in October 1991, permitting life forms to be patented (the first patented life form was the Onoco genetically-engineered mouse, produced by scientists at Harvard University and patented in 1988). Co-operative ventures combining government and private funding remain widespread and continue to extend the bounds of intellectual property.

The Glaxo gene bank is likely to be one of the more important of such ventures; where the intellectual property exists, literally, only in a frozen form. This highlights one of the more difficult aspects of judgement in scientific intellectual properties – the layman's capacity to understand the purpose of the work in hand and the usefulness of his or her investment to the process. Unlike the USA, where many individuals cross readily between science and commerce, promoting the importance of scientific applications to a wider public (one major example is Mitchell Kapor, founder of the software house Lotus and a former DJ), this talent remains thin on the ground in the UK, notwithstanding several government White Papers seeking to promote understanding between the business and scientific community.

One of the more evident efforts to bridge this gap has been the growth of university-based businesses. Oxford University goes further than most, running its own intellectual property initiative. Increasingly the historic concept of a general benefit for the world community from scientific breakthroughs has been supplanted by scientists taking out commercial patent rights and protection first. This new set of priorities for the scientist proved too much for some; in December 1995 a British judge lamented this change of priorities from public benefit to individual profit. The attitude is, however, understandable, since the vast majority of scientific papers published elicit no financial return. Arguably, scientific papers were the means by which Robert Maxwell made his first substantial sums, publishing such papers at little cost and charging substantial subscriptions for a broad range of scientific journals.

Intellectual Investment Property through Third Parties

Though a few scientific properties can exist in their own right (computer software being the most familiar), many require syndication or application to realize their value. This is especially the case where substantial investment is required to develop the process. In common with much music or writing, this involves sub-licensing – the sale of specific territorial or type rights on a planned basis – to recoup the original investment. The individual may acquire such properties and then sell on the sub-licensing rights or, if appropriate, move into the third category for intellectual property investment: the company or agency. The company or agency spreads a risk, and commonly represents many properties, which may be scientific or creative or both (the British food group, Booker, for example, controls the rights to the estates of Agatha Christie and Ian Fleming, among others, as well as administering rights to scientific processes, and since 1975 it has funded Britain's foremost literary prize, named after the company). The function of the agency or company is to transfer the potential into the actual, calling on shareholders (who may be individual investors) to participate in the risk that is spread over its basket of properties, and to exploit the rights substantially more effectively than an individual could. Since the life of some artistic properties may be over a century, and that of scientific applications from 15 to 45 years or more, their life may extend beyond the life of their originator, and in such cases third-party involvement can be particularly effective for the succeeding generations.

These entities are very diverse, with different relationships to the marketplace. They encompass the entire spectrum of activity and size, from single-owner, single-shareholder companies to multinational conglomerates, and many have their own specialities. Given its corporate legal status, a company or agency also serves as a bulwark for the owners of properties, not least for tax and administration purposes. Another advantage is that it can accommodate both short-term and long-term views. The investor/owner of intellectual properties may lodge a property or properties with such concerns by formal agreement and see a regular return from his initial input. An investor/owner may also take a shareholding in a concern that deals with intellectual properties, or indeed he may establish a company to clear or administrate income from the exploitation simply of his own properties.

The latter approach is now commonplace, and, even allowing for not-entirely-reliable estimates of net worth, musicians and composers who use their companies to deal with their intellectual property income, such as Phil Collins or Eric Clapton, regularly feature in tables of UK wealth leaders. These companies licence their owners' output to major multinational concerns, such as EMI (Thorn-EMI), Sony, BGM and Polygram (Philips), which have the capacity to manufacture and sell their musical product throughout the world. (Incidentally, the very format used – CD – is protected by intellectual property rights as a scientific process.)

Publicly quoted companies active in the intellectual property field provide the individual investor with a straightforward method of holding an intellectual property investment. Other methods present problems because of the sheer diversity of choice. Any decision on investment should be made either on sound proven criteria or on a significant personal interest and acceptance of absolute risk. However, the individual investor in Britain is not alone in facing a dilemma over how to approach this area; the UK government White Paper on science of 1993 noted the same problem in respect of Government investment in science research. Nevertheless, despite the risk element, investment in some form of intellectual property, directly or indirectly, is likely to be the norm by the millennium, not least because such material is now recognized as the 'raw material for wealth creation' in the twenty-first century, and hence integral to the functioning of an advanced economy and culture. The status of intellectual property is now so significant for the British economy that some form of government encouragement of such investment appears to be inevitable. The means of such encouragement – be it by tax breaks on ownership and retention, by extending the Business Expansion Scheme approach beyond the idea of business 'angels', or by some other means – remains a matter of speculation.

Brands as Intellectual Property

Company accounts do not, as yet, adequately deal with intangible assets. Beyond individuals and rights to processes, the most readily identified intangible asset in a corporate context is a brand name: Coke, Typhoo tea, Mars, Walkman and so on. The US concern Philip Morris, having once declared the notion of brands 'dead', had changed its mind by 1995, when its Marlboro cigarette brand captured a record 31% of the US market. Each year, the American research magazine *New York Financial World* publishes a listing of the world's leading brands and their values; a consistent leader in the UK listing to 1995 was Persil (though the debacle over the introduction of the Persil Power detergent considerably damaged the image and share value of the brand-owner, Unilever). At first sight, British companies may not appear to own or control many original brand names, but closer inspection reveals that they have been particularly adept at acquiring such assets. These now range from Lucky Strike cigarettes (owned by BAT) to Colt revolvers (owned by Tomkins), from Haig Whisky (owned by Guinness) to Dr Pepper's (owned by Grand Metropolitan). A number of leading brands remain associated with their originators; Disney and Ford are probably the world's best known, but British examples include Harpic, Kenwood mixers and Twining's teas. Brands can also be generic and cover a range of assets – the Harrods, Forte, Courage or, more recently, Virgin names typify this type of brand. Strong brand names, which carry customer loyalty and goodwill, are universally preserved. Among British examples of brand names that remain intact after takeovers are Brook's Brothers, New York (taken over by Marks & Spencer); the Hilton chain (taken over, outside the US, by Bass) and the Virgin record label (taken over by Thorn-EMI).

Evaluation of a brand name is as subjective as the evaluation of works of art, for it may be significant on a variety of levels. It can be important within a particular product field (such as the Zantac drug from Glaxo, or Pampers disposable nappies), or it may be significant locally (Sir Terence Conran's Quaglino's restaurant), nationally (Homepride bread) or internationally (Forte hotels). The language and nature of the name itself can be valuable, and throughout the world this gives rise to frequent actions to protect product names and identities (over and above measures to tackle counterfeiting). The regulations in this area affecting the UK market are detailed in Kurly's *Law of Trade Marks and Trade Names*. It appears that short names and initials have the edge, with the phonetics of the English language appearing to make for the most adaptable names (in 1994 'Coke' was rated as the world's second-best-known word, behind 'OK'!).

The significance of the names and identity of products or their associations was recognized by a UK government Act, in operation from 1 April 1995, giving new powers to owners to defend likenesses, names and associated elements (such as smell, in the case of perfumes) against copycat products. Its effectiveness was proved during the summer of 1995, when major British supermarket chains withdrew a number of copycat own-brands. The defence of a brand, whether by an individual or company, goes beyond the protection of promotional budgets or related investment and seeks to maintain integral value, or worth. Such defences can sometimes seem unusual, as in the case brought in 1993 by the *Financial Times*, which sought to prevent the *Evening Standard* from publishing daily financial information on pink paper. This case stretched the bounds of proprietary claims and failed, but the principle that erroneous or unintentional infringement of proprietorial rights can significantly affect share prices remains. Such claims and counterclaims are now so frequent that the concerned investor will find them more effectively covered by electronic news sources, such as Bloomburg Information (US) or the UK's Reuters Financial Service information, than by broadsheet newspapers. In the United States, the interpretation of 'likeness' was broadened by a case in March 1994, in which the Supreme Court ruled that 2 Live Crew's version of *Oh, Pretty Woman* was a fair parody and could not be blocked by the copyright owners Acuff-Rose Music. The case was significant for both its judgement and for the potential sums at risk, estimated to be over $13 million in royalty payments.

There are other ways of devaluing brands that, though fortunately rare, can also be significant. Apart from piracy, unregistered production can occur. The most frequent form is an abuse of licensing, the licensor extending the production run without rendering due account to the licensee (royalty and associated audits exist to deal with this). Spoiling or 'dirty-tricks' campaigns intended to degrade or 'see off' a competitor also happen. In the 1980s Associated Newspapers conducted a very public spoiling campaign against Robert Maxwell's twenty-four-hour newspaper the *Daily News*, while the British Airways 'dirty-tricks' campaign to undermine confidence in Virgin Airlines led to an undisclosed damages settlement in the UK and court action for violation of anti-trust legislation in the US. The arrival of new competition can also substantially affect the value of a brand, particularly where the status of the company and brand are virtually indivisible. In March 1995, after the introduction of the UK National Lottery, the British betting concern Ladbrokes made a £100 million write-down of the value of its brand name Vernons (football pools), describing it as 'a cry of pain in a business that is hurting'. Similarly, in a six-month period in 1994 Sainsbury's own-label Classic Cola accounted for 75% of the chain's cola sales, leading to accusations from brand leaders over copycat products. Sainsbury's was obliged to redesign its packaging. By the end of the year Pepsi had taken the step of a complete redesign and change of colour scheme (blue, as opposed to the predominant red) to make certain of a distinct appearance.

9 Land, Forestry and Historic Properties

Land

There are five types of land in Britain: commercial, recreational, agricultural, residential and non-utility. The last is divided into various sub-types, including contaminated, redundant (usually awaiting development or new use, for example, military property), waste and unsound land. Unsound land is often so termed for geological reasons, an example being the coastal area near Scarborough, Yorkshire, where landslips and land subsidence are frequent. Sites previously used for industrial or military purposes, such as the former US airbase at Upper Heyford in Oxfordshire, have now been given the unappealing official designation of 'brownfield sites'.

The designation of land and its use is governed by a host of primary legislation and local, parish or by-law regulations. Ownership of land in the British Isles is recorded in the Land Registry, and title deeds, confirming the extent and form of the property, are issued to cover each sale or acquisition. Ownership can be in abeyance or in dispute as a result of loss, accident or even negligence, and such cases are most familiar from notices in local newspapers concerning estates and wills, through which claimants to property or clarification of ownership are sought. Some holdings are of no fixed ownership, being common land or subject to default or intestacy, and in due course the Treasury, or some other government body or institution, may take over the land.

Since 1945 land ownership in the UK has changed substantially. Large tracts of recreational land are now controlled by national or quasi-national bodies, among them the Ministry of Defence, the Forestry Commission, the National Parks Commission, the National Trust, the Railtrack element of British Rail and local councils. Much of the acreage acquired by these bodies over the past fifty years derives from the ancient Three Estates – Church (its land is now held by the Church Commissioners), Aristocracy and Crown – which also still retain huge tracts of land. In addition, legal changes have given powers to central government departments, ranging from the Department of Energy to the Department of Transport, and local government to acquire land by compulsory purchase. This has been used to acquire land for a broad range of purposes, from firing ranges to motorways, from sites for British Nuclear Fuels to observatories, as well as wayleaves (the right to run cables or pipes above or below a property). Land has been bequeathed or handed over to the authorities by individuals and trusts. Only in the 1990s has central Government sought to divest itself of some of this vast land bank, most publicly as a consequence of the controversial 'peace-dividend' reduction of the armed services and the privatization of industries, notably British Coal. Details of the ownership of land in the UK can be gained by applying to the Land Registry.

Land Use in Britain

Britain, the third most densely populated nation in western Europe, has seen a continued movement of population away from major cities and towards the south of England from the late 1970s. This combination has caused land to become closely associated with political aspirations. The retention of large tracts of land by government or national institutions has exaggerated the value of land in a manner exceptional for a developed country, and the ring-fencing of specific areas designated as green belt or Sites of Special Scientific Interest (SSSIs) has also limited the potential availability of land. From 1986, almost thirty years after the maintenance of green spaces was first legislated for, the process began to break down. Limitations on property dimensions (known as Halsbury Rules) were abolished in 1985, flood-plain restrictions along river courses were lifted, and commercial and residential developments on previously sacrosanct green-belt land were approved at both local and national level. By 1994 some 48% of all land undeveloped in 1914 had been developed, and out of a total of 50,000 square miles of England 2,700 square miles had been given over to development since 1945. In addition, substantial areas had been flooded to provide reservoirs. In 1991 the Government introduced provisions to assist the protection of Environmentally Sensitive Areas, the number of which is due to reach 22 by 1996.

There remain potential gains for the investor in agricultural, recreational and commercial land. From the mid-1970s British farming underwent considerable structural change. In the twenty years to 1994 the number of full-time farmers fell from 618,000 to 172,500, while at the same time the optimum size for a profitable cereals farm increased (in 1995 sizes ranged from 1,500 to 2,000 acres, with an average across the UK of about 1,200 acres). The process of consolidating agricultural holdings into larger units, instigated by individual landowners, was augmented through investments by pension funds and institutions, including major insurance companies.

The CAP and its Consequences for Agriculture

After Britain joined the European Community (EC) in 1971 its farmers enjoyed considerable amounts of subsidy under the Common Agricultural Policy (CAP). Up to 1989 this related to productive capacity only, and it was directly responsible for changes in use of agricultural property. The ubiquity of oilseed rape (subsidy: £1,500 per acre), acreage of which increased by 500% in the decade to 1988, was one consequence of exploitation of the detail of subsidy conditions, though, by contrast, both dairy and pig producers suffered substantial cuts in subsidy or permitted capacity; from 1983 dairy farming was affected by the introduction of milk quotas, which meant that a newcomer could only enter milk production by buying or leasing land with an existing quota. The value of EC subsidies is based on what is termed the 'green pound' which is related to the value of the ECU (European Currency Unit), so the devaluation of sterling in September 1992 increased the value of subsidies to British farmers. However, such gains were affected by restrictions on productivity, with the result that cereal, potato and dairy farmers gained, while sheep and cattle farmers in upland areas lost out – as, again, did pig farmers. The level of subsidy for grain production reached £1,900 an acre, and farm subsidies of £190,000 a year became possible. In 1994 farmland prices in Britain had risen 29% in 18 months and a number of institutional investors began selling off their holdings. Under the GATT agreement of December 1993 farm subsidies were to be reduced (in a process the National Farmers' Union said would mean 'painful adjustments'), but figures from the government watchdog, the National Consumer Council (NCC), in April 1995 revealed that EU subsidies for British farmers had actually increased to a total of £2.3 billion because of the devaluation of sterling, a 20% increase from 1992. This rise in subsidy has been instrumental in encouraging further sales, notably by local authorities, backed by Government incentives to encourage more young farmers by offering inducements to farm-management concerns.

From 1989 the CAP was revised and, to combat overproduction, a new 'set-aside' policy introduced under which a percentage of a farmer's land could be taken out of productive use and either left unused or used, within specific parameters, for recreation. Payment of £1,750 an acre per annum was awarded for 'set-aside' land. This policy was a short-term measure applied to a long-term industry in a piecemeal attempt to deal with the long-standing issue of overproduction arising from oversubsidy. It put particular pressure on investors with longer-term objectives, including pension funds and major farm-management concerns such as Velcourt, which struggled to live up to its motto 'be profitable'. There were, however, many beneficiaries of this policy, among them Captain Mark Phillips who admitted receiving a reported £400,000 under the scheme in the five years to 1994, but called it 'crazy – there is no sense to it, although financially we are doing very well out of it.... Our profit, or 90% of it, comes from Brussels'. The Queen was estimated to have received £1 million from set-aside over the same five-year period. The regulations were altered in December 1994, creating a dispensation for 'market' set-aside that allowed farmers to count woodland and conservation areas as part of the 15–18% of land required to be taken out of food production. In January 1995, under more new regulations, set-aside land could not be used for charity events or for any purpose that raised money for third parties. However, it could still be used to grow 'oilseed rape for industrial use', for which farmers were to receive the standard oilseed rape subsidy on top of the set-aside sum of £300 plus an acre! Set-aside schemes also exist on a local basis, such as those to encourage conservation. Nonetheless, by 1995, with substantial reductions in productive capacity, 40% of farms had at least one source of earned income other than from food output, according to Produce Studies. In reality all this has led investors in agricultural land to look for both subsidies from set-aside and subsidized farm production and also ways to earn ancillary income from the reuse of all non-farming land.

The operation of EU regulations can have a significant effect on specialist markets. One of the most controversial moves caused the grubbing up of nearly 7,000 acres (or some 15%) of Britain's orchards by 1995 in return for compensation of £12 million, or £1,800 an acre. Such relatively fast and large-scale alteration to the profile of agricultural production in the UK makes forward planning exceptionally difficult. Among recent long term investors in agricultural land in the UK have been the Mormons, now said to own over 10,000 acres; it is estimated that 48% of their profit per acre is generated through grants and other public subsidies!

Ownership and Investment Opportunities

Ownership of agricultural property in Britain is mixed. Individuals, trusts, management companies with individual and corporate shareholders, institutions, local and national government, all own such property. The benefits of company ownership of agricultural land, which carries certain tax advantages, were reduced in 1984 when the ownership of farmland under the Business Expansion Scheme was abolished. Among the more recent phenomena in corporate land holdings have been golf-courses, 68 of which were opened on former agricultural land in 1993. The prospects for these remain weak, and many such leisure investments have foundered, usually as a result of inadequate capitalization, over-optimistic forecasts or unforeseen competition. Diversification of land use is encouraged by the Countryside Commission under the Countryside Stewardship Scheme, which offers grants and capital assistance for six sectors, including archaeological sites and historic features, to create new opportunities for enjoying the countryside. This scheme involves public access, alongside the re-creation of features or original habitat, and is open to any manager of suitable land who enters a ten-year agreement. Details of the scheme are available from regional offices of the Countryside Commission; assistance with entry to the scheme, and access to other rural grants, is offered by Rural Action, based in Cirencester, Gloucestershire.

Collective investment in agricultural land may be made through a management or other commercial company with agricultural interests. The level of initial investment in such companies averages about £10,000. For these specialist commercial investment concerns, management accounts should be examined and reviewed in the same manner as those of any other business. Tax liabilities on income and gains on landholdings in the UK can be complex, since there are various choices and allowances available to landowners; specific professional tax advice should be obtained where any situation is not simple. Among the regular guides to investment in farming land is the Midland Bank's *Forward Planning* guide, published annually.

Land may be sold by private sale, by sealed tender bid or by auction. Information on properties for sale, detailing points such as acreage, buildings, use and the number of lots available (many agricultural properties being sold in parcel, rather than single, lots) is given in trade publications, such as the *Estates Gazette*, on electronic information systems, in retail magazines (including *Country Life*) and in newspapers. It is now common for farm estates to be sold as parcel lots, comprising a number of farms. Details of the acreage and type of farmland is specific to each, as is the output per annum; the income produced may vary widely, but can be examined in detail by the potential purchaser. Ownership is transferred either by means of one or more payments under contract, or by payment of a deposit with the balance provided through a commercial mortgage. A buyer should request detailed accounts for the past management of the land, documentation on any limitations or restrictions on its use, and details of any potential or actual planning permissions. It is also advisable to check on other obligations, such as conservation, pest control, water extraction and other factors that can affect agricultural properties.

One of the more potentially difficult areas has been the increased sale of reclaimed land; in 1994 it was estimated that 100,000 plots of land that had been contaminated and subject to clean-up were on, or coming to, the market. The 1992 Environmental Information Regulations allow potential buyers of such land to investigate fully the land's type and past use, and guidance is offered by the Department of the Environment. Also in consequence of the rationalization of government and institutional property holdings, an increased number of what are termed 'white-elephant' properties are coming to market. These are largely redundant institutions, such as schools or hospitals, which include land. The future usage of such properties is unclear. Where such properties are considered, three key points should be addressed:

1. The area of both the property itself and the surrounding land. Consideration should be given to previous land usage and the prospects for getting planning permission.
2. The quality of the buildings. Many entail obligations as a consequence of listing.
3. Location (including access).

Some other features may make land unsound as a long-term

investment. Among these is the existence of the natural radioactive gas radon, which is emitted by certain types of rock and is particularly prevalent in Cornwall. The health hazard that this poses remains unclear, and studies to determine its effect have yet to be completed. Another extensive study, on the incidence of ill health in areas subject to electrical radiation (notably in areas dotted with pylons) – begun after the High Court rejected a test case alleging a link between power lines and childhood leukaemia in October 1993 – is due for completion about the turn of the century. This long-term study was obscured by controversial headlines in February 1996 that claimed there was a link between radon and leukaemia. This potential problem already has some effect on the availability of mortgages and the valuation of land close to areas possibly affected.

Title to Land and Mineral Rights

There are opportunities for investment in titles, such as lordships of manors, related to land in Britain. The re-creation of titles arose in the 1950s in consequence of a Royal Commission which determined that all common land and its owners, the lords, be registered. Over 16,000 pieces of land were registered under this legislation, but only about 6,000 were identified with a specific owner. The majority of titles are now bought and sold like shares. The title, such as a lordship of the manor or a barony, may still be associated with the original land or property from which the title derives, and the property sold with the encumbent title. This is exceptional, most titles are now divorced from any specific property and will be bought for status alone. However, there remain titles which still entail ownership of mineral rights, in consequence of the abolition of the copyhold system in 1922, when all land became freehold and mineral rights were deemed to be retained by the landowner unless specifically sold or assigned. In a number of cases the nominee owner was the title holder rather than the landowner (albeit they were in large part one and the same). In these cases, the title carried right of access to mineral exploitation, commonly by royalty arrangement. The title, therefore, had a value over and above its nominal status and could confer other historic (if not archaic rights) such as the grazing of sheep or appointment of certain local officials. This covered what had long been held common land, along with recognized privately owned land. There were exceptional cases where determination of ownership was so obscure, that land and the titles that went with it might, after due passage of time, be acquired through 'squatter's rights'.

It took some decades for the potential of titles and their associated rights, primarily that of implied status, to be realized. By the 1980s the sale of titles became an adjunct to property sales, organized under the auspices of the Historical Records Agency, London. By 1990, by dint of considerable research, most of the important – and lucrative – prospects had been accounted for. Curiously, the documents relating to the acquisition of a title (the rolls) remain unsaleable, and remain the property of the Master of the Rolls in perpetuity.

The determination of ownership of mineral rights by way of a title, can, rather like treasure trove, be a complex process. Though it may be clear that the Royal Family controls the rights to the potential oil under parts of the Windsor estate or the UK Government controls rights to offshore drilling in national waters, the question of a title and its relation to specific mineral rights does require research where a considerable investment is being considered. Prices for titles can vary extensively, but can be substantial. In December 1994 the Earldom of Arran, one of three titles held by Lady Jean fforde, was sold for £400,000.

Certain historic titles will permit extension of a property to adjoining common land. The title can often include what are termed wayleaves (the rights to run cables and pipes above or below property). The Acts of 1989 and 1991 changed provisions as to who may propose work involving wayleaves (for example a privatized utility) and what notice is required. Any damage must be underwritten by the utility company concerned, and compensation of up to 80% of the freehold value can be sought, subject to agreement between the utility company, the National Farmers' Union and the Country Landowners' Association.

Sporting Land

Since 1990 the valuation of sporting land has been increasingly tied to conservation and employment, above and beyond the value of the sporting rights attached to the land. The three types of sport most commonly involved are deer-stalking, game shooting and fishing. Each has a value tied both to the location and to past records of the numbers of quarry killed or caught. The tax paid on land used for field sports in Scotland was abolished as from 1 April 1995, bringing Scottish land in line with that in the rest of the UK.

This tax had stood at between 50p and £1 per acre per annum, and could often be quoted in equivalents of head or brace of game.

Stalking land is calculated per deer, and grouse moors per brace (two birds) shot, based on written records for the previous ten years. From 1990 to 1995 the price of grouse moors was about £1,500 per brace, but this has been affected by competition from shooting opportunities available in Eastern Europe. Land with pheasant or partridge shooting rose from £750 to about £1,000 between 1988 and 1990, but fell back to the lower figure for the following five years. Shooting (rough) rights have values in the region of £50 to £100 an acre, up from the £20 to £50 in 1989.

Fishing is calculated on the yardage of river bank, except in the case of salmon fishing, which is valued on the basis of catch records. The substantial increase in farming of salmon has not unduly affected values, and in 1991 the price for rivers was about £10,000 for each salmon caught (an exceptional £18,000 per salmon was realized for one Scottish estate in 1990) falling to £6,250 in 1993. Trout fishing fell from some £150 a yard in 1991 to £80, or even £50, a yard by 1993. (Some rivers carry a premium, however. Part of the Test in Hampshire reached a price of £800 per yard in 1988.) In Scotland trout fishing rights are not usually sold separately from the land itself, since trout fishing rights carry both bank and riverbed ownership rights.

It is an integral aspect of the valuation of a sporting estate that past records of grouse, deer or other quarry taken are identified, to provide a guide to future sporting prospects. The major demand from British and European shooters is red grouse; in 1994 one moor was calculated at up to £2,750 per brace. The grouse moor was a Victorian innovation, stemming from the invention of driven shooting in 1850. It was not until 1954 that the first national analysis of game bags was undertaken, revealing that, on average, a brace was shot for every eight acres of ground on Scottish moors, and a brace per four acres in northern England; exceptionally, on some Yorkshire moors the figure could be as high as a brace per acre. For red deer, the stalking value is currently put at between £15,000 and £20,000 per stag, a substantial fall from 1991, when prices close to £50,000 per stag were realized.

There are commonly three general types of estate, defined by their terrain: low ground, moorland or upland. In terms of size, a small estate is in the range from 3,000 to 5,000 acres, a medium one between 6,000 and 20,000 acres, and a large one 20,000 acres or more. In 1995 the 32,155-acre Gunnerside Estate in Swaledale, Yorkshire, was sold for about £10 million to the US tycoon Robert

Miller, while the 20,000-acre Tulchan estate in Morayshire, changed hands for about £12 million, making it one of the most expensive estates on record. In price-per-acre terms, though, some southern estates are even more expensive. In 1991 the 850-acre Longparish estate in Hampshire was sold for £6 million, while the 1,200-acre Watergate estate in Sussex realised £5.5 million at the end of 1990.

In recent years one of the attractions of such estates, above and beyond their sporting potential, is the appeal of secure privacy within a large area of one's own land. Many sporting estates will be mixed, offering both shooting and fishing, like the Halladale estate, Caithness, which was offered in May 1995; it had 52 fishing pools and three sporting leases covering over 4,300 acres. The vast majority of estates will offer a main and secondary property. Such secondary property may sometimes be unusual; the Glen Lyon estate, Perthshire, covering some 6,000 acres, was offered with its own hydro-electric power station when it came on the market in January 1995. Under the policy of the National Rivers Authority, rivers are subject to inspection, and all inland fishing is regulated under the rod-fishing licence scheme. By June 1995 there were few good investment opportunities involving fishing, given that many of the estates had been overfished, and their declining catch record bore this out.

Land Investment for the Future

From 1990 to 1995 the prospect of investment in land or estates providing a return above the rate of inflation has been limited by weak demand, a surplus of land available (partially due to industrial recession and the after-effects of the Lloyd's insurance market problems) and a lack of quality estates on the market. However, the continuance of widespread management subsidy for properties and an increase in the acquisition of sites for non-agricultural use – ranging from environmental protection to leisure development – is likely to cause a rise in demand. In addition (although estimates vary greatly), there will be substantial increases in the use of land for housing – perhaps 1.7 million new dwellings by the year 2000 – and there is the prospect of some of the 1996 proposals for 21 new towns being realized.

On a broader scale, continued adjustment of the CAP and the reduction of EU surpluses is likely to benefit agricultural producers, not least through substantial anticipated flow of funds from the emerging nations, notably China, where demand for foodstuffs for human and animal consumption will increase. This reflects the state of world food output in 1995, when demand outstripped supply for the first time in a generation – a trend which is set to continue.

Forestry

It can be argued that for over a thousand years, until the mid-twentieth century, the course of British history was influenced by the existence of native woodlands and forests as much as it was by any other national asset or characteristic. Investment in, and care of, this asset was encouraged over many centuries. By the eighteenth century allowances or grants were given to stimulate the production of timber for building naval or commercial vessels and to provide charcoal for smelting. In 1918, at the end of World War I, regeneration of the native woodlands and forests became imperative after their decimation to provide timber for ammunition boxes. The main public body charged with promoting forestry, devising policy for afforestation and maintaining the reserves of growing trees was the Forestry Commission. In 1924 it absorbed the Crown woods and forests (except for those areas personally owned by the Royal family). Its annual purchase grant from the Exchequer has allowed the Forestry Commission to acquire a considerable acreage of growing or potential forestry from private owners and government departments.

Forestry in the UK since 1970

The body of private estates, including farms, that maintained woodland remained substantial until the beginning of the 1970s. Between 1970 and 1974 a number of significant changes took place in the structure of forestry which were to give us the woodlands and forests we see today. The 1970 Trees Act laid down that tree-preservation orders were to apply to dedicated woodlands (as opposed to coppices or haphazard tree growth), and to those woodlands in receipt of grants that were no longer managed under a plan of operations approved by the Forestry Commission. These provisions were to encompass replanting and, in effect, increased Government involvement in the pattern of the forestry industry as a whole. Common to measures from 1970 onwards was the distinction between two types of woodland and forest – conifer and broadleaved – with native species increasingly preferred. This preference became more pronounced by the 1990s, when the impact of imported species – ranging from the Douglas Fir to the Maple – on the local and national ecology was better understood. (Such importation carries additional risks. In 1995 the highly destructive spruce bark beetle was accidentally imported to the UK, causing enormous damage.)

The Trees Act proved timely, for private woodlands were to shrink substantially: from 60,500 acres in 1971 to a mere 21,475 acres by 1977. In an effort to halt this decline, the acreage of woodland on which grants were paid was doubled over a six-year period, and in October 1973 the Ministry of Agriculture proposed a wider policy on forestry. A higher grant would be paid for growing hardwoods (the import of which became both increasingly costly and restricted), and the Forestry Commission was to take a more flexible attitude to the amenity or land-use aspects of schemes proposed by private owners. In an effort to offset the decline in private holdings, the Commission was charged with planting 55,000 acres of woodland a year on its own account. In the 1980s incentives were introduced to foster private investment in woodlands and forests by management companies, investment companies or individuals.

The problems (some actual, some imagined) affecting the private sector forestry industry by the 1990s caused a substantial review of policy for the new decade. A leading objective was to curb what was termed the UK's 'hopeless dependence' on foreign timber, and a series of measures, some of them the result of undertakings given at the Rio Environmental Summit in 1992, were introduced. The most tangible new measure was the establishment of ESAs (Environmentally Sensitive Areas) and related NSAs (Nitrate Sensitive Areas); by March 1994 these were to cover 10% of the total agricultural land of the UK. The Community Woodland supplement followed, under which 250 local planting schemes were proposed for the end of 1994, to redress local depredation or environmental damage. In April 1992 the Farm Woodland Scheme was launched, allowing woodland to be brought into set-aside (though the UK government only won EC support for this at the end of 1994). This scheme offered annual payments to farmers, in addition to Forestry Commission grants, to encourage the planting of trees. The basic structure of the Forestry Commission itself was altered, with the establishment of the Forestry Authority to implement Government policy, including the control of tree-felling, advice to private woodland owners and administration of grants. From 1981 the Forestry

Commission itself was permitted to sell forests and woodlands into the private sector, with 10,104 hectares being sold in 1994.

Woodland Grant Schemes

The Woodland Grant Scheme of 1994 set out the framework for private investment in forestry, whether through a syndicate or company or as an individual. Investment in timber remains a unique prospect, involving the combination of a long-term commitment and an illiquid asset (the minimum time-scale involved is eight to ten years for softwoods, and up to 120 for hardwoods), and it was against this background that the scheme aimed to reinvigorate private sector planting, which had fallen 8.4% in a year. In addition, there was a new tendering scheme to stimulate the planting of new woodlands in what was termed the National Forest, in the west Midlands, and the generation of local 'Community Forests'. As these provisions are the context for private investment in the sector, they are a useful reference.

The rate of grant for new planting is £700 per hectare for conifers and, for broadleaved trees, £1,350 per hectare for woods under 10 hectares or £1,050 per hectare for those of 10 hectares and over. The grants are paid in two instalments – 70% after planting and 30% after five years. For the full grant, planting density has to be 2,500 or more trees per hectare, though in some circumstances a density of 1,100 may be accepted. These conditions include new native woodlands on appropriate sites, or small-scale planting of broadleaved trees as part of predominantly coniferous planting schemes. The Better Land supplement is paid for both conifers and broadleaves in eligible areas (as listed by the Forestry Commission or Forestry Review Group). The rate is £400 per hectare for planting set-aside and £600 for other land, and the grant is payable in a single instalment. Areas to be planted are restricted to 1,250 hectares per year on set-aside land and 1,000 hectares per year on other land, and the scheme runs for five years. This is the Short-rotation Coppice. A grant of £325 per hectare is payable for restocking conifer plantations, and £525 per acre for broadleaves; the required densities are 2,250 trees per hectare for conifers and 1,100 per hectare for broadleaves. Natural regeneration grants are possible for both tree types, at £325 per hectare for conifers and £525 per hectare for broadleaves. An annual management grant for woodlands and forests is payable at £35 per hectare where the management aims for wider environmental benefit, including public access (this provision now includes woodland under ten years old). In appropriate cases a Livestock Exclusion annual premium of £80 per hectare per year is payable to farmers to exclude livestock for up to ten years from old-established or native woodlands whose long term survival is considered to be threatened by grazing. In addition to the above grant aid, funding was also made available for woodland in priority areas covering the National Forest and twelve Community Forests.

While woodland or forest are generally understood, the concept of short-rotation coppicing requires some explanation. It involves the planting of willows or poplars that are cut back to a stump after a year or so. This causes the stump to produce a number of off-shoots that are later harvested and made into fuel (they can, for example, appear as wood-chip fuel for barbecues).

The level of compensation offered by English Nature for the preservation of woodland can be substantial. In August 1995 Viscount Cranborne was said to have been paid over £250,000 for preservation of trees in an SSSI. The compensation level, which had stood at £20,000 for the first year, rising annually, was under review by the end of the year. Other schemes of benefit to investors exist at a local level. From November 1994 the Isle of Wight introduced an assistance scheme offering £14,000 per acre for the planting of deciduous species, especially hazel, partly to encourage the survival of one of the last pockets of the native red squirrel in Britain; an additional grant was made available for owners who left such woodlands unused for a five-year period. English Nature offered assistance of up to £50,000 for a similar scheme. The largest such sanctuary scheme was launched in the Kielder Forest, Cumbria in 1995, accounting for an estimated 12,000 acres out of the 125,000 acres of this forest. Kielder, the largest man-made forest in northern Europe, is supported by local trusts, the Forestry Commission and local councils. Initially it was planted mostly with Sitka spruce, a fast-growing species, but from 1993 it was decided to increase the proportion of Scots pine and Norway spruce, along with the broadleaf species of birch, alder and willow. In certain areas, approved species may vary. Planting of the yellow-leaved *robinia*, for example, was discouraged, because of the colour of the foliage.

Tax and Risks in Forestry Investment

From April 1993 the occupation of commercial woodlands was removed from income tax unless woodlands were occupied for the purpose of felling or removing timber in connection with a proper trade. Even given the number of incentives, investment in timber requires a minimum initial investment of £100,000 by an individual to be viable. There are specialist forestry unit trusts that make it possible for smaller investors to participate in this area, and these are listed in the financial pages of broadsheet newspapers.

The risks of forestry investment are considerable. Insurance is needed against storm, fire or pest (although, in south-west England the Countryside Commission offers grants to offset storm damage dating to 1990). Other risks include the possibility of a fall in demand for timber (and hence in its price), changes in demand for growing plantations and the consequences of poor husbandry (the quality of the management of the asset has to be considered). However, under proper management and specialist guidance, investment in timber can prove tax-effective over an eight- to ten-year period, as an alternative to equities or in combination with property and other agricultural investment.

Historic Properties

For many of moderate wealth, one of the more appealing prospects for investment in Britain is a historic property. Such properties require considerations beyond those for other property investment – after all, it was the difficulties of maintaining them as family homes which led to the sale of some 400 such properties in the eighteen years to 1991. Nonetheless, against the general background of declining property values in Britain from 1989, many historic properties have held or increased their value.

Such properties come on to the market in a variety of forms, one of which is multi-occupancy conversions. During the 1980s an astute realization of the problems of maintaining substantial properties, led to the conversion of a considerable number of historic buildings into self-contained flats or wings by restorers and developers, among the most notable being Kit Martin; from 1980 to 1991 33 were converted. This created units within these properties that were both secure and affordable, and inspired a range of shared tenancies. Details of such shared tenancies throughout the country appear regularly on the books of estate agents or are advertised in the press. Each deal will be individual, because of the specific nature of each historical property, but should, nevertheless, be considered in the same way as any other property deal, particularly in respect of contractual terms and value.

Other substantial historic properties appear on the market that have not been converted in this way. Properties in central London command a premium, in part as a result of overseas investment by both individuals or corporations (some of the more notable recent buyers in London have been wealthy Russians, whose interest has caused substantial price rises in areas such as W2). The sale documents or advertising will detail the general condition and status of the property, which may range from the derelict to the pristine.

Among the leading sources of detailed information on historic properties in the British Isles in a run-down state is the organisation SAVE (Britain's Heritage), which has campaigned for the rescue and reintegration of historic buildings for over a generation. In addition, the Heritage Department maintains a Buildings at Risk register. A number of estate agents specialize in historic properties, among the better known being John D. Wood, Knight Frank & Rutley and, more recently, Condé Nast property and Sotheby's Realty (the property offshoot of the leading auction house). For many historic properties fully illustrated catalogues are produced, and these can prove an invaluable source of information on the status of the property, particularly where it is not in one of the major cities, including some detail of its history. One of the most comprehensive guides to historic buildings in Britain is the 'Buildings of England' series (and its companion series on Scotland and Wales) published on a county-by-county basis, originated by Sir Nikolaus Pevsner. These series are available in many reference libraries and describe virtually all major historical buildings in Britain.

Two of the most important considerations in relation to the acquisition of a historic property in the British Isles are the questions of listing (covered in the next section of this chapter) and the grants available for upkeep and repair. Taking on a historic property – which should ideally be a matter of personal affinity, rather than the acquisition of a mere status symbol – often requires professional management and careful planning for its acquisition and use. Identifying a means by which the property can generate income and be self-sustaining, rather than simply devouring capital, is an important aspect of such an investment in the longer term (many an aristocrat has become impoverished by the considerable costs of keeping up the 'historic pile'), and this will apply even where the property is not to be a sole residence. Scrutiny of the journal of the Historic Houses Association will reveal the wide variety of means employed, under an equally wide variety of circumstances, to achieve this object. These now include such diverse activities as film-making and product launches. The Historic Houses Association drew up the standard contract for filming in historic houses in 1980; current fees for filming at an historic property are typically £600 a day outside and £1,200 a day inside. The 1960s approach of opening the property to the public or developing a theme park is no longer the most appealing option, since there is now considerable competition, as well as a seasonal variation in income. Government has sought to take a more positive attitude to historic buildings, acknowledging the responsibility imposed on the private-sector custodians of the national heritage by introducing conditional support for such properties at both national and local level. In part this has reflected broad public dismay at the vandalism and destruction of the national fabric up to the 1980s by speculation and neglect – often stemming from a lack of interest at government level itself.

Listing

By mid-1995 some 443,000 buildings or sites were listed by the Department of National Heritage under the 1990 Act that covered historic property in the UK (the term now includes buildings dating from as late as the 1960s). Some of these properties can be unusual: medieval rabbit warrens, piggeries or, in one mistaken case, a 1960s slab of concrete. Listing forbids alteration or demolition (as in the case of a building) without prior consultation with, and permission from, the Department of Heritage and other bodies, notably the local planning authority. The listing classification covers three grades: Grade 1 (6,000 properties, 1.4% of the total listed); Grade II* (18,000 properties, 4.1% of the total listed); and Grade II (419,000 properties, 94.5% of the total listed). In addition local authorities restrict the alteration and development of certain unlisted properties under by-laws, termed 'townscape' measures. It is a criminal offence for an owner to demolish, alter or extend a building without consent in a way which would affect its character.

Not unusually in Britain, certain government departments and agencies (which owned over 600 historic properties in 1991) still enjoy immunity from such prosecution. There are several incidents annually where permission is sought for the demolition of historic buildings in 'public' hands – for example, the John Rylands mansion, Longford Hall, Stretford, which was left to the local residents 'for all time'. There is therefore an apparent conflict between the government's action in respect of its own historic buildings and the sensitivity it expects of private individuals. This has to be resolved if the Government's views on heritage are to be consistent.

If a listed building or site is considered for purchase, it should be remembered that the onus for its proper upkeep rests with the owner, and notices served for dereliction of this responsibility (which may be subject to criminal proceedings) can be 'inherited' from previous owners. Repair notices from the proper authorities are served in expectation of compliance, and continued neglect can lead to compulsory acquisition of the property (appeals against this can be made to both magistrates' courts and to the Department of Heritage). Councils have powers to carry out urgent repairs to a building that is unoccupied (usually to make it weatherproof) and then recover the costs from the owner; in such cases, one of the grounds for appeal is financial hardship. For properties of Grade II status and higher, the local authority is to be consulted (unauthorized work may attract a £2,000 fine or three months' jail, or both). If consent for alteration is granted, this is valid only for a five-year period. If the work is an alteration this is zero-rated for VAT; repairs or maintenance attract VAT.

The acquisition of an historic property must be approached with some caution, since there are buildings where protection covers features and fixtures as well as the fabric itself. The Planning and the Historic Environment controls of September 1994 seek to prevent the destruction of a building's special interest – its value in the community – by inappropriate development. They encompass the setting of the property, and the range of items they cover is wide, including lamps, verges and signs. Developers can apply for immunity from listing for five years, but having expert advice is a must. Interpretation of the regulations may be subject to prevailing taste, so determining the true status of the property in all its details before purchase may involve unexpected expenditure and effort. There have been instances where items, such as fireplaces or gates, which have been added to a property, or been altered in the twentieth century, are considered to be part of the original property – even though the 'new' fixture may date from several hundred years after the original building. In the 1990s cases have been brought against owners to recover, repurchase or replace such fixtures if they have been altered or sold. In 1994 George Sassoon, the son of the poet Siegfried, was fined £10,000 for removing the gates to his historic property, Heytesbury House in Wiltshire; partly as a result of this, the property was sold to developer Brian Cox. The problems entailed in taking on an historic property are clearly demonstrated by subsequent events in this case. By October 1995 the property was described as semi-derelict, as the local council insisted that 'a developer needs to make a profit in order to restore an important listed building is not a good enough reason to overrule planning objections'. In another landmark case, in early 1994, architect John Melvin was fined for partially demolishing a Grade II house in Doughty Street, London, by removing the second-floor and first-floor partition walls; as a result he was threatened with expulsion from the Architects' Registration Council, which would have prevented him from making a living.

These extreme cases of the possible effect on owners of legislation interpreted at a local level, emphasize the need to obtain extensive and expert legal advice on acquisition of an historic property. In effect, all matters relating to the listing should be set out in the purchase contract, after being checked and confirmed in writing by the relevant Government authorities. In this way the possibility of exceptional interpretations of current legislation is removed. Mr Proby of the Historic Houses Association is clear about what a potential or new owner needs to do: 'The great secret is to get the local planning inspector on your side'. Some owners take a very direct route. After buying the Grade I Wardour Castle at Tisbury in Wiltshire in November 1991, Nigel Tuersley commissioned English Heritage to do extensive research on the building and to act as consultant for the ensuing restoration work.

Grants for Historic Properties

The potential financial demands of a historic property have long been recognized in the UK. In 1946 a considerable fund (equivalent to several hundred million pounds) was raised from sale of war surplus to establish the Land Fund, which was intended to assist owners of properties with repairs and maintenance, as well as funding the purchase of properties or prospects for the nation. The Land Fund evolved into the National Memorial Heritage Fund (the same body now responsible for distributing the heritage element of National Lottery monies). Questions remain over the expenditure of the money and cases of 'lost opportunities', but the level of grants to private owners has been broadened. On a national level, the incidence of grants from English Heritage is small. In 1994 only 23 (of an estimated 400) owners of historic houses received grants towards repair bills; in 1988 the figure was 69, and in 1992 a mere seven. This incidence compares very unfavourably to other EU nations.

At present grants are awarded and administered by the Department of Heritage or its subsidiary bodies, such as English Heritage, local county or district councils or London Borough Councils. Grants are largely limited to Grade I and Grade II* properties, and applications can only be made before the work commences. The appropriate body can vary according to the property concerned; in the case of traditional farm buildings the arbiter is the Ministry of Agriculture or the Countryside Commission. There can be an extensive element of bureaucracy in the application for a grant, and the theoretical 'unlimited' funding available at a local level was abolished in 1993, resulting in only a proportion of costs being covered by grants.

The costs of running a stately home remain substantial. A detailed analysis of the Longleat estate in 1995 revealed an annual running cost of just under £3.4 million and an annual profit of only £100,000. With a substantial increase in competition for the public's patronage from other leisure attractions, the profit margins of historic properties are likely to continue to decrease as visitor numbers fall, unless additional means of raising revenue can be used. In many cases this means golf courses, sporting or leisure complexes or hiring out the property for commercial or tourist groups.

Generally Britain has a more extensive intact heritage than many European countries. Consequently it has a proportionally greater problem of protection at a time when private and public funds are both in limited supply, and when the regulations relating to protection are onerous and therefore costly to meet. The government has yet to find a completely satisfactory way of reconciling the cost of protection with commercial reality.

10 Small Business

It is a general misconception that the roles of finance and management in business are somehow interchangeable. Providers of finance – investors, shareholders, owners – provide (and stand to lose) money to help a business trade and/or grow, and they look for an above-average return in response to an above-average risk; a manager runs far less of a personal financial risk, being paid a salary to run the business, with perhaps the possibility of an equity stake and profit share as additional incentives. An investor has to differentiate between a small business that is purely proprietorial in nature and outlook and one that has good growth prospects and will eventually cease to be 'small'.

Proprietorial businesses are those in which the owners and managers of the business are one and the same. They tend to be family-owned and controlled and to exclude participation by outsiders, and they can often stagnate when the interested family members have died or left the business. (Many UK small businesses pay salaries or dividends to family members who never set foot in the workplace and never contribute directly to either the finance or the management of the business. Such arrangements, which may go back many years, are often the result of inheritance from the original owner-operators of the business.) They are not usually attractive propositions to an investor – the shares are too tightly held, the trading results are patchy, the level of investment poor and the process of modernization (if any) woefully behind the times.

What interests investors is a dynamic business with an identifiable market, identifiable products or services, and high-quality staff and management. They like to see the ownership of existing shares spread among a variety of people who all contribute to the business. They look for a steady increase in turnover and profits, good planning, targets, investment in new equipment and technology, competitive margins and possibilities for expansion. The essence of good business is quality – quality earnings and quality assets, including human resources. These attributes are easy to list but hard to identify in real life (many businesses are patchy through no fault of their own; the economy at large, the type of market, unfair competition, all these can contribute to a less than satisfactory result).

An investor offers financial resources in return for a share in the business, but there are many stories of well-established businesses sold cheap because they go through a difficult time and find that they have lost the support of their main backers, usually the bank. This is because much funding for small business is essentially short-term. Indeed there are also investors who are after a 'quick buck' – they can go in and strip out the choice assets ('cherry-picking'), making a profit for themselves in the process but leaving the business worse off than before. Both in the US in the 1980s and in the UK in the 1970s such processes destroyed many a family concern and put thousands of people out of work; this is not an investment strategy for small business, but one that works against it.

A real investor in small business is a financial nanny: helping the business to grow, showing it the way. This involves getting and keeping the right people, critically appraising all aspects of current operations and getting out of unprofitable or inappropriate lines – but with the overriding aim of keeping the best of the existing business and inflicting the minimum of damage in the process. (The former chairman of ICI, Sir John Harvey-Jones, has made a very large and public reputation out of his ability to advise relatively small business in this way.) What is involved is a positive attitude where the investment is real, purposeful and professional. Prudent investors do not invest in small business as a hobby.

What is Small Business?

A small business may be defined in terms of various combinations of turnover, headcount and capitalization. Dun & Bradstreet, the debt-grading concern, defines a small business as one with a turnover below £10 million; the UK government uses a combination of turnover, numbers employed and net assets; under the Companies Act 1985 a small company is defined as one with a turnover of not more than £350,000 and a balance sheet total of less than £1.4 million. The European Community defines small businesses by the numbers employed in two ranges: less than 10, and 10 to 499.

In the UK small businesses can take three different forms: sole trader; a business under joint individual ownership and with or without employees (a partnership); or a limited-liability company, a legal entity established by registration with Companies House, London, with its specific areas of activity defined by articles and a memorandum (from 1994 a limited company may function with only a single share, owned by a single shareholder). Each of these forms of small business is subject to government regulation, liable to amendment in each Budget, covering the wide variety of responsibilities of the individual or individuals concerned.

The element of risk in the sector is widely acknowledged (27% of small businesses failed between 1991 and 1993), but the small-business sector remains an important element of national and EC trade. In Britain small business represented 24% of all business activity in 1993, which corresponds to the EU average for the number of small businesses in relation to the total number of businesses. This figure, however, falls well short of the EU average of 45% of small businesses employing 10–499 persons. Many observers perceive this lack of 'growth' in the UK small-business sector as a fundamental problem. There are, however, a number of conflicting views as to why it should be so particular to Britain, and what cause and effect it has on the economy as a whole. The UK government has sought to encourage small business through policies aimed at reducing the risk for investors by means of tax incentives or by making it easier for small enterprises to seek outside capital – for example via the 'business angels' scheme inaugurated by the DTI from 1994.

The profile of small business start-ups is related to (1) personal preference for self-employment; (2) a service or product concept perceived as more effectively undertaken by a small concern (possibly a spin-off from a business of medium or large size); and (3) a creative concept that can inspire confidence and generate external capital support. The basic document for any small business is a prospectus – although, over time, the direction and progress of the business may vary substantially from this. For the outside investor the prospectus, the structure of the company and its personnel will become a basis of choice for investment, augmented by suitable independent financial advice. A personal affinity for, or experience of, the type of business involved is not a necessary prerequisite for an investor, though in broad terms it is recommended that an investor should buy shares in a sector that he knows quite well. However, this safety-first approach is not always appropriate, and in the UK it has probably caused loss of both new skills and wealth in the long-term, especially in technology-driven areas.

In the case of start-ups, as opposed to mature businesses, the company may be set up as a private company, or it may seek flotation from the outset on the Alternative Investment Market, which was established in 1995 with ten small companies listed. In the past decade a number of new companies have been backed by larger concerns which have put up the greater part of their capital, with a number of small shareholders completing the issue. Many of these fall into the category of 'blue-skies' companies at the leading (and experimental) edge of a technology or process. There also exist a number of investment trusts that specialize in investing in certain types of small business. The best known is 3i (formerly known as Investors in Industry), whose shares rose by 53% between the trust's flotation in 1994 and February 1996. Another leading trust for small business is the Mercury and Kleinwort Europrivatisation Investment Trust. Small companies can offer inducements to encourage private funds, such as warrants giving an option to take up additional shares, to take account of likely trading conditions and allow for a margin of error/contingency provision.

There is no proof that a company with ten or more employees is more effective than one with fewer, yet through the 1990s the UK government has tended to ignore very small companies (it was implied, in a parliamentary debate on small business in late 1995, that companies with under ten employees could be disregarded for official purposes). This completely overlooks the 'virtual company' – one of the major developments in small business, largely originating in the United States. Such a company may consist only of a single employee, with all other personnel subcontracted to function within a structured framework of an entirely temporary and flexible nature. Some UK small companies with less than ten employees have long had this 'virtual' structure, and several of the 300 leading wealth-generators in Britain operate companies on this basis. For dealing with certain intellectual properties or artefact-based wealth (art, for example) this structure is highly efficient and non-bureaucratic. It is thus no longer true that the personnel structure of a company necessarily reflects either its aspirations or its ability to create wealth, nor need it be a key indicator for investors. Indeed, the current corporate emphasis on 'downsizing' suggests that size can cease to be an advantage and start to be damaging.

Profit

One way to assess a small company is on the basis of its profitability. Profit can be defined as the difference between income and expenditure over a given period, normally six months or a year. In many small companies the figures as they stand are distorted by the fact that the profit largely represents the salaries of management, leaving only a small sum for reinvestment in the business or distribution to shareholders. The reason may be one of practicality (the management have to be paid) or of tax planning (it is better to distribute profit than to keep it in the business).

Capital and Debt

Another benchmark for evaluating a small business is the relationship between its capital – the sum of its assets – and its debt or long-term liabilities. This equity/debt relationship, or gearing, will fluctuate, and may, indeed, be seasonal. On start-up state there will often be a negative balance between the level of borrowings and the capital base, until sufficient trade is generated to maintain a positive cash flow. The quality of assets of small companies and their realizable value can be very variable, and in the UK there is a persistently low capital base ('chronic undercapitalization') which has been noted by successive political commentators and government ministers. Lack of access to long-term financing at the outset puts many small concerns in the position of depending on bank overdraft funding; the variations of interest rates and the incidence of delayed receipts can then exacerbate this dependence, which in turn undermines confidence in many new concerns. The shareholder therefore has a responsibility to augment the capital base of the company (his investment could well be rebalanced from profits at a later date, since any excess capital can always be repaid to shareholder).

The capital-to-debt ratio of many small businesses in Britain is actually better than some would suggest. Indeed, the majority of small businesses have no borrowings. Recollections of past experience (their own, or that of other firms) has led to the elephant-never-forgets principle largely supplanting the desire to borrow from institutions at all. This state recalls the situation in the early 1960s, when the vast majority of small enterprises sought access to private funds, and even then only when they were needed.

To monitor the balance of capital to debt, shareholders should obtain and examine accounts on a periodic basis, at least twice a year. Regular conversations with senior management are also recommended where the shareholding represents a substantial (15% or more) stake in the business.

Debentures and Loans

One of the means by which small businesses raise capital is through debentures. These are effectively loans raised by the company from investors at a fixed rate of interest, with the assets of the business being used as security. In Britain, some 60 debentures are traded on the Stock Exchange, and they can be bought through stockbrokers or unit trusts that specialize in fixed-interest securities. Details of these debentures, which may entitle the owner to a variety of concessions or privileges, are available from the office of issue. Among the more publicized forms of debenture are those issued by sporting companies, Wimbledon, the All-England Lawn Tennis Club, the Scottish Rugby Union, the English Rugby Union (named the Rose Debenture Scheme) and Rangers Football Club among them. One of the more common forms of sporting debenture on offer is that issued by golf clubs; the Oxfordshire Golf Club, near Thame, Oxfordshire, offers a debenture at £26,000 for seven-day membership and a £78,000 corporate debenture. Other debentures cover entertainment. The Royal Albert Hall offers these in the form of rights to a box for a specific period of 999 years; in 1995 a box at the Hall was reportedly for sale at close to £300,000.

Venture Capital Investment

Under regulations applicable from April 1995 the Venture Capital Investment Trust was established to encourage more people to invest in small companies in return for tax breaks. The new trusts are listed on the stock market and will invest in unquoted companies with assets under £10 million. The investor receives up-front tax relief of 20% provided the shares are held for five years. In addition, an allowance of up to 40% 're-investment relief' is given if they sell existing investments with a capital-gains-tax liability. With the objective of improving the standing of small companies, the UK government introduced the Business Links initiative in May 1995, which consists of a network of 600 recommended personal business advisers. The Government offered to pay 75% of the costs of the advice they give. Among the aims of the initiative was to improve joint-venture alliances between small business and local public services, and one of its longer-term objectives was to pursue the establishment of a UK equivalent of the German 'Mittelsstand', a sector of prosperous medium-sized firms, often family-run. A commentator from a leading high street bank stated in late 1995 that one of the problems with small business was a 'lack of long-term planning – two out of three very small firms never plan more than a month ahead'.

The Dynamics of Small Business

There are 2,000 or so companies quoted on the London Stock Exchange, ranging in market value from over £20 billion (Glaxo Wellcome, BP and so on) right down to £10 million or less; most are within the range £50 million to £500 million. With UK price-earnings ratios at around 20 this means that the smallest quoted companies have profits of some £500,000 a year – a figure very much within the reach of a smaller company. Such companies often seek a Stock-Exchange quotation as part of an expansion plan, under which the major owner relinquishes some of his shares for the public sale, thus realizing a substantial sum for himself and enabling the company to raise further funds on its own account. Typically, the major shareholder's share might be valued at twenty times their original cost (which explains why so many people have become paper millionaires by this means), and the holding he retains after the public offering usually shrinks to between 10% and 15%.

One frequent reason for seeking a quotation is to buy out a minority shareholder who originally provided finance to the company. This is the role of the serious investor in small companies, and it is most satisfactory for such an investor to be able to sell his holding at perhaps twenty times its original cost, knowing that his finance contributed to the company achieving what it has. There are serial investors in small companies, who are continually looking for new businesses to invest in and have very clear criteria for the provision of their funds. One of the best known UK examples, although unquoted, is Richard Branson's Virgin group of companies. Such investors are often only known through an examination of sizeable minority holdings in small quoted companies – though they often use nominees (possibly based offshore) to protect their interests and maintain anonymity.

The merits of a quotation are debatable. It is a costly exercise, and the reporting requirements for quoted companies are strict. The stock market is also sometimes accused of being 'old-fashioned' and often does not understand new businesses and new business areas. It may get very excited about 'special situations' such as British Biotech or M.A.I.D., but the enthusiasm often wears off when analysts start wading through reported figures. The company that shows steady growth and is easy to understand is the essence of the London market, though it is unlikely to be part of the dynamic of twenty-first-century investment. London has no equivalent of the US NASDAQ (National Association of Securities Dealers Automatic Quotation) and does not take as long-term a view as the Japanese. In falling between two stools (neither enthusiastic about small business nor taking a longer-term view) we can sometimes scare off small companies that might have sought a market quotation; this seems a pity. Although the number of quoted companies continues to increase, and the fortunes made by some individuals continue to prove the value of selected small-business investment, the marketability of the newly-quoted shares is sometimes very limited.

11 Portfolios

The preceding chapters have covered, in some detail, the considerable range of options available for investment in both conventional and non-conventional areas. There are essentially only three legitimate means by which to acquire sufficient disposable wealth to consider a portfolio of £100,000 or more. These are winning the money (the National Lottery and Premium Bonds create between 100 and 200 new millionaires a year); earning it (this requires earnings of at least £170,000 after tax and normal living expenses); or inheriting it. For many of us perhaps the last is the most likely method, and even then it will probably only happen when we are aged 50 or more.

There is vast scope for investment, and even the world's richest people would find it virtually impossible to invest at the top end of each of the markets outlined in this book. Investors eventually settle down to areas they are comfortable with, and that require only the effort they are prepared to make. Few people have sufficient knowledge to investigate many promising investment areas at any one time, and even fewer have the time (time is indeed money). You could employ agents to do all the research for you, but the world's most successful investors maintain a hands-on approach: they need to have a feel for the market they concentrate on. Wealth also implies leisure – after all, money of itself is sterile – and many wealthy people feel they have paid the necessary dues and want (possibly need) to relax in their good fortune.

There follows an outline of approaches to, and the composition of, investment portfolios from £100,000 to £10 million. The division of the amounts is deliberate, since the approach does depend on the sums involved. However, it follows that there are grey areas between each of the portfolio sums as given, and there are alternative approaches. The attitude taken here is positive and medium-risk; due consideration of enjoyment and leisure has been included.

1. A £100,000 Portfolio

The amount of £100,000 is not enough to provide anything other than a relatively small amount of additional income. However, if invested fully it could, over the long-term, grow sufficiently to necessitate a change in the pattern of investment, perhaps more in line with the £250,000 portfolio (see below).

With a dividend yield of 3% (net), a £100,000 portfolio fully invested would return income of £3,000 annually – if invested in a high-interest account it would possibly even double this, but there would be no potential for capital gain. The major brokers do not feel a sum of £100,000 is large enough to interest them, since the investment fees (at 1%) are too small an incentive. The safe option for £100,000 is to invest at least 25% of the money in short-term deposits with a building society or a bank at the highest available rate. The balance could then be invested in blue-chip equities through your existing bank or a small broker. Given the size of the portfolio, the equities purchased should be very safe, almost entirely FT100 stocks, subject to annual review and confirmation of strategy, and all investments should remain in the investor's ultimate ownership. Only over a long period of time would a portfolio of this size grow large enough for sophisticated diversification.

If you have outstanding liabilities at the time you receive your £100,000, it would be sensible to repay all sums which can be repaid out of income. For most people this will involve repaying a mortgage, thus ensuring that future earnings from the portfolio are not subject to month-on-month mortgage repayments that can often reduce net earnings by 25% to 30%; this will increase subsequent net income, which will then be available for investment in its turn. Even for a mortgage where tax relief is available up to a maximum of £30,000, this would only leave £70,000 for investment purposes.

With a sum such as £100,000, gifts to family or friends could also be made, which might use a further £10,000. Where such payments reduce the amount available for investment, it might be reasonable to avoid equities altogether and simply keep the balance in high-yielding bank and building society accounts, to be used for family holidays or other specific occasions (such as weddings), rather than in the form of any real investment structure. Despite its apparent desirability the sum of £100,000 does not really encourage a serious investor.

£100,000 PORTFOLIO

	Capital £	Income p.a. £
Building Society & Bank Deposits	25,000	1,250
FT100 Shares	60,000	1,800
FT mid-250 Shares	15,000	450
	100,000	3,500

2. A £250,000 Portfolio

With an amount of this size to invest the circumstances change sufficiently for a division to be made between 'fun' money and investment money. Perhaps £50,000 could be set aside to buy things you always wanted – a new car, holidays and so forth – with the remaining £200,000 used for investment.

Once more, at least 25% of this sum should be put somewhere completely safe such as a high-interest bank or building society account. Perhaps a longer-term view could be taken, since the money would not be required immediately, and this would make an investment earning a higher rate of interest possible – perhaps even a bond with a 3–5-year maturity. The remaining £150,000 could then be invested in equities for growth and income, producing approximately £5,000 per year (after basic-rate tax).

Again, depending on your view, it is possible to use some of this money to repay liabilities, including the mortgage, and to make gifts to relatives and friends as desired. However, the size of this portfolio also is too small to involve any decisions of a broader nature or to open up the entire spectrum of investment possibilities.

A number of families in the UK will inherit sums of £250,000 in the next few years, since it equates to the value of a reasonably-sized house in an urban centre with the mortgage already repaid. It is therefore not an exceptional sum in terms of investment potential, but nonetheless gives sufficient security to

£250,000 PORTFOLIO

	Capital £	Income p.a. £
Building Society & Bank Deposits	20,000	1,000
Bond Investment	20,000	1,000
FT100 Shares	130,000	3,900
FT mid-250 Shares	30,000	900
Personal Possessions	50,000	0
	250,000	6,800

ensure a permanent increase in standard of living and an element of cash for pure enjoyment.

3. A £1,000,000 Portfolio

With a sum of £1 million there is an immediate change in perspective. This is a sum that would interest major investment houses, being well in excess of their normal minimum portfolio value of £250,000. To be a millionaire by itself no longer carries the cachet it once did, since there are over a million millionaires (albeit dollar millionaires) in the USA alone. The Inland Revenue estimates that there are at least 10,000 UK millionaires and this figure is likely to double in the next five years.

A true millionaire in today's terms could be seen as someone who has cash or near-cash resources of a million pounds, and this sum only just fits this category. It has always been said that acquiring the first million is the hardest, and thereafter a millionaire's resources render the next million easier to make (the expression 'money goes to money' does have a certain truth!). Having a million pounds to invest also means that the fixed costs diminish in relation to the sums invested and cease to be a critical part of the equation: in other words the investment and broking fees are not high enough to affect any single investment decision.

The availability of a million pounds concentrates the mind – and usually concentrates the minds of everyone else around you as well. By virtue of being a millionaire you may become a target for envy and begging, and old relationships may come to be questioned as a result of the presumption that you have become one of 'them', rather than still being one of 'us'. Since the degree of objectivity required when investing sums of a million pounds or more is high, this makes impersonal investment decisions difficult. It is therefore advantageous and necessary to employ agents, such as experienced, qualified accountants and solicitors, to ensure that a professional and objective approach is maintained, and that, where tax investment or personal circumstances change, new opportunities are exploited as they become available.

It is always sensible to make a will and review it on a regular basis, but where funds of this size are involved it is essential that their owner has a very clear idea of where they will go when he dies – and this should be considered at an early stage in the investment planning. With a sum of this size you can make lifetime bequests that will effectively implement a thought that may have been in your mind for some time. In other words, if there is a charity or an individual you always wanted to help, this is the time to do so; giving away £100,000 out of a total of £1,000,000 might perhaps seem to be reasonable. However, once money is available on this scale such gestures can become either too rare or too frequent, and the money can be squandered or withheld to an unreasonable degree. A balanced approach is needed.

As before, this sum will enable liabilities, including a mortgage, to be repaid but will leave enough money to make a balanced investment strategy possible. If you are left with £850,000 after repaying debt and making gifts, you might very well want to buy a better house, which could require (at least) £200,000 for the house itself and £50,000 for contents. You could then use a further £100,000 to £150,000 to buy a property abroad, which you could rent out to cover its costs between your own visits. This option has its drawbacks, though. You may not want to go back to the same place for your holiday each year, and there can be problems with tenants or agents, particularly where a foreign language is involved. Owning a property abroad combines a currency risk with real-estate investment, generally is not income-producing and is immoveable; it therefore breaks several of the rules of flexible investment. Moreover, equivalent (or better) hotel accommodation may often be cheaper than annual maintenance costs. In the end, whether or not to own foreign property is a matter of personal preference.

A certain amount of personal indulgence is obviously possible with a million pounds, and £50,000 could just be wasted on experiences and purchases that are of questionable value but personally enjoyable! (There is a rather likeable human tendency to 'go a bit mad' when we first have money – and why shouldn't we? Normally this phase is short-lived, though; reality soon takes hold again, and the desire for a static, normal existence reasserts itself.) That would leave a balance of £550,000 for retention and long-term investment. Of this, £100,000 could be earmarked for alternative investments, possibly spread over five different areas to provide a small number of valuable pieces that give personal pleasure as well as having lasting intrinsic worth that could make them resaleable for an increased price at some point in the future. Such items would also provide a framework for a conservative 'millionaire' lifestyle and would help to maintain a sense of perspective over the entire net worth.

This would leave £450,000, of which £150,000 might go into non-risk or risk-averse assets, such as bonds, annuities, gilts and high-interest deposits (the sum involved is not high enough to make more than three such investments). The remaining £300,000 should be invested in equities, based on 60% in UK investments and 40% in other markets, putting emphasis on mature stock markets such as the USA and European markets. This will ensure stability and ready realization in case of need. Only a small proportion of this sum – up to 10% – should be invested in emerging markets such as those of south-east Asia.

In current terms these investments should generate a gross income of approximately £12,000 from the non-risk areas and £9,000 from equities, together with an annual target of £9,000 in realized gains. In other words, the invested total of £450,000 would generate income of some £30,000 before tax, which would help to maintain a steady if not spectacular lifestyle for a normal family and remove long-term insecurities about financial matters. However, even a million pounds, approximately 50% of which is non-income producing, does not provide sufficient income to sustain a non-working lifestyle, which is why even modest millionaires have to carry on working. A £1,000,000 portfolio is well short of current criteria for the 'serious' money needed to produce what most people would consider a life of leisure, living off investment income. Such a lifestyle tends to require a net worth of £40,000,000 or more!

£1,000,000 PORTFOLIO

	Capital £	Income p.a. £
Building Society & Bank Deposits	50,000	2,500
Bond & Gilts Investment	100,000	5,000
FT100 Shares	140,000	4,200
FT mid-250 Shares	40,000	1,200
Overseas Shares	120,000	3,600
Personal Possessions & Alternative Investments	100,000	0
Gifts & Debt Repayment	100,000	0
UK Property	200,000	0
Overseas Property	100,000	0
'Fun' Money	50,000	0
	1,000,000	16,500

4. A £5,000,000 Portfolio

With a net worth of £5,000,000 you enter an environment peopled by successful businessmen, highly-paid directors of public companies, well-known sportsmen and entertainers who have had the good sense not to blow their money. This is the sort of level of wealth where multi-millionaires start to become involved in charities and are generally known simply for being rich. They are beyond the day-to-day cares of most, but will still have to protect and nurture their incomes if they are to maintain a millionaire existence and a life of reasonable leisure.

There are approximately 200 people in the UK who are regularly paid over £500,000 a year – which is what it takes to achieve this level of net worth. About a third of these have salaries in excess of £1 million. They range from Bernie Ecclestone of F1 Promotions, doyen of the Grand Prix track, to pop star Phil Collins, to Christopher Ody, the commodity dealer and hedge fund manager. These people operate in high-risk, high-reward areas, where the earnings of one year might never be repeated. To make the top 500 wealthiest in the UK your net worth (possibly grossly exaggerated) might be £40 million, which (even if only 50% is income producing) would give a yield of £600,000 after basic-rate tax; this represents approximately 30 years' average male earnings and seven times the average director's earnings.

With a sum such as £5 million, debts can be paid off, including the mortgate, as before. A bigger, better house can be bought, possibly with land if it is in the country; hobbies can be indulged, and holidays and personal pampering are all affordable. If you take the flight on Concorde, a cruise on the QE2 and a round-the-world trip as a way of easing yourself into this new lifestyle, you have already spent at least £20,000, without including hotels and spending money – it is not inconceivable that your first bout of hedonism will cost at least £100,000. At the same time you will be acquiring such 'essential' items as the (tasteful) gold wrist-watch, gold jewellery, pearls, diamonds and other precious objects; jewellery alone could easily come to a further £150,000. Status-symbol cars, such as a Rolls-Royce, Bentley, Ferrari and Aston Martin (his and hers of course) could also cost a further £200,000, and if the new house is centrally located in a prestige area of a major city it is likely to cost between £500,000 and £1.5 million, depending on the location. With this level of wealth a second home is likely to be attractive. Obviously this is a matter of personal choice, but even a modest luxury apartment in the sun or snow would cost at least £250,000. If your properties are to be furnished and decorated to a high standard, the furniture in the main house is likely to cost £250,000 and that for the second house at least £50,000. So far you have spent £2.5 million – half the total. Easy, isn't it?

We have seen that prime London property can cost £1 million or more, before running costs. A good apartment in the south in France would cost £400,000 (a house would cost twice as much or more), and such levels of property prices are repeated around the globe, wherever the rich and famous congregate. Limited-edition luxury cars cost the same as an apartment or house: the Lamborghini Diablo 30SE is priced at £160,000; the McLaren F1 at nearly £600,000; the Jaguar XJ220 at £200,000 plus (reduced from nearly double); the Bugatti EB110 is similar, while the Ferrari F512LM is a relatively 'cheap' £130,000. A Monet (*Rouen Cathedral*) sold for £7.5 million in 1995, twice the price of Stubbs' *Portrait of a Royal Bengal Tiger*, while a Picasso oil will cost £2 million to £18 million, or a Matisse up to £9 million; Alan Bond foolishly bought Van Gogh's *Irises* for over £30 million at the height of the 1980s art boom. In such a context a net worth of £5 million would seem to be too small for the full range of millionaire accoutrements to be affordable. Indeed, there is a well-known US art fund available for private collectors where the minimum value for the collection has to be $2 million, and the minimum annual investment in art and other collectables $1 million.

If, after a bout of luxury consumerism, a certain guilt feeling emerges, then £500,000 can be earmarked for good causes and relations as well as the payment of liabilities. Since gifts made during one's lifetime are potentially tax exempt, there should be no problem with even substantial gifts (provided you survive for seven years), but if your aim is long-term then it may be worthwhile to set-up a charitable trust that, invested fully, will produce income for annual charitable donations. The basic legislation on charitable investment requires that 50% of all investment should go into 'narrow-range' and 50% into 'wider-range' investments. Narrow-range investments are virtually risk-free, such as building societies or bank deposits, National Savings and government gilt-edged stocks. Wider-range investments cover all other types of investment, principally equities. There are strict criteria for the trustees of charitable trusts that require them to make prudent investments; this implies that any equity investment is likely to be geared towards blue chips and the FT 100 index.

So, after immediate requirements are taken care of and a multi-millionaire conscience has been salved, there remains

£2,000,000 for pure investment. With a sum of this size it is sensible to hire two competing brokers who have responsibility for a portfolio of £1 million each. Their instructions should be identical: to maintain the real value of the investments and also to seek to equal or beat a relevant index, such as the FT100 or FT All-share Index. With sums such as this you would pay financial advisers (an accountant and a solicitor) to ensure that the brokers' performance is properly controlled and reviewed. Normally you should expect quarterly summaries showing performance, and it is important to ensure that reviews take place as soon as possible after the end of the quarter, so that any necessary amendments to the portfolio can be made to minimize any losses that might have arisen. The foregoing implies that the portfolios will run on a full discretionary basis, so the broker will make the decision as to how to invest the money. The danger of this approach is that the brokers may change investments on too regular a basis, making a commission as they do so; to avoid such 'churning', the professional advisers should make it abundantly clear to the brokers that this is unacceptable.

Since the portfolios are now of some substance, diversification into non-UK stocks and shares is desirable. Although there are theories that advocate such diversification should follow the size of the different world markets, it is likely that 60% of the portfolios will always be UK-based; of the 40% left, 25% of this is likely to be in the USA and Europe, with the remainder in the Far East and other emerging markets. With the criteria for performance established, the portfolios should, if properly managed and reviewed, perform according to plan and provide substantial growth in the long-term. Where wealth is large there should be no immediate necessity to call upon capital, and this should make the task of achieving growth in the portfolios easier.

With £2,000,000 invested there should be a yield before tax (SIB net) of some 3% or £60,000 a year. This is still not sufficient to provide a family with a 'millionaire' lifestyle without having to continue in some form of employment; such a sum could be spent on air fares for a family of four in one year alone! A millionaire lifestyle 'requires' a long summer holiday, a winter break in the sun and another in the snow as well as the odd weekend jaunt – not to mention trips to Ascot, Wimbledon, Henley and Lords for the traditional London summer season. (With an income of only £60,000 you would start to worry about the price of champagne at these events!) To sustain such a lifestyle you need to work on income as much as capital; if you allow yourself to use up capital to supplement your income, such a spending pattern will certainly erode your remaining wealth rather quickly.

What does it cost to 'live like a millionaire'? If the main house costs £20,000 a year to run, including services and general maintenance, having live-in staff would add another £20,000 p.a. for a reliable, experienced couple. (This assumes that the house has been renovated to a high standard and that it and the garden are maintained at that level.) Car expenses, including insurance on the high-risk vehicles, would probably run to £20,000 per year. The holidays described above would probably account for a further £90,000 for two adults and two children at full price for six weeks a year. School fees for the children might run to £20,000 p.a., and personal items, such as clothes and general entertainment, might add another £40,000. Professional fees would be some £10,000. If you add all these expenditures together you will find that over £200,000 net per year is required to sustain a care-free, fully enjoyable, no-normal-expense-spared lifestyle. If the investments bring in £60,000 p.a., a further £160,000 net is required, or approximately £250,000 gross at current 40% income-tax rates: if this shortfall were met by spending capital, the total capital invested could be spent in 10–15 years. (The above figures assume that the second home pays for itself by rentals when not in use, and that there are no huge extravagances, such as the hiring of aeroplanes or yachts or the running of horses. This sort of outlay could easily wipe out the capital much more quickly.)

Undoubtedly this sort of earning and spending is beyond reality for all but very few people. However, as can be seen above, even those who have the money initially and wish to enjoy it while they can will find it can soon disappear if they 'live the life' – a habit that, once formed, is difficult to break. Moreover, the figures above assume no change in relationships – divorce or separation could remove a substantial part of the capital – and do not allow for alcohol, drug, or gambling addictions, any of which could cripple all but the wealthiest.

Daft though it may seem, this logic indicates that even £5,000,000 does not guarantee what most people would perceive as the best of lifestyles. If you came into the money at the age of 35 and lived in such a style you could be broke in cash terms by age 50, with no pension to look forward to and no choice but to continue working. It is ironic that there are calls to limit the amount paid out by the National Lottery to a maximum of £5,000,000, because that sum is not nearly as Croesus-like as might first be imagined. There are examples of immature and gullible pop stars who have earned (grossed) £5 million and spent it within two or three years.

£5,000,000 PORTFOLIO

	Capital £	Income p.a. £
Building Society & Bank Deposits	250,000	12,500
Bond & Gilts Investment	500,000	25,000
FT100 Shares	700,000	21,000
FT mid-250 Shares	200,000	6,000
Overseas Shares & Emerging Markets	600,000	18,000
Personal Possessions & Alternative Investments	650,000	0
Gifts & Debt Repayment	500,000	0
UK Properties	1,250,000	0
Overseas Property	250,000	0
'Fun' Money	100,000	0
	5,000,000	82,500

5. *£10,000,000 Portfolio*

Although £10,000,000 is well short of the sum required to join the five hundred richest individuals in Britain, it is still very substantial and provides opportunities that the £5,000,000 portfolio does not give. With a sum of £10,000,000 it is possible to diversify the investments to a very large extent, and so minimize risk at the same time as maximizing opportunities for income and personal pleasure from assets acquired, without the probability of running through the capital in a single adult lifetime.

Of the £10,000,000, some £2,000,000 could be invested in property. One large house in the UK, possibly in the country, together with an apartment in an urban area, would cost up to £1,000,000; in addition overseas properties could be bought, one for summer and one for winter, for up to £500,000 each. This suggests a lifestyle of weekends spent in the country, with a month overseas in the summer and another in the winter – plus, very likely, other holidays for winter sun and weekend breaks. Someone with this level of wealth would probably spend at least three months a year abroad for pleasure, be permanently (naturally) sun-tanned and be described as one of the 'jet set'. The downside of so much leisure might be an inclination to gain weight and an air of dissolution – which might need to be counteracted by periodic visits to health farms, and maybe a visit or two to a plastic surgeon for a cosmetic 'nip and tuck'. It should be said that such a life can be luxuriously boring! However, the primary advantage that such money gives is the ability to order one's own life without the need to refer to others (except family, of course).

The international emphasis of this sort of lifestyle is very strong, which has both investment and taxation implications. It is possible to base one's life in a tax haven, or to spend so little time in any particular country that a taxation profile is minimized, and possibly legally avoided. In general, spending half a tax year (usually a calendar year) in one country qualifies you as a taxpayer in that country. (Theoretically you could be resident in two countries, in which case a 'tie-breaker' between the contesting tax regimes would be determined by other factors, such as your preferred location, the place where you spend most time, where your doctor or dentist operate, and so on.)

When a net worth of £5 million is involved, and corresponding levels of capital and potential income, greater care is usually devoted to ensuring that inheritance is properly controlled through the use of trusts, and that the wealth itself is protected from both relatives and outside forces. There are many examples of families of this wealth, and more, surrounding themselves with a series of barriers that cloaks their dealings in virtual secrecy and makes any casual searching for their wealth virtually impossible. The key to enjoying the greatest wealth is usually anonymity, and most people in the highest echelons of wealth in any particular country are unlikely to be well-known to the gossip columns, or even the business pages.

If £2,000,000 is invested in property, a further £2,000,000 could be invested in non-risk assets – divided between an annuity, to provide an income for an early retirement at the age of (say) 45 or 50, and £1,000,000 invested at the highest rates with a bank or building society, with the interest being re-invested. This will ensure both liquidity and certainty. It may be advantageous to split the invested cash between sterling and other currencies, particularly where overseas properties are in use. Keeping a certain level of funds in local currency is always helpful, both from the point of view of establishing a profile in the towns or villages, where the properties are located and also as a hedge against any weakness in sterling. The commonest currencies that UK residents would invest in are US dollars and German deutschmarks, although French francs are also popular. Bear in mind that, at least in recent years, there has been a tendency for the pound to shadow the dollar, and for the French franc and Swiss franc to shadow the deutschmark. This apparent natural 'equilibrium' was upset with disastrous results for the UK, when, after Britain entered the Exchange Rate Mechanism (ERM), sterling attempted to shadow the deutschmark; the pound rose to a value of DM3, but Britain's embarrassing withdrawal from the ERM in 1992 caused it to fall to DM2.2 in 1995, a drop of 25%.

Given the international profile of a £10,000,000 portfolio-owner, a further £2,000,000 should be invested in offshore investments (outside UK tax jurisdiction), managed by a reputable broker; the most common offshore location used by UK citizens is the Channel Islands. These are long-term funds not intended for repatriation to the UK and can be seen as a source for ready money, should their owner take a sudden and extreme dislike to, for example, a particular government, or the British weather. They might be invested 60% in non-UK holdings and 40% in UK stocks. As a *quid pro quo*, £2,000,000 should be invested in onshore investments in the UK, divided between equities and bonds in a 75:25 ratio, with perhaps 60% in UK stocks.

Because of the size of the portfolios a managed fund is desirable, but subject to the same caveats as before, that they should be regularly reviewed by qualified financial advisers appointed by the owner. In addition two brokers should be used for the onshore portfolio and two for the offshore portfolio, to ensure an element of competition and comparison. Since these funds are not for risk the investment criteria should be for growth, not income, and the performance should aim to match or beat both inflation and a relevant index. For the onshore funds the relevant index might be the FT100, and for offshore the FT World Index, to take account of the likely international emphasis of such a portfolio.

A portfolio of £2,000,000 should yield approximately 3% to 3.5% a year (£60,000 to £70,000) before high rate tax (an additional 20%), and this income should be sufficient to enable the day-to-day expenses on the offshore and UK properties to be met. The income from the annuity and from the cash should enable other personal expenses to be met without requiring any immediate use of capital. Where possible, unused income should be reinvested, since the compound value of reinvested income is significant over longer periods of time; for instance £100 of income reinvested at a yield of 3% over 10 years will be worth £134 by the tenth year, and £2 million will grow to £2.68 million simply through reinvestment of the income. Over a lifetime the impact of reinvested income will be even greater, as capital gains are added to the simple compound interest calculation.

The £2,000,000 remaining from the original £10,000,000 could be seen as a combination of 'fun' money and money for charitable and family gifts, as well as other types of investment. The 'fun' money element would pay for the around-the-world trip and expenditure to ease oneself into a life of comparative leisure. Between £200,000 and £1,000,000 might perhaps be used as gifts and to pay off existing debts. The remainder could be used to buy house contents, jewellery and other types of alternative investments, including collections. A limited sum could also be put at risk in a business investment where the returns are expected to be higher than average – possibly this could be an already existing family company (it is inadvisable to make such an investment in a completely new business, since new businesses have a high rate of failure in early years, and you would stand to be the main loser). There are tax incentives available for making such venture-capital investments, but all such decisions should be carefully vetted by a knowledgeable, experienced professional.

If such a net worth as £10 million is properly managed, and assuming a degree of good fortune, the amount should double over seven years, based on an average return of 10% a year (3% yield and 7% growth). This would mean that an individual with £10,000,000 at the age of 40 would have £40,000,000 by the age of 54, and might be worth £100,000,000 on retirement. With the prospect of sums of this size, and of the income from them also increasing, there should be considerable emphasis on an investment structure that makes any possibility of dispute about the wealth, whether in the owner's lifetime or afterwards, minimal. This can be achieved by hiving off the money into various trusts, both to protect the assets themselves and also to depersonalize the ownership.

The rules concerning the establishment and structure of trusts can become complex, but it is usually beneficial for anyone of high net worth to ensure a certain level of disinvestment of personal property, so that a neutral approach adopted by the trustees can ensure continuity of ownership and of wealth. Since the trust structure is more subtle than personal ownership, it acts as a deterrent to spurious claims and is likely to make any attack on the wealth contained in the trust more expensive and difficult. (Such claims will inevitably arise – it is part of the process of wealth-creation.) In addition, the incidence of divorce among those of considerable wealth would appear to be unusually high, and careful planning is needed to cope with this contingency, despite the personal odium this may involve. Often couples will not even consider such planning, since they believe it is unnecessary.

£10,000,000 PORTFOLIO

	Capital £	Income p.a. £
Building Society & Bank Deposits	1,000,000	50,000
Bond & Gilts Investment	1,000,000	50,000
FT100 Shares (Onshore)	1,600,000	48,000
FT mid-250 Shares (Onshore)	400,000	12,000
Overseas Shares & Emerging Markets (Offshore)	2,000,000	60,000
Personal Possessions & Alternative Investments	800,000	0
Business Investment & Venture Capital	500,000	50,000
Gifts & Debt Repayment	500,000	0
UK Properties	1,250,000	0
Overseas Properties	750,000	0
'Fun' Money	200,000	0
	10,000,000	270,000

Income is based on net amounts received per annum as follows:
- 3% on stocks and shares
- 5% on bank and building society deposits, bonds and gilts
- 10% on business and venture capital investments

The portfolio divisions are based on a conservative approach for the long-term.

12 Wealth Today

Individual Wealth in the UK

In 1994–5, less than 1% of UK taxpayers fell into the band with an annual income of £40,000 and over – and an average income tax bill of nearly £21,000. The percentage of wealth owned by adults (aged 18 and over) fell by 3% between 1976 and 1992, while the estimated net worth of the wealthiest 25% of the population has remained constant at around 70% of total national personal wealth from 1976 to date. The greatest rise in the proportion of UK net wealth held in any particular investment sector was shown by life assurance and pension funds, which rose by 18% between 1971 to 1993, to account for 33% of UK net wealth. Despite consistent and continuing efforts to widen the ownership of shares (one of the objects of privatization issues from 1980), the percentage of net wealth held in stocks and shares fell by 15% in the decade from 1971 to 1981, and by a further 4% from 1981 to 1993.

Holdings of savings in interest accounts, National Savings, shares, TESSAS (Tax Exempt Special Savings Accounts), PEPs (Personal Equity Plans) and other forms of investment, chiefly unit trusts and government securities, essentially reflect income levels. Those with incomes above £25,000 have the highest percentage of shareholdings (29% in December 1993) and the highest percentage of other forms of investment. There is therefore consistent evidence to suggest that there is a formidable 'entry barrier' to investment, arising, rather obviously, from a shortage of income available after tax and immediate consumption. Government incentives to lift this barrier will plainly be self-defeating if incentives to invest are counteracted by higher taxes, whether levied directly on income or indirectly on consumption.

What is Wealth?

If you live in Nigeria, your average life expectancy will be 40 and your average annual income some $200; if you live in Switzerland your life expectancy will be 70 and your annual income $40,000; and around and between these averages there is a vast gulf between those who earn nothing and those who, like George Soros, can earn $300 million in a year. In 1993 the late Steve Ross, of Time Warner, had a total remuneration package (including stock options) in excess of $200 million, and in 1988 the now-disgraced junk-bond king Michael Milken earned a disclosed $600 million. To earn such vast sums you need to be a certain person in a certain place at a certain time. Those who would glibly assert that there is no such thing as the 'deserving' rich should examine the workload and ability of many of those who create billion-dollar enterprises from scratch. Very, very few politicians have ever done this, with the one exception of the Europhobic financier turned politician Sir James Goldsmith – who has a distinctly low opinion of his fellow politicians.

Wealth creates jobs, which create more wealth; it also attracts taxation, which enables society to reallocate a proportion of national income to the disadvantaged. In 1994 Peter Wood, founder and chief executive of Direct Line insurance, was paid £24 million, which was the highest identified pay in the UK in that year and was criticized by the opposition front-bench spokesman Robin Cook. (The payment was in fact exceptional and arose largely from the sale of Mr Wood's business to the Royal Bank of Scotland; his salary was seen to be £360,000, once the proceeds of the sale were stripped out.) Mr Wood took umbrage at the politician's view: 'Robin Cook is rude about me, and my attitude is "Well, what have you done?" I've brought cheaper, better insurance, better mortgages, better loans, and my tax has probably built a few roads and hospitals. So what have you done, Mr Cook? Nothing.'

The politics of envy have no place in a modern society. There is now a more general acceptance in the West (and the East) that reward follows actual achievement, whatever the field of such achievement. Nobody has yet managed to cap the rewards at the top of the tree, but this does not make the tree less fruitful for others – rather the reverse, since capitalism has generally made the world better off, at least materially. Rewards are hard to compare, though. Is a nurse more valuable to us than a film star? Is a skilful manual labourer better than a commodity dealer?

We reward intelligence and entrepreneurial skills to a greater extent than other qualities, partly because they are rarer. We give preference to professions over trades, reflecting specific knowledge and background. We pay men more than women (men make most of the earning rules). We pay disproportionately highly for the short-lived careers of sports stars and pop stars. We pay low for vocational workers, and we expect charities to be largely staffed by volunteers. In short, rewards follow the preferences of society at any one time; there is no explicit intention to pursue fairness or social justice, just an amorphic interaction of stimuli and responses, with money as the method of keeping score. Politicians may seek to change the rules and make the game fairer, so as to give each player a chance; but, as in all games, play has moved on by the time the referee has a chance to check it.

The government employs hundreds of thousands of citizens in its day-to-day administration, but, fundamentally, they are financially unproductive. Since 1965 the proportion of Gross Domestic Product (national income) that has gone to the government has varied between 35% and nearly 50%. Conservative governments over the last fifteen years have sought to reduce the level of UK government expenditure, but the proportion of national wealth it soaks up has remained stubbornly around the 45% level in the 1990s (after a temporary fall to below 40% in the late 1980s). Now that the impact of privatizations and North Sea oil revenues has worn off the UK Public Sector Borrowing Requirement (PSBR) has crept up to some £40 billion a year, after being in credit from 1987 to 1991. This expenditure and this borrowing has to be paid for by those who earn and those who consume, through taxes and duties, and, despite the apparent culture clash between business and government, there is a mutual interest in enlarging the Gross Domestic Product and the per capita income of the country as a whole.

Some politicians feel the need to extract from high earners as great a proportion of their wealth as possible, so as to assert a moral imperative and to make society 'fairer'. It is certainly true that Conservative governments from 1979 put considerable emphasis on reducing taxes, and that this has tended to favour the highest earners. However, the opportunities for the legal avoidance of tax have diminished at the same time, so it is difficult to make simplistic comparisons between regimes. High-tax regimes encourage avoidance and illegal evasion, and they may also create a disincentive to some earners (though this is not proven). On the other hand, the possibility of dividing all wealth equally, according to a 'pure' Communist thought process, is spurious. (Where Communism has not been rejected it survives largely because of a combination of coercion and poverty.) Even a toned-down version has been rejected by virtually every country in the world, and the cost of comprehensive welfare-state provision is today acknowledged as unsustainable. To want to help those who are not as fortunate is human nature, but so is the desire to be better off.

According to *Forbes* magazine in 1995 there were 388 families and individuals with a net worth of $1 billion or more; about half were in the USA, over 50 in Germany, and Japan had 40. The 40-year-old Bill Gates, founder of Microsoft, was the wealthiest, at $13 billion (£8 billion). Most of this represents the value of his shares in Microsoft – but this changes from day to day and in any case does not represent actual disposable wealth, since, if he sold his interest, the company's value would be likely to plummet. Warren Buffet, the 'sage of Omaha' is valued at $11 billion, but this may exaggerate the true value of his shares in Berkshire Hathaway (it is his ownership of the stock that sustains its value, so there is an element of double-counting). Outside the USA Yoshiaki Tsutsumi, whose Japanese real estate makes him the third wealthiest, is reliant on the probably exaggerated property values of Japan to underpin his position. Hans Rausing, of Tetra Laval, is next with $9 billion: a fortune based on the packaging that has taken over consumers' lives, such as the milk-carton. Most of these individuals of huge worth lead 'normal' lives in a very abnormal context – they want for nothing and have command of their destinies (to an extent that most of us can never emulate), but they still work, take responsibility and keep regular hours. The image of a playboy billionaire is in fact distinctly misleading. Most billionaires are rather old; they certainly don't look glamorous, and they have a strong conservative, even cautious, streak. If they didn't their money would probably have been blown a long time ago.

The American author of *More Than Money* felt 'isolated, embarrassed and encumbered,' when he inherited $500,000 at the age of 22; since two million Americans are estimated to have a $1-million net worth, he may not have been alone. US wealth is concentrated in the top 1% of the population, where, according to Hancock (author of *More Than Money*) it 'creates a lot of stress and unhappiness'. This seems to be an entirely negative attitude, although it is true that wealth creates its own problems (even if you can afford to be miserable in comfort). In 1994 a 44-year-old factory worker won £18 million on the UK Lottery; he subsequently fell out with his friends and stated the win had made his life 'a misery'. The estranged wife of another winner said she would try to get half his £11-million jackpot (without first reading the divorce laws). There are some people who are ill-prepared for the positive side of such wealth, but to a large extent they can employ someone else to deal with it (as suggested here), which will relieve many of their burdens. The publicity and clamour quickly die away where professional stonewalling is used, a trust structure can remove legal ownership, and they can then go back to a normal life. In most cases this is what happens: people adapt quickly to their luck, don't abuse it, and live rather better but not exaggeratedly. Their friends bless their good fortune (what sort of friend would curse it?). If they still feel hassled or guilty, they can always give their wealth away.

Most people would consider the sums discussed in this book to be in the realm of fantasy. However, let us put them into context. Ten million pounds would buy 8% of a jumbo jet (yet there are people who do own jumbo jets), or it would buy five Patriot missiles, which, when fired, would last thirty seconds; it represents one-fifth of the money raised by Live Aid to relieve famine in Ethiopia – and, ten years later, famine is starting to return. 'Vast personal wealth' of this order arouses envy, and yet governments will spend (and possibly waste) £10,000,000 in a day – but one rarely hears of a civil servant or an MP fired for misuse of funds.

In the twentieth century vast bureaucracies, at local government, central government and supra-government (e.g. UN or EC) levels have grown up. Their purpose is to shape and mould our lives by increasing regulation and intrusion into every individual's lives, whether those individuals are conscious of it or not, with the objective of the greater good. Where such bureaucracies do not exist to the same extent the level of deprivation and poverty of the local population tends to be considerably higher than in the western world. The growth of emerging economies on the one hand and the increased legislation of commercial actuality in mature economies on the other has meant that wealth has to be created within a more restrictive set of rules even as growing populations in emerging countries demand higher living standards. Inevitably this means that proportionately fewer wealth creators have to create greater wealth within narrower confines. Surely this should be a reason for greater encouragement of wealth creation, which seems to be the antithesis of bureaucratic regimes. That is why any individual who has created very considerable net worth should at least be given the benefit of any doubt as to their ability to use it as wisely as their fellow human beings. This rather Victorian view does, however, presume that one thing Government is meant to be good at is ensuring that the vulnerable in society are protected from the sharks – an assumption that is being constantly challenged.

Without the capitalist culture man would have missed out on a vast number of experiences and positive actions which money was required to stimulate. The opening of world trade from the earliest centuries has required finance from private merchants willing to risk capital in cargoes to new lands. Philanthropic, a charity is reliant on private funding; much prime research comes from commercial sponsorship; exploration is still largely an area for personal input; sport has developed from the effects of private individuals, both on and off the sports arena; entertainment relies on the individual inspiration of talented stars. Many areas of human endeavour are not directly connected to the State and are financially supported by wealthy individuals. Indeed many of these areas may have developed only because the State has little involvement with them. In other words there are indirect as well as direct benefits arising from wealth creation that can add to the quality of life. Inevitably there are areas where only a cohesive, powerful body, such as Government, can regulate excesses and run 'natural' monopolies (such as defence) in conjunction with private enterprise. Only an ascetic will consider money to be the root of all evil. It should be seen rather as a means for potential good. In the fifty years since the end of World War II the general standard of living in the UK has improved dramatically for most; in terms of health, education and consumption it has improved far beyond what our great-grandparents would have believed was possible. For a minority (discounting those who can make an effort, but do not do so), though, conditions have regrettably not improved. In addition, the downside of a material age has become increasingly apparent in drug and alcohol abuse, unemployment and crime. The challenge for the future is to encourage and use wealth to solve the problems that lie at the edges of the capitalist system. This surely must be the aim of twenty-first-century socialism.

Bibliography

Art at Auction 1970–1995 (Sotheby's)

Ash, Russell, *The Top Ten of Everything, Years 1991–1996* (Headline & Dorling Kindersley, 1996)

Bennett, David and Mascetti, Daniela, *Understanding Jewellery* (Antique Collectors Club)

Bosworth, Tony, *Buying Vintage and Classic Cars for Profit* (Robert Hale, 1996)

Browne, T., & Partnow, E., *Dictionary of Photography: Photographic Artists and Innovators* (Macmillan, 1982)

Carden, Philippe & Huntley, Bee, *Investing in West End Theatrical Productions* (Robert Hale, 1992)

Christie's Yearbook: Review of the Season

Cottle, Sidney, Murray, Roger F. & Block, Frank, E., *Security Analysis* (McGraw Hill, 5th edn, 1988)

Curtis, Tony, *The Lyle Price Guide to Printed Collectables* (1984 & 1994)

Duthy, Robin, *Guide to the Antique Shops of Great Britain 1996* (Antique Collectors Club, 1996)

Focal Encyclopaedia of Photography (Caxton Press, 1958)

Forestry Commission, Annual Report 1995 (HMSO, 1995)

Gabardi, Melissa, *Art Deco Jewellery* (Antique Collectors Club, 1994)

Gardiner, G. & Morris, A., *The Automobolia of Europe* (Antique Collectors Club, 1994)

Gernsheim, Helmut, *Creative Photography* (Faber, 1954)

Graham, Benjamin, *The Intelligent Investor* (Harper & Row, New York, 1980, 4th edn)

Graves, Charles, *None But the Rich* (Cassell, 1963)

Guiliano, Geoffrey, *The Beatles* (Sidgwick & Jackson, 1986)

Hamilton, William, *The Stock Market Barometer* (Fraser Publishing Co., New York, 1993)
Hangstrom, jun., Robert, *The Warren Buffett Way* (John Wiley & Sons Inc., 1994)
Information Economy (US Department of Trade, 1977)
Lefevre, Edwin, *Reminiscences of a Stock Operator* (John Wiley & Sons, Inc., 1994)
Loke, M., *The World as It Was, 1865–1921: A Photographic Portrait* (Summit Books, New York, 1980)
Miller, J. (Ed.) & Gleeson, J., *Millers' Guide to Pop, Rock and Film Memorabilia* (Reed, 1996)
Poynder, Michael, *The Price Guide to Jewellery* (Antique Collectors Club, 1995)
Reitlinger, Gerald, *The Economics of Taste* (Barrie & Rockliff, 1961)
Soros, George, *The Alchemy of Finance* (John Wiley & Sons, Inc., 1987 & 1994)
Sotheby's Yearbook: Sotheby's Season
Thompson, Alan G., *Buying and Selling Pictures Successfully* (Robert Hale, 1997)
Train, John, *The Money Masters* (Harper Business Books, 1980)
——, *The New Money Masters* (Harper & Row, 1984)
Wall, John, *Dictionary of British Photographic Collections* (Royal Photographic Society, 1977)
ArtNews
Art Newspaper
Antique Collector
Antiques Gazette
Apollo
Billboard
Book and Magazine Collector
Bookdealer
Camera
Coin Monthly
Country Life
Daily Telegraph
Estates Gazette
Field
Financial Times
Fortune
Music and Video Week Directory
New York Financial World
Record Collector

Screen International
Stage and Television Today
Stamp Monthly
Statesman's Yearbook
Sunday Times
The Times
Treasure Hunting
Variety

Appendix I

Prices and Inflation in the UK, 1980–1995

	Mortgage rates %	Bank rates%	Average earnings (% increase)	Retail prices (% increase)
1980	15.0	14.0		
1981	15.0	14.5		
1982	10.0	10.0		4.8
1983	11.3	9.0		5.2
1984	11.9	9.8		4.7
1985	12.8	11.5	10.2	5.3
1986	12.3	11.0	9.3	3.5
1987	10.3	8.5	10.5	3.3
1988	12.8	13.0	12.0	6.8
1989	14.5	15.0	10.0	7.0
1990	14.5	14.0	11.0	8.7
1991	11.5	10.5	8.2	4.2
1992	9.3	7.0	6.1	3.0
1993	8.0	5.5	4.7	2.9
1994	8.1	6.3	5.6	3.3
1995	8.0	6.5	4.6	3.2

The above figures show inflation and financial costs moving steadily down into single figures in the 1990s. Price increases lag behind wage increases, indicating consistent growth in real incomes for those in work.

Source: *The Economist*. (Calculations by authors.)

Appendix II

Exchange Rates, 1990–1995: The Value of the Pound in Selected Foreign Currencies

		$	Change (%)	DM	Change (%)	Yen	Change (%)
1990	January	1.61		2.76		236	
	June	1.74	8.1	2.90	5.1	269	14.0
1991	January	1.93	10.9	2.89	–0.3	262	–2.6
	June	1.63	–15.5	2.93	1.4	226	–13.7
1992	January	1.82	11.7	2.87	–2.0	234	3.5
	June	1.86	2.2	2.92	1.7	240	2.6
1993	January	1.57	–15.6	2.45	–16.1	193	–19.6
	June	1.50	–4.5	2.55	4.1	165	–14.5
1994	January	1.48	–1.3	2.58	1.2	168	1.8
	June	1.55	4.7	2.45	–5.0	155	–7.7
1995	January	1.56	0.6	2.46	0.4	156	0.6
	June	1.58	1.3	2.19	–11.0	133	–14.7

The above figures show a steady devaluation in sterling against the major currencies, particularly strong on the UK's exit from the ERM. It is no wonder that sterling is now bracketed with other 'weak' currencies, such as the Italian lira.

Source: *The Economist*. (Calculations by authors.)

Appendix III

US, UK & Japan: Stock Market Index Comparisons, 1990–1995

		FT100	Change (%)	Dow Jones	Change (%)	Nikkei	Change (%)
1990	January	2434.1		2810.2		38915.9	
	June	2399.8	–1.4	2842.3	1.1	31571.8	–18.9
1991	January	2143.5	–10.7	2633.7	–7.3	23848.7	–24.5
	June	2461.2	14.8	2910.1	10.5	23907.4	0.2
1992	January	2432.9	–1.1	2902.3	–0.3	22736.3	–4.9
	June	2560.6	5.2	3285.6	13.2	16107.0	–29.2
1993	January	2789.7	8.9	3313.3	0.8	17680.7	9.8
	June	2907.6	4.2	3497.5	5.6	19538.3	10.5
1994	January	3444.0	18.4	3895.3	11.4	17369.7	–11.1
	June	2909.0	–15.5	3669.6	–5.8	20639.2	18.8
1995	January	3034.4	4.3	3790.7	3.3	19271.0	–6.6
	June	3313.2	9.2	4542.6	19.8	14759.0	–23.4

The Nikkei has been particularly volatile in recent years as the effects of recession and property loans have been felt on the market (much Japanese borrowing is based on quoted stocks, often without reference to underlying asset values).

Source: *The Economist*. (Calculations by authors.)

Appendix IV

Unit and Investment Trusts: Highest Returns from £1,000 Invested after 5 Years From 31/3/91 to 31/3/96

Fund	Value (£)	Increase (%)
UK Growth		
Jupiter UK Growth	2,329	132.9
Schroder UK Enterprise Accumulation	2,284	128.4
Fidelity Special Situations	2,129	112.9
Fidelity Recovery	2,171	117.1
Perpetual UK Exempt (3 years)	1,689	68.9
(Sector Average)	(1,688)	(68.8)
International Growth		
Prolific Technology	4,805	380.5
Framlington Health Fund	3,732	273.2
HTR Global Technology	2,815	181.5
PM Overseas Growth	2,437	143.7
Scot Equitable Technology	2,446	144.6
(Sector Average)	(1,841)	(84.1)

Table V
Investment Trusts

UK Capital Growth		
Welsh Industrial	2,013	101.3
Fleming Enterprise	1,752	75.2
Kleinwort Endowment Policy (3 years)	1,308	30.8
Broadgate (3 years)	1,231	23.1
(Sector Average)	(1,882)	(88.2)
International Capital Growth		
RIT Capital Partners	2,424	142.4
Primadona	2,407	140.7
Murray Smaller Markets	2,213	121.3
Electric and General	2,325	132.5
British Empire Securities	2,073	107.3
(Sector Average)	(2,044)	(104.4)

N.B. All income was reinvested
Source: *Micropal*. (Calculations by authors.)

Appendix V

PEP-Linked Investment trusts: Highest Returns Over One and Five Years

	Value (£)	Increase (%)	Fund Size (£m)
Over 1 year			
Law Debenture Corporation	4,927	64.2	225
Schroder UK Growth Fund	4,277	42.6	146
Personal Assets	4,253	41.8	19
Mercury Keystone	4,249	41.6	117
Kleinwort Charter	4,188	39.6	218
Scottish Investment	4,101	36.7	765
Scottish Eastern	4,080	36.0	634
Foreign & Colonial Eurotrust	3,996	33.2	170
Brunner	3,974	32.2	175
Electric & General	3,966	32.2	217
Over 5 years			
Personal Assets	12,247	308.2	19
Law Debenture Corporation	11,221	274.0	225
Electric & General	8,931	197.7	217
Mercury Keystone	8,801	193.4	117
Fleming Fledgeling	8,744	191.5	51
Finsbury Growth	8,591	186.4	66
Lowland	8,453	181.8	83
TR European Growth	8,379	179.3	116
Dunedin Enterprises	7,808	160.3	45
Finsbury Trust	7,780	159.3	15

The above figures a £3,000 lump sum, with gross income reinvested. Values are as at 3 March 1996.

Source: *Micropal*. (Calculations by authors.)

Appendix VI

Commodities, 1990–1995

		All-commodity Sterling-rated index (1985 = 100)		North Sea Brent Crude Prices		Gold Prices	
		Index	Change (%)	$ per barrel	Change (%)	$ per troy ounce	Change (%)
1990	January	97.2		20.60		401.10	
	June	100.3	3.2	16.45	–20.1	367.50	–8.4
1991	January	79.4	–20.8	27.80	69.0	391.50	6.5
	June	81.6	2.8	19.45	–30.0	361.00	–7.8
1992	January	72.8	–10.8	17.83	–8.3	351.75	–2.6
	June	78.1	7.3	20.80	16.7	338.75	–3.7
1993	January	90.0	15.2	17.75	–14.7	329.15	–2.8
	June	85.9	–4.6	18.72	5.5	375.25	14.0
1994	January	101.0	17.6	13.57	–27.5	394.25	5.1
	June	126.5	25.2	16.36	20.6	387.80	–1.6
1995	January	141.1	11.5	16.23	–0.8	380.30	–1.9
	June	133.3	–5.5	17.37	7.0	384.90	1.2

Sources: *The Economist* and *The Times*.

Appendix VII

Marriages and Divorces in the UK, 1980–1989

	Marriages	Divorces	Ratio (marriages:divorce)
1981	397,800	155,000	2.6:1
1982	387,000	159,000	2.4:1
1983	389,300	162,000	2.4:1
1984	395,800	158,000	2.5:1
1985	393,100	175,000	2.2:1
1986	397,900	169,000	2.4:1
1987	351,761	151,633	2.3:1
1988	348,492	152,633	2.3:1
1989	346,697	150,872	2.3:1

Source: Office of Population and Censuses and Surveys. (Social Trends.)

Appendix VIII

Art at Auction

Gains on Paintings sold at Auction, 1980–1995

Artist	Average gain/loss (£)	School
Renoir	1,662,750	Impressionist
Pissarro	748,000	Post-Impressionist
Rauschenberg	660,000	Contemporary
Chagall	492,500	Modern
Magritte	196,000	Surrealist
Vuillard	96,000	Post-Impressionist
Corot	65,000	Romantic
Picasso	−10,300	Modern
Monet	−104,400	Impressionist
Sisley	−106,600	Impressionist
Matisse	−277,000	Fauve
Bonnard	−382,000	Modern
Toulouse-Lautrec	−620,000	Post-Impressionist

Based on data compiled from auction records and the *Daily Telegraph* Index. The *Telegraph* Index rates the central 80% band of actual prices at auction as a mean. Some specialist sectors recorded substantial falls – the New York index for contemporary art fell an average of 48% in 1993.

Paintings sold at Auction, 1970–1995

Year of sale	Artist	Title	Price (£)
1984	Canaletto	*The Old Horse Guards, London*	9,200,000
1985	Mantegna	*Adoration of the Magi*	7,500,000
1991	Titian	*Venus and Adonis*	6,800,000
1986	Rembrandt	*Portrait of a Girl*	6,600,000
1992	Goya	*Bullfight*	4,500,000
1984	Stubbs	*Hound attacking a Stag*	432,143
1984	Breughel	*Landscape with St John*	218,943
1984	Turner	*Off Ramsgate*	140,000

The above prices are indicative of the range of values for world-renowned artists. None of the above prices rank in the top ten auction prices for paintings, which range from £49.1 million for Van Gogh's *Portrait of Dr Gachet* (sold in 1990) to Manet's *La Rue Mosnier aux Drapeaux* sold for £16.7 million in 1989.

Sources: *Daily Telegraph* Index and *The Times*.

Appendix IX

Photographs: Prices Realized, 1970–1995

Year of Sale	Photographer	Title	Price (£)
1993	Edward Curtis	*The North American Indian*	427,419
1995	Edward Curtis	*The North American Indian*	290,312
1993	Alfred Stieglitz	*Hands of Georgia O'Keeffe*	260,458
1993	Alfred Stieglitz	*Hands of Georgia O'Keeffe*	257,097
1989	Alfred Stieglitz	*Equivalents*	249,056
1994	Man Ray	*Noir et Blanche*	239,952
1992	Edward Curtis	*The North American Indian*	211,764
1993	Man Ray	*Demain, Aujourd'hui*	143,548
1993	Man Ray	*Glass tears*	122,500
1993	Tina Modotti	*Two Callas*	122,258
1990	Anna Atkins	*British Algae, 1843*	98,200
1992	Alexander Rodchenko	*Girl with Leica*	97,032
1989	Man Ray	*Primacy of Matter Over Thought*	76,582
1991	El Lissitsky	Untitled	73,537
1990	Paul Outerbridge	*Self Portrait*	61,491
1990	Paul Outerbridge	*HO Box*	54,660
1985	Anna Atkins	*British Algae, 1843*	44,000
1994	Man Ray	Untitled	24,200
1990	Gustave Le Gray	*Seascape*	20,000
1994	Gustave Le Gray	*Seascape*	18,700
1980	Albert Southworth	*Self Portrait*	15,720
1981	Edward Weston	*Nautilus*	15,052
1981	Edward Weston	*Nautilus*	11,818
1988	Joe Rosenthal	*Iwo Jima*	10,599
1994	Lewis Carroll	*Irene*	9,900
1980	Edward Weston	*Shells, 1927*	8,277
1984	Paul Outerbridge	*Toilet Paper Advertising, 1936*	7,857
1977	Anon.	*Photograph of Photography, 1842*	5,800
1978	Julia Margaret Cameron	*Mrs Herbert Duckworth*	5,500
1978	Roger Fenton	*Odalisque*	5,400

Appendix IX (continued)

Year of Sale	Photographer	Title	Price (£)
1980	Edward Steichen	*Garbo*	5,240
1977	Lewis Carroll	*Alice Liddell*	5,000
1982	Gustave Le Gray	*Seascape*	4,200
1980	Julia Margaret Cameron	*Philip Stanhope Worsley*	4,000
1978	Gustave Le Gray	*Seascape*	3,500
1977	Gustave Le Gray	*Seascape*	3,400
1975	Henry and T.J. Dixon and A. and J. Boot	*Images of Old London*	3,150
1975	Julia Margaret Cameron	*Idylls of the King*	2,835
1977	Julia Margaret Cameron	*Hershel*	2,600
1995	André Kertesz	*Satiric Dancer*, 1926 (reprint)	2,156
1995	Joe Rosenthal	*Iwo Jima*	2,013
1981	Man Ray	*Study of Hands behind a Veil*	1,800
1980	Peter Henry Emerson	*Gathering Water Lilies*	1,455
1978	Julia Margaret Cameron	*The Dream*	1,300
1994	Julia Margaret Cameron	*Sappho*	1,065

The above are indicative of the range of prices for photographic material and show the changes in prices through time, as well as identifying the most sought-after images. Non-sterling prices are translated at rates prevailing at the time of sale.

Sources: Authors' archive together with 'Top Ten of Everything 1996'.

Appendix X

Rock 'n' Roll memorabilia
Total Annual Sales at Sotheby's, London, 1981–1994

	Value (£)	Change (%)
1981	97,660	
1982	104,506	7.0
1983	147,617	41.3
1984	251,155	70.1
1985	222,277	–11.5
1986	307,345	38.3
1987	225,604	–26.6
1988	375,920	66.6
1989	277,288	–26.2
1990	635,151	129.1
1991	602,085	–5.2
1993	138,085	–77.1
1994	917,777	564.6

The above figures show the fluctuations of an emerging market. Despite the general upward trend it remains to be seen whether this is a genuine market or a 'baby-boomer' phenomenon that will decline in time.

Excluding cars (not strictly memorabilia) the highest-priced pop memorabilia items are guitars, such as Jimi Hendrix' Fender Stratocaster sold for £198,000 in 1990 and Buddy Holly's Gibson acoustic sold for $242,000, also in 1990.

Sources: Authors' archive together with *Christie's* and *Sotheby's Yearbooks* 1981–1996. (All prices converted to sterling at prevailing rate.)

Appendix XI

Classic Cars: Prices Realized 1970–1995

Year of sale	Model	Sale location	Price (£)
1990	Alfa Romeo 2.9-litre 1941		7,600,000
1990	Ferrari GTO, 1962	Monaco	6,870,000
1990	Ferrari 250 GTO, 1962	Monaco	6,410,000
1987	Bugatti Type 41 Royale sports coupé, 1931	UK	5,575,000
1986	Bugatti Type 41 Royale, 1929	USA	4,300,000
1991	Ferrari 250 GTO, 1962	USA	3,230,000
1990	Ferrari Dino 196SP, 1960	Monaco	2,574,591
1989	Aston Martin DBR2, 1957	Monaco	2,178,000
1990	Ferrari 250 GT Berlinetta, 1957		2,000,000
1989	Alfa Romeo Tipo B, 1934	Monaco	1,971,000
1989	Mercedes-Benz 500K roadster, 1934	Monaco	1,956,237
1985	Rolls-Royce Phantom V (John Lennon's), 1965	USA	1,768,462
1989	Alfa Romeo Tipo 8C 2300 Spyder	Monaco	1,763,000
1990	Rolls-Royce Silver Ghost, 1907	USA	1,720,000
1988	Mercedes-Benz 500K special roadster, 1936	UK	1,595,000
1991	Mercedes Simplex Sixty, 1903		1,562,000
1989	Jaguar D-Type Lord Louth	UK	1,200,000
1989	Rolls-Royce Pullman limo, 1912		1,020,000
1995	Jaguar D-Type	UK	1,000,000,
1987	Ferrari 330 GTO Berlinetta, 1963	Monaco	940,752
1987	Ferrari 250 Testarossa 3-litre, 1958	Monaco	901,320
1991	Alfa Romeo Rinoldi 8C-2300 Spyder, 1933		615,285
1989	Porsche 935, 1977	UK	440,000
1987	Ferrari 250 GT 3-litre, 1960	Monaco	338,000
1995	Aston Martin DB35	UK	275,000
1988	Ferrari 400 4-litre, 1963	Monaco	258,862
1991	Ferrari 275 GTB		243,465
1990	Rolls-Royce Silver Ghost, 1911		231,110
1995	Porsche 959	UK	224,995
1979	Mercedes-Benz 500 K roadster, 1936	USA	210,526

Appendix XI (continued)

Year of sale	Model	Sale location	Price (£)
1995	Ferrari F40	UK	199,995
1989	Bugatti Type 49 coupé, 1932	UK	198,000
1989	Aston Martin DB3, 1953 chassis	UK	198,000
1981	Packard Twelve model 1108, 1934	USA	184,210
1979	Mercedes-Benz SS38 two-passenger, 1929	USA	168,421
1989	Aston Martin DB3 drophead coupé, 1953	UK	165,000
1990	MG Ulster Magnette, 1934	UK	165,000
1991	Bugatti 328 cabriolet type 7		158,000
1990	Bentley 4.5-litre sports tourer, 1928		143,807
1985	Packard Twelve model 1107, 1934	UK	129,000
1995	Aston Martin V8 Vantage Volante	UK	111,500
1986	Jaguar C-Type sports two-seater, 1953	UK	108,000

The above prices indicate the range of prices for classic cars and the changes over time, as well as identifying the most sought-after marques. Prices have fallen considerably since the 1989/1990 peak. Non sterling prices are translated at rates prevailing at the time of sale.

Sources: Authors' archive together with *Christie's* and *Sotheby's Yearbooks* 1981–1996.

Appendix XII

Representative Prices of Important Jewellery, 1970–1995

	Description	Maker	Carats	Price (£)
1989	Ruby and diamond ring	Chaumet	32.08	2,869,560
1989	Diamond necklace with five huge sapphires	Van Cleef & Arpels		2,100,000
1980	The Polar Star (cushion-shaped diamond mounted as a ring)	Boucheron	41.28	1,960,784
1991	Suite of 1936 Art Deco jewellery	Cartier		1,500,000
1979	Emerald and diamond diadem		605	771,428
1991	Ruby and diamond necklace, *c.* 1935			601,500
1987	Jewel hand ornament designed by Mucha for Sarah Bernhardt, 1899			426,538
1978	Diamond ring set with emerald-cut diamond	Harry Winston	26.95	397,222
1979	Diamond ring set with pearl-shaped diamond	Harry Winston	15.26	284,000
1991	Pair of sapphire and diamond bracelets, *c.* 1930	Cartier		220,000
1980	Diamond ring	Boucheron	9.13	205,714
1983	Blue diamond set with navette cut	Bulgari	4.61	195,161
1985	The June Briolette pendant and diamond set		48.42	177,419
1973	Ruby and diamond necklace	Cartier		120,000
1973	Antique diamond and sapphire tiara			109,333
1974	Emerald and diamond brooch	Cartier		105,642
1980	Emerald and diamond bracelet	Van Cleef & Arpels		102,803

The above indicate the range of prices for gemstone jewellery and the changes over time, as well as identifying the most sought-after makers. Non-sterling prices are translated at rates prevailing at the time of sale.

Prices Realized for Important Diamonds, 1970–1995

	Description	Carats	Price (£)
1990	Flawless D pure white (Mouawad Splendour)	101.84	7,890,000
1990	Uncut from Aredor mine, Guinea (sold by tender)	255.61	6,230,000
1995	Begum Blue		5,100,000
1988	Pear-shaped white	85.91	4,856,383
1991	Rectangular-cut white (Jeddah Bride)	80.02	4,181,287
1990	Agra pink	32.24	3,999,827
1988	Rectangular-cut white	52.59	3,978,723
1988	Pear-shaped pink (Mouawad Pink)	21.06	3,855,576
1987	Pear-shaped white	64.83	3,752,941
1984	Pear-shaped blue	42.92	3,548,387
1988	Pear-shaped white (Star of Abdel Aziz)	59.00	2,957,713
1990	Rectangular-cut blue	19.41	2,820,513
1990	Golden Drop yellow	18.49	2,200,000
1988	Aga Khan III diamond	33.13	1,807,143
1973	Pair of pear-shaped diamonds	44.93/42.2	640,000
1987	Red diamond	0.95	550,000
1982	Maximillian diamond		427,050
1977	Unmounted pear-shaped	25.07	340,909
1972	Unmounted pear-shaped	55.91	335,196
1970	Emerald-cut blue-white, rare type 11b	47.40	263,692

The above prices indicate the range of prices for the highest-quality diamonds and the changes over time. Non-sterling prices are translated at rates prevailing at the time of sale.

Average Price One-Carat Flawless White Diamond, Antwerp, 1974–1985

	$	Change (%)
1974	6,000	
1975	5,500	–8.33
1976	6,000	9.09
1977	7,500	25.00
1978	16,000	113.33
1979	33,000	106.25
1980	55,000	66.67
1981	25,000	–54.55
1982	13,000	–48.00
1983	10,000	–23.08
1984	12,000	20.00
1985	13,000	8.33

Sources: *Christie's* and *Sotheby's Yearbooks* 1981–1996.

Appendix XIII

Land Values in the UK, 1990 and 1995

Strutt & Parker/MAFF Land Index

Category of farm	Mean price per acre (£) 1990	1995	Change (%)
Mainly dairy	3,410	3,210	–5.9
Mainly arable	2,335	2,270	–2.8
Mainly beef/sheep	2,390	2,124	–11.1
All commercial farms	2,445	2,171	–11.2
Mainly residential	2,695	1,964	–27.1

Sunday Times Land Valuation Tables, 1990 and 1995

Category of farm	Land quality	Mean price per acre (£) 1990	1995	Change (%)
Scottish Highlands	Poor	300	40	–86.7
	Good	1,000	1,100	10.0
Scottish Lowlands	Poor	600	600	0.0
	Good	2,000	1,250	–37.5
Northern England	Poor	1,600	700	–56.3
	Good	2,000	1,200	–40.0
South-east	Poor	1,500	400	–73.3
	Good	2,200	1,500	–31.8
South-west	Poor	750	1,250	66.7
	Good	2,750	2,300	–16.4
Wales	Poor	200	1,600	700.0
	Good	1,700	2,750	61.8
West Midlands	Poor	1,400	1,250	–10.7
	Good	3,200	2,500	–21.9
East Midlands	Poor	1,600	1,250	–21.9
	Good	3,125	1,750	–44.0
East Anglia	Poor	2,100	1,000	–52.4
	Good	1,000	1,750	75.0

Source: Adapted from MAFF/*Sunday Times* 1990–1995 figures. (Calculations and résumé by authors.)

Index